Future of Business and Finance

The Future of Business and Finance book series features professional works aimed at defining, analyzing, and charting the future trends in these fields. The focus is mainly on strategic directions, technological advances, challenges and solutions which may affect the way we do business tomorrow, including the future of sustainability and governance practices. Mainly written by practitioners, consultants and academic thinkers, the books are intended to spark and inform further discussions and developments.

Anne Katrine Lund • Mette Refshauge

Mastering Corporate Communication

A Modern Guidebook for Future-fit Strategies, Tools and Skills

Anne Katrine Lund
Værløse, Denmark

Mette Refshauge
Vedbæk, Denmark

ISSN 2662-2467　　　　　　　ISSN 2662-2475　(electronic)
Future of Business and Finance
ISBN 978-3-031-50231-6　　　ISBN 978-3-031-50232-3　(eBook)
https://doi.org/10.1007/978-3-031-50232-3

Translation from the Danish language edition: "Strategisk kommunikation i praksis. Viden og værktøjer til at skabe værdi" by Anne Katrine Lund and Mette Refshauge, © Samfundslitteratur 2023. Published by Samfundslitteratur. All Rights Reserved.

© The Editor(s) (if applicable) and The Author(s), under exclusive license to Springer Nature Switzerland AG 2024

This work is subject to copyright. All rights are solely and exclusively licensed by the Publisher, whether the whole or part of the material is concerned, specifically the rights of reprinting, reuse of illustrations, recitation, broadcasting, reproduction on microfilms or in any other physical way, and transmission or information storage and retrieval, electronic adaptation, computer software, or by similar or dissimilar methodology now known or hereafter developed.

The use of general descriptive names, registered names, trademarks, service marks, etc. in this publication does not imply, even in the absence of a specific statement, that such names are exempt from the relevant protective laws and regulations and therefore free for general use.

The publisher, the authors, and the editors are safe to assume that the advice and information in this book are believed to be true and accurate at the date of publication. Neither the publisher nor the authors or the editors give a warranty, expressed or implied, with respect to the material contained herein or for any errors or omissions that may have been made. The publisher remains neutral with regard to jurisdictional claims in published maps and institutional affiliations.

This Springer imprint is published by the registered company Springer Nature Switzerland AG
The registered company address is: Gewerbestrasse 11, 6330 Cham, Switzerland

If disposing of this product, please recycle the paper.

Contents

1	**Introduction**...		1
2	**Strategic Organisational Communication in a New Era**............		5
	2.1	Strategic Anchoring as a Foundation........................	6
	2.2	The Multiple Roles of the Professional Communicator.........	9
	2.3	Organisational Anchoring................................	15
	2.4	Situational Anchoring...................................	16
	2.5	Case 1. In Maersk's Communicative Engine Room............	20
		2.5.1 A Changing Communications Function................	22
		2.5.2 The DNA of a Communicator at Maersk...............	25
		2.5.3 The Viral Maersk Shoes...........................	27
		2.5.4 Relational Work of Strategic Producers................	31
		2.5.5 A Communicative Quantum Leap in Progress..........	35
	2.6	Interview. With Symmetry as a Goal.......................	36
		2.6.1 Organisational Positioning Needed...................	36
		2.6.2 It Took a War..................................	37
		2.6.3 Essential Receptiveness...........................	38
		2.6.4 Be Curious and Inquiring..........................	38
	References..		40
3	**Credibility and Trust as a Field of Work**........................		43
	3.1	Trust Can Be (Re)Won.................................	45
	3.2	Elements of Credibility.................................	48
	3.3	Trust Is Challenged....................................	50
	3.4	Case 2. When Credibility Is Challenged.....................	51
		3.4.1 The Ethical Commitment Was Clear..................	52
		3.4.2 The First Communicative Handling...................	54
		3.4.3 Long-Term Preventive Organisational Work............	58
	3.5	Interview. Watch Closely!...............................	60
		3.5.1 Be the Credibility Sheriff in Your Organisation...........	60
		3.5.2 A Historical View of the World.....................	61
		3.5.3 Create Joint Action...............................	61
		3.5.4 Train Your Observation Skills.......................	62
		3.5.5 Mind Your Own Ethics............................	63
	References..		64

4 Corporate Citizenship in a Changing World 65
- 4.1 Build Social Licence to Operate 66
- 4.2 A Strong Purpose as a Starting Point...................... 67
- 4.3 Positioning Potentials in a Changing Media Landscape 69
- 4.4 With the CEO as a Cross-Platform Channel 71
- 4.5 The Practical Work of CEO Activism 73
- 4.6 Case 3. With New Fuel in Sight............................ 76
  - 4.6.1 Action Behind the Ambitions 78
  - 4.6.2 'Maersk Channel'................................. 81
- 4.7 Interview. Be a Stakeholder Capitalist...................... 85
  - 4.7.1 The Meaning of It All 85
  - 4.7.2 Credibility Is the Core 86
  - 4.7.3 From Shareholders to Stakeholders.................. 86
  - 4.7.4 Communication in a Changed World................... 87
  - 4.7.5 Communication Drives the Work..................... 88
- References... 89

5 Communication Must Create Contact 91
- 5.1 Mental Shortcuts as a Tool................................ 92
- 5.2 Changing Criteria for Selecting Content 93
- 5.3 Cross-Cutting Story Universes............................. 94
- 5.4 Communication in Dialogue with Stakeholders 96
- 5.5 Training Others for Contact............................... 98
- 5.6 Communication in Contact 99
- 5.7 Case 4. In Touch with the World 99
  - 5.7.1 Catch the Eye................................... 100
  - 5.7.2 Eye-Catching Infographics and Facts 101
  - 5.7.3 A Step Forward as a 'Thought Leader' in a New Field..... 102
  - 5.7.4 Training Managers with Sharp Data from Students......... 105
  - 5.7.5 Guerrilla Journalism at Eye Level with Stakeholders 106
- 5.8 Interview. Have High Ethical Standards and Take Note!.......... 109
  - 5.8.1 Create Solid Credibility.......................... 110
  - 5.8.2 Social Media Are Not a Channel..................... 111
  - 5.8.3 Listen Very Carefully............................ 111
  - 5.8.4 The Visual Turn 112
- References... 113

6 The Data-Driven Communicator............................... 115
- 6.1 Data-Driven Stakeholder Knowledge 118
- 6.2 A Measurable Basis for Communication Work................... 119
- 6.3 The Theoretical Basis for Evaluation........................ 120
- 6.4 An Agile Evaluation Model................................ 121
- 6.5 AMEC Recommendations for Measurement in Practice.......... 122
- 6.6 When an Audit Is the Ambition............................. 126
- 6.7 Data as Driver, Feedback and Mandate....................... 126
- 6.8 Case 5. Being Data-Driven Must Be Useful 127

		6.8.1	KPIs as Direction and Motivation	128
		6.8.2	'Social Listening' on Social Media	129
		6.8.3	Data-Driven Processes	131
		6.8.4	Data Related to Events	131
		6.8.5	Data in Channel Work	133
		6.8.6	A Data-Driven Future	135
	6.9	Interview. Choose Communication!		135
		6.9.1	Drop the Recipients – and Rethink 'Audiences'	136
		6.9.2	Learning Is Essential	136
		6.9.3	Lift the Heavy Weights	137
		6.9.4	Interpret Data Wisely: Even on the Move	137
		6.9.5	Skills of the Future	138
	References			139
7	**Internal Stakeholders in Focus**			141
	7.1	Communication with Internal Stakeholders		142
	7.2	The Culture of Communication as a Field of Work		144
	7.3	The Organisation's Communication Infrastructure		145
	7.4	The Strategy as an Anchor in Internal Communication		148
	7.5	Case 6. A Shoe Ready to Make Its Mark		149
		7.5.1	A Visual Framework for the Strategic Narrative	151
		7.5.2	Virtual Leaders' Meeting as a Kickoff	152
		7.5.3	Continuous Strategic Communication	154
		7.5.4	Keeping Your Nose to the Grindstone	156
	7.6	Interview. With the Individual as Key		157
		7.6.1	Forget About the Suggestion Box in the Corner	157
		7.6.2	Strategic Acumen and Communication Skills Are Not Enough	158
		7.6.3	Listen, Interpret and Understand	158
		7.6.4	The Internal Communication Elements	159
		7.6.5	Not Cosmetic, but Necessary	160
	References			161
8	**Facilitating Change**			163
	8.1	Linear Perspectives of Change		165
	8.2	The Agile Change		166
	8.3	The Human Factor		167
	8.4	Facilitator of Change		169
	8.5	Case 7. Orchestrating Effective Changes		172
		8.5.1	The Right Mandate for the Communicator	173
		8.5.2	An Analytical Starting Point	174
		8.5.3	A Unifying Growth Narrative	175
		8.5.4	An Advanced Channel Mix	176
		8.5.5	Data-Driven Change	178
		8.5.6	Integration Continues	180

	8.6	Interview. Involvement Is Key	180
		8.6.1 Step into the Change	181
		8.6.2 Away from the Campaign Trail	182
		8.6.3 We Must Not Fear Authenticity	182
		8.6.4 Psychological Safety as a Foundation	182
	References	184
9	**When the Crisis Is Triggered**	187
	9.1	Risks and Crisis Types	188
	9.2	The Strategic Crisis Communicator	190
	9.3	The Rhetorical Arena	192
	9.4	Response Strategies in Crises	195
	9.5	Proactive Crisis Management: 'Stealing Thunder'	196
	9.6	The Internal Stakeholder in Times of Crisis	198
	9.7	Crisis Awareness of the Professional Communicator	199
	9.8	Case 8. Global Balancing Act in Times of Crisis	200
		9.8.1 One Step Forward	201
		9.8.2 The Internal Balancing Act	203
		9.8.3 With Facts at the Core	204
	9.9	Interview. Keep Focus on Those Affected!	206
		9.9.1 Digital Change: And Yet Not	207
		9.9.2 The Hierarchical Fallacy	208
		9.9.3 Intuitive Decisions Guided by Strategy	208
		9.9.4 Nothing Like a Good Crisis	209
	References	210
10	**Skills of the Future**	213
	10.1	From the Point of View of the Communication Industry	220
	10.2	Prioritised Skills Development	222
	10.3	Case 9. Future Skills at Maersk	228
		10.3.1 Strategic Producer Academy	230
		10.3.2 A Stradivarius in Play	232
		10.3.3 Quality in Production	232
		10.3.4 To Be Continued	233
	10.4	Interview. You Must Link Knowledge, Skills and Personality	235
		10.4.1 Listen Actively	236
		10.4.2 Crack the Data Code	237
		10.4.3 Drop the Technology Dazzle	237
		10.4.4 Develop Your Understanding of People	237
		10.4.5 Look Inwards	238
	References	239

Introduction

Communication is at the heart of every organisation today. More than ever before, it is about being a credible organisation in the eyes of *all* stakeholders. No longer can an organisation be content with addressing one agenda or one group of stakeholders at a time. The requirement is to be visible and accessible all the time, to everyone, everywhere. This is no small challenge. It requires good trust-building communication on all platforms, internally and externally. At the same time, the frequency of both change and crises has increased significantly, and there is no reason to believe that this will change. This means that organisations are challenged as never before, and all these factors call for skilled communicators. Society, customers and investors are holding organisations accountable in new and more ways. Employees are demanding more and more meaning, direction and engagement, as are the talents of the future, for whom there is intense competition. The mediatised reality requires round-the-clock focus, calling for transparency and smart interaction. This means that the professional communicator must master multiple channels and orchestrate the organisation's own voices wisely.

Major challenges and new opportunities for the skilled professional communicator who can and must make a difference in organisational success. In this book, we try to identify what all these changes require of the professional communicator and to inspire how to approach the challenges. Based on current research from around the world and insight into Maersk's communicative engine room, we identify requirements, pitfalls and potential, and we try to identify key communicative approaches. For example, what do the new demands require of an organisations' communicators in terms of content, pace, formats and orchestration of the organisation's voices?

We believe that communicators are at a crucial crossroads. For decades, the focus has been on playing a role in strategic advice, which has certainly brought much good. But it has, in part, moved the communication profession too far from its true raison d'etre: delivering tangible communication that effectively bridges the gap between sender and receiver. In a time when anyone with a smartphone can be their own communication channel, the professional communicator must more than ever be aware of the levers that differentiate professionally sound communication from the overwhelming and constant flow of messages from everyone, everywhere, at all times. This is the challenge if the profession is to remain relevant. Accelerated pace, artificial intelligence and the disintegration of traditional communication processes threaten to 'disrupt' the discipline as we know it. If we are able to adapt quickly and seize the new opportunities, however, there is potential for renewed relevance and ground-breaking developments in the role of the professional communicator. These days, communicators in companies, organisations, educational institutions, media and agencies are contemplating how to master the role in the future. This has prompted us to come up with a book aimed at the communicators of the future, the many students who will soon find their way from well-read theorists to professional practitioners.

In the book, we seek to establish the necessary link between the strategic perspective and the craftsmanship, exemplified by cases from Maersk, because the communicator of the future will have to master it all and at a pace never seen before. At Maersk, this work has resulted in the definition of a completely new role for communicators, that of 'strategic producer'. A role that requires the professional communicator to anchor all activities in the overall strategy of the organisation and at the same time be able to follow through on strategic recommendations with concrete, creative, quality solutions. The role implies that the professional communicator is not only responsible for being a concrete strategic advisor and for producing communication, but also for being a 'producer' inspired by the meaning of the word in the film and music industry, where the producer is responsible for organising a production. A strategic producer is responsible for orchestrating the best communicative solutions—sometimes by creating the communication themselves, sometimes by carefully staging others, choosing the right team of organisational voices and ensuring that they deliver a good product.

The book provides a solid theoretical foundation based on central parts of communication theory. Always with the ambition to include the most qualified perspectives and with quotations from the primary sources to make the book as useful as possible for the communication student. Communication theory ranges from Aristotle's definition of rhetoric as the art of finding the most persuasive arguments over 2500 years ago to today's researchers looking at everything from mediatised trust to effective social media or public relations. In this book, we do not allow ourselves to belong to one direction or school but rather to eclectically draw inspirational theory from across the board and bring it together in a hopefully inspiring and application-orientated fusion. It is always debatable whether something has been left out or whether it is cheeky to merge across disciplines and schools, but the ambition has been to inspire as much as possible and as far as possible to include research-based approaches. The individual researchers are of course credited along the way, but the merger must be at the authors' own 'expense'.

It has been a great privilege when working on the book to not only draw on theoretical publications but to also talk to the world's leading researchers in the field.

These dialogues have provided nourishment and direction for the work on the book, with excerpts included as interviews in each chapter, so our readers can also get a sense of what the world's leading communication researchers see as the biggest challenges right now. What was striking was how much everyone agreed. They may have researched very different fields, from crisis communication to the use of data or communication on social media, but they all agreed that the biggest challenge right now is to understand that communication is not just about passing on information. It is about active listening and communicating with stakeholders symmetrically and in a trust-building manner. Each and everyone talks about how the professional communicator must understand stakeholders even better, use data wisely and manage communicative interaction rather than 'performing' with a perhaps overconfident campaign approach.

All chapters in the book thus have three elements. First, introductory pages to the chapter's theme with an application-orientated selection of theory and approaches to navigating as a communicator. Second, a case study from Maersk, where each chapter's theme is illustrated with examples and reflections from the global organisation. In this context, one of the authors of this book, Anne Katrine Lund, PhD in rhetoric and strategic advisor, has interviewed Maersk employees, followed work processes for several years and assumed the role of the curious and critical interviewer, whilst the book's other author, Mette Refshauge, Director of Communication at Maersk, is interviewed as a practitioner in several of the case descriptions. The aim of these pages is to provide a real insight into the engine room of a large organisation's communications function. What is important? What is difficult? And what have they been working on? In a personalised interview at the end of each chapter, the floor is given to one of the world's leading researchers, who will draw on their research to provide perspective and advice on what communicators need to pay attention to in order to make a difference.

The book is structured in a way that seeks to cover the entire field of work of the professional communicator.

- Chapter 2 focuses on the changing reality in which communicators have to work and the roles this calls for.
- Chapter 3 identifies the foundations of the communicator's work in establishing credibility as an organisation and building trust with all stakeholders.
- Chapter 4 looks at the demands on organisations today to not only deliver good financial performance but also to take responsibility as corporate citizens.
- Chapter 5 takes a closer look at the demands of communication today. For example, what are the changing news criteria and formal requirements that the professional communicator has to fulfil?
- Chapter 6 looks at how the communication task is made both easier and better if the professional communicator works systematically in a data-driven way.
- Chapter 7 focuses on the internal stakeholder particularly and looks at how communicators orchestrate communication to support the success of the organisation.
- Chapters 8 and 9 look specifically at how communicators can help manage change and crises, respectively.

- Chapter 10 takes a close look at the communicator's own competences. What do today's communicators need in terms of knowledge, skills and personal qualities to succeed in the difficult and important art of helping organisations communicate well?

Many thanks to all the many researchers who have made us wiser. Special thanks to Ana Tkalac Verčič, Ángeles Moreno, Ansgar Zerfass, Chiara Valentini, Helle Kryger Aggerholm, James Grunig, Jim Macnamara, Lars Thøger Christensen, Linda Putnam, Mats Heide, Mark Ørsten, Marianne Wolf Lundholt, Mie Femø Nielsen, Ralph Tench, Robert L. Heath, Rupert Younger, Sine Nørholm Just, Vibeke Thøis Madsen, Timothy Coombs, Winni Johansen and Øyvind Ihlen.

Also, a big thank you to all the students who have put into words what they would like input on—and to all the communicators and managers at Maersk who have put up with the many curious questions and have always been ready to provide insight into what they do and explain why.

Last, but not least, a big thank you to our families who have supported us through endless hours of writing and book meetings along the way—and to the constructively critical readers who have helped us find the right form: Christina Tønnesen, Frederik J. Preisler, Helle Kryger Agerholm, Mette Green, Pernille Steensbech Lemée, Sascha Amarasinha and Timme Bisgaard Munk.

We hope that the book will help to sharpen the relevance of the professional communicator and inspire even better strategic communication in practice.

Strategic Organisational Communication in a New Era

2

The world is changing at a dizzying pace. It challenges communicators to navigate in new ways, with new challenges and new demands. Communication is no longer about sending a message when there is something new to tell but about being in open, authentic contact: about being present. This chapter takes a closer look at the new reality of the communicator: From the comprehensive communication theory, what can help us to understand our challenges, role and shared responsibilities?

The case study in this chapter provides an insight into how the global company Maersk works professionally with communication. How have communicators organised themselves in recent years to meet a new reality of major changes, new ambitions and over 100,000 employees worldwide?

The chapter's international expert is pioneering researcher Professor Emeritus James Grunig, who has been a central figure in the development of the communication profession for 60 years. He offers his views on what is particularly important to pay attention to in the context of communication right now.

The professional communicator has an increasingly important role in a modern organisation. In the past, when organisations were more closed and the outside world less demanding, the first professional communicators were content to sit in 'text offices', where their task was largely to convey the organisation's messages to a specific recipient. Today, the reality is very different. For example, it is impossible to have full control over all communication, so the communicator must not only communicate but orchestrate the communication of the rest of the organisation, which places entirely new demands on the roles of the communicator and the communications function in order to succeed in ensuring effective communication with all stakeholders.

Basically, it is the responsibility of the communications function to create a credible perception of the organisation both internally and externally and to help the

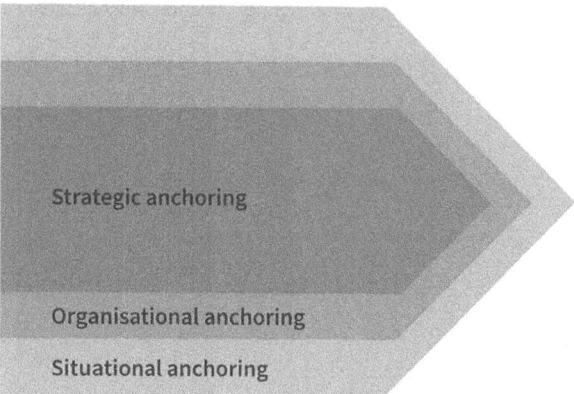

Fig. 2.1 The professional communicator's three approaches to anchoring an initiative. Source: Lund and Refshauge (2023)

organisation achieve the goals it has set itself as strategies, visions, or purposes. The professional communicator thus always works with a strategic anchoring of all communication, ensuring coherence between words, expressions and ambitions. The professional communicator must also ensure that the communication is organisationally anchored so that it is credible and sustainable communication and not, for example superficial spin or a polished and unreliable version of reality. In addition, the professional communicator must ensure that all communication is situationally anchored in a constantly updated understanding of what is going on outside the organisation.

It may sound simple, but it is a complex and important task that requires strong analytical, strategic, psychological and communicative skills. Figure 2.1 highlights the three main approaches to the work of the professional communicator, namely strategic, organisational and situational anchoring. In the following sections, all three steps are analysed, drawing on leading theoretical inputs and industry experience.

2.1 Strategic Anchoring as a Foundation

Communication is never an end in itself but is intended to support the organisation, i.e. it must be strategically anchored in the organisation's mission: 'Strategic communication is the purposeful, normative use of communication functions and discourse processes by organisations to accomplish their missions, visions and core values' (Heath et al., 2018: 1).

The communicator's complex task is to orchestrate the organisation's many expressions so that the strategy is as successful as possible—from the controlled expressions in the organisation's own channels such as websites and newsletters to the more complex tasks, such as training managers for press contact, moderating commentary tracks on social media or managing crises and change.

2.1 Strategic Anchoring as a Foundation

Falkheimer and Heide (2018) summarise the objectives of strategic communication's contribution to creating value for the organisation as follows:

The professional communicator must contribute to **organisational efficiency** by supporting direction and meaning. Employees need to know and understand the organisational direction, and they need to be able to translate it into something that can guide their task performance and their communication with all stakeholders.

The professional communicator must also contribute to **transparency** and openness, so what the organisation does for internal and external stakeholders is clear and accessible, and the communicator must contribute to protecting and clarifying the organisation's **image**.

Falkheimer and Heide (2018) also point out that the professional communicator shares the responsibility for clarifying, co-creating and maintaining the **organisational identity** (134). Understood in the sense that the communicator, precisely by putting the organisational identity into words and, for example talking about the corporate culture, giving examples of values, approaches and results, is a co-creator of the internal self-understanding and identity.

If strategic communication is to be successful for the professional communicator, there must be no distinction between internal and external communication, but rather integrated communication across all channels and platforms. This perspective has also been called 'integrated communication' (Cornelissen, 2020), precisely because it does not distinguish but integrates and harmonises. It is an important focus in practice and has meant that many communications functions today work across channels and also in many places with a so-called 'newsroom approach', where you constantly think across all stakeholders and channels. Regular editorial meetings across, e.g. the press team, internal team, branding and management teams would ensure that coordination, versioning, timing and reuse are carried out wisely. In the 'news-room', every single content element must thus be discussed in terms of relevance across the board. The starting point is that it no longer makes sense to dedicate individual channels or formats to individual stakeholders, because the pace and transparency of the media landscape means that everyone sees everything all the time, at the same time. Of course, employees need to know what is being communicated externally and are also important ambassadors for communicating messages to the outside world. At the same time, all employees are also potential 'leakers' in a transparent reality where sharing content is both easy and common. That is why external perspectives must also be activated in the assessment of what should go out internally. Does an internal story have the potential of landing in external media, and would you want it to? Furthermore, companies that are listed on the stock exchange must adhere to strict rules regarding who knows what and when.

Another perspective on the professional communicator's field of work can be drawn from the research tradition of organisational communication or CCO (**C**ommunicative **C**onstitution of **O**rganisations) (Feldner & Fyke, 2018). This summarises four communication flows that are important to be aware of, each linked to and reaching into the organisation: membership negotiation, self-structuring, activity coordination and institutional positioning.

The first flow is **'membership negotiation'**, where you can already see from the name that the focus is on relationships and how they are constantly (re)negotiated in communication. The professional communicator must develop and maintain relationships with members of the organisation and potential members. For example, what is the level of commitment, identification and leadership? And how can communication support these relationships?

The second flow is the **'self-structuring'** of the organisation, i.e. the complex structure that the organisation itself has created to distinguish itself from others. It is the way in which the organisation has decided to organise itself by assigning leadership roles, defining an organisational structure, creating fixed procedures and meeting forums. These structures are largely created through communication about and within the organisation. But even the more informal communication is part of the self-structured flow that maintains the structures, e.g. feedback and more formal control processes. Communication guides the processes and thus helps to constitute the organisation. Here, the role of the professional communicator is to diagnose, set norms, develop and train. A concrete example could be large-scale meetings with the management of an organisation. The professional communicator may consider how the current formats work and make a professional assessment of whether they are appropriate and support the organisation's ambitions in the best possible way, or whether something needs to be adjusted. Changes may require new norms for what constitutes a good large-scale meeting, the development of a new concept and training of managers to be part of it.

The third flow is **'activity coordination'**, which covers all the activities that connect and drive progress towards organisational goals. This may, for example be the many processes with communicators as facilitators but also communication as a tool for other actors in the organisation. For example, change processes where the professional communicator helps to drive change by ensuring that activities are coordinated so they are always in line with the needs and ambitions of all stakeholders.

The fourth flow is **'institutional positioning'** as a communicative flow. It covers how the organisation positions itself at macro level with actions in relation to e.g. suppliers, customers, competitors, partners or legislators in order to legitimise itself.

CCO is based on the idea that communication is a force that creates connections in a system and that organisations interact rather than being isolated structures (Robichaud & Cooren, 2013). Legitimacy must be built, and only then will the organisation have real agency in relation to stakeholders.

Both Falkheimer and Heide's objectives for strategic communication and Feldner and Fyke's four flows show how widely ramified the communicative work can be for the professional communicator. The responsibilities of the communications function vary from organisation to organisation—in some places it is exclusively PR, in others internal communication or perhaps integrated communication. Regardless of local organisational differences, it is the responsibility of the professional communicator to take an interest in the four strategic perspectives as well as the four flows in order to identify how best to support the organisation's direction and meaning within the given framework.

Fig. 2.2 The excellent communications function. Source: Brockhaus et al. (2022)

The strategic anchoring of communicative work requires the professional communicator to know and act in accordance with the organisation's strategy at all times and to ensure consistency of expression. This is often an overlooked task, but it is crucial for supporting the organisation's success in the best possible way. It is not enough to know the buzzwords and the main features of the strategy. The communicator needs to step into the strategic space and understand both the choices and the opt-outs of a strategy in order to support not only the strategy narrative internally but strategy execution in general.

When Brockhaus et al. summarise the requirements for the excellent communications function today (2022), it is about a communications function that both has influence in the organisation and creates effective communication, as shown in Fig. 2.2.

Figure 2.2's dual focus on influence and performance shows the complexity of communication work. The professional communicator must not only be skilled at influencing, advising and orchestrating organisational voices but must also be able to excel at good communication on numerous platforms. So it is not an either/or, but a both/and.

2.2 The Multiple Roles of the Professional Communicator

The fact that a communicator is not exclusively a communicator is often a surprise to other professionals, who may tend to think that the communicator is just there with pen and paper to take notes for the next communicative product. But the roles of the communicator are many, from the classic producer to trend analyst, trainer,

Table 2.1 Overview of the four roles of the head of a public relations function

Role	Main attributes
Orienter, societal	Leadership support & Brand
Catalyst, value chain	Brand & Core Competencies
Implementer, functional	Core Competencies & Planning
Navigator, corporate	Planning & Leadership support

Source: Gregory and Willis (2013)

moderator of internal events, facilitator of change and strategy messages or crisis manager. There are many theoretical operationalisations of the roles. The following section describes two key approaches that can help to get an overview of the many nuances of communication work today.

Indeed, the first theoretical approach expands the communicator's roles to much more than producer. Gregory and Willis (2013) present four roles as suggestions for tasks that a manager of a public relations function should fulfil, shown in an overview here and discussed in Table 2.1.

Gregory and Willis emphasise that communication is as much about understanding and orienting as it is about catalysing, navigating and implementing. As shown in the list above, they point out that the communicator has an important role in orientating themselves: '**the orienter**'. The task is to know and understand what is going on in the surrounding society and with all stakeholders. It is an analytical role that ensures that the organisation's communication may be positioned wisely in the context. The knowledge gathered must then be communicated to the right people in the organisation so decisions can be made on the right foundations.

Thus, the next role is already underway: '**the catalyst**'. The role of the catalyst is to ensure that the knowledge gathered is used to make a difference in all the relevant places in the organisation. The word originally comes from the world of chemistry, where a substance that is a chemical catalyst makes processes happen—it is precisely the job of the communicator to bring knowledge into the organisation and set processes in motion. Some people catalyse processes by communicating something themselves, but many acts as catalysts by setting other parts of the organisation in motion with something that is not in itself outwardly communicative. For example, knowledge from responses to posts on social media can provide insight into criticism or wishes from a customer group that must be conveyed to a customer department or product development department. Gregory and Willis point out that the catalyst must work throughout the value chain, from input on raw materials to production and customer experiences, to sharpen the entire organisation's deliverables and positioning. 'Embedding a value chain, stakeholder perspective in the design, creation and delivery of products and services requires the communications function to provide vision-critical intelligence, engagement capability and evaluation to ensure the delivery of organisational objectives. Here the function is as catalyst for the organisation ensuring values are lived and changing realities rather than changing perceptions' (Gregory & Willis, 2013: 43).

The third role, '**the implementer**', is more functional. The implementer is functionally executing and manages the necessary activities and communicative products. It may be that a diagnosed reputational crisis, after a discussion with management, has turned into a renewed decision to change behaviour, which now needs to be communicated across platforms. The communicator thus takes responsibility for implementing the renewed position in communication with key stakeholders across platforms.

The last role, **'the navigator'**, is what Gregory and Willis call a key role for the communicator. It builds on the knowledge and agency of the previous three roles and is the role of navigator for the organisation. Through their insight into the external environment, internal ambitions and challenges, the professional communicator is uniquely positioned to help navigate wisely to ensure a strong and credible reputation.

The overall role as navigator and reputation manager of the organisation can be elaborated and concretised utilising the concepts of James Grunig to clarify the communicator's work with concrete strategic management.

He clarifies how the professional communicator in reputation management must navigate a complex landscape with many stakeholders. The communicator must be close to management. There must be close contact between the communicator and management so their decisions can be based on key knowledge from the communicators, just as the communicator must initiate the relevant communication based on management's wishes. Communicators must obtain this knowledge by, amongst other things, maintaining close contact with stakeholders and the public. In other words, the knowledge that Gregory and Willis' orientation role ensures that the communicator has.

Grunig also describes how the behaviour of stakeholders and the public can often create situations that call for action. It is the communicators' job to recognise these challenges or issues and bring them back to the management table so they may be dealt with. They can be positive—simply evidence of a strong relationship, or they can be critical challenges that need to be handled with crisis management. For example, communication about the company's work on gender equality may be strongly criticised because it is not perceived to be in line with the composition of the board. The communicators must bring these issues to the attention of key stakeholders and perhaps even develop a crisis management contingency plan with specific messages and suggestions for spokespersons on all relevant platforms.

These efforts have an impact on relationships that is important for management to understand, because it affects both the organisational reputation and the achievement of organisational goals.

This shows the complexity and multi-faceted nature of the work of the professional communicator responsible for the reputation of the organisation. For further studies, you may wish to seek out James Grunig's more detailed model of these highly complicated processes (Grunig, 2018). Similar process models could be created focusing on internal processes such as change, strategy implementation or maintaining organisational commitment. But the core is the same in all of these. The professional communicator must gather important knowledge from outside and inside the organisation and manage complex interactions to ensure that the organisation addresses and acts communicatively to key challenges.

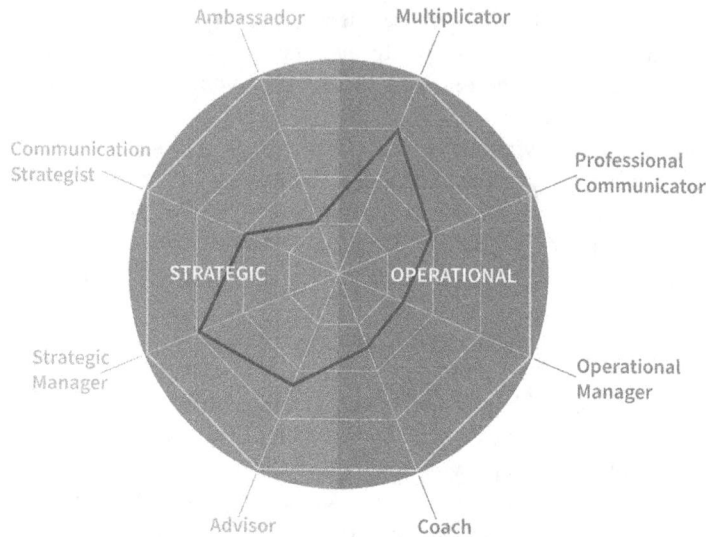

Fig. 2.3 Strategic and operational roles of the communicator. Source: Berger et al. (2017).

A slightly more detailed and practical operationalisation of the communicator's roles can be found in Berger et al. (2017). They divide the eight different roles of the head of communication into strategic and operational roles, as shown in Fig. 2.3.

According to Berger et al., the strategic roles are:

- '**Ambassador**'. The ambassador is the role of the public face, where the communication professional has the mandate to act on behalf of the organisation, which is supported by Mykkänen and Vos (2015) and van Riel (2012), amongst others.
- '**Communication strategist**'. The role of the communication strategist is to define concrete communication objectives that ensure that the organisation's strategy is translated into concrete action in communication across all platforms. The communication strategist ensures coherence.
- '**Strategic manager**'. The role of the strategic manager is to think strategically and to lead effectively, using relevant management tools to manage/develop both internal forces and external deliverables.
- '**Advisor**'. The advisor role is partly about ensuring that management is aware of risks and expectations from stakeholders and partly about advising management on strategic decisions. It is a role that requires that 'the CCO has to be able to offer serious, frank and even bold consultation to top management as well as to maintain a good relationship with key stakeholders (e.g. Zerfass & Franke, 2013). In this role, the CCO draws the attention of top management to potential communicative risks, societal expectations and critical issues and provides advice on strategic decisions. The advisor has a trust-based relationship with

2.2 The Multiple Roles of the Professional Communicator

senior managers. He is valued by internal partners for the ability to span corporate boundaries' (Berger et al., 2017: 10).

The operational roles, according to Berger et al., are:

- **'Multiplicator'**. The multiplicator role covers the function of ensuring that the organisation's strategy reaches both internal and external audiences. The communicator must ensure that platforms and channels are available and take co-responsibility for concretising abstract strategies that make sense and are easy to remember for internal and external stakeholders.
- **'Professional communicator'**. The professional communicator is the role that creates effective communication across all channels and platforms. A role where the communicator works tactically to deliver what has been decided strategically. 'Skills such as improvisation and editing are important aspects of the operational communicator repertoire (e.g. Gregory & Willis, 2013; Steyn & Everett, 2009)' (Berger et al.: 11).
- **'Operational Manager'**. Operational Manager is a more administrative role where the communicator ensures good processes and routines for implementing, executing, evaluating and measuring all relevant activities. It is also a practical administrative role with responsibility for budgets and staffing and, not least, decisions on channel infrastructure and coordination across all platforms and channels to ensure: 'integrated messaging processes across shared, earned, owned and paid media (e.g. Dozier, 1984; Macnamara et al., 2015; Moss & Green, 2002)' (Berger et al., 2017: 11).
- **'Coach'**. The coach role is the one that ensures that the communicator is able to step in and orchestrate all the organisational voices (Falkheimer et al., 2016), both in terms of ensuring the right contingency plans and, more specifically, by training and sparring with the individual to ensure that both form and content are well in hand. This is a role that requires insight into rhetoric, psychology and pedagogy.

The model is set up as a grid to inspire individuals to take stock, as exemplified by the yellow highlighting. What roles is the communicator taking on and is it expedient?

A study amongst Danish counsellors (Gravengaard et al., 2022) further nuances the roles by asking the counsellors themselves what they actually do. This leads to even more nuances with, for example the roles of analyst, problem solver, sparring partner and boundary setter.

Since 2007, European researchers organised in the European Public Relations Education and Research Association (EUPRERA) have been monitoring the communication industry's self-assessment of the state of strategic communication. Working with the European Association of Communication Directors (EACD), they gauge the self-perception of over 30,000 communication professionals each year (see Fig. 2.4).

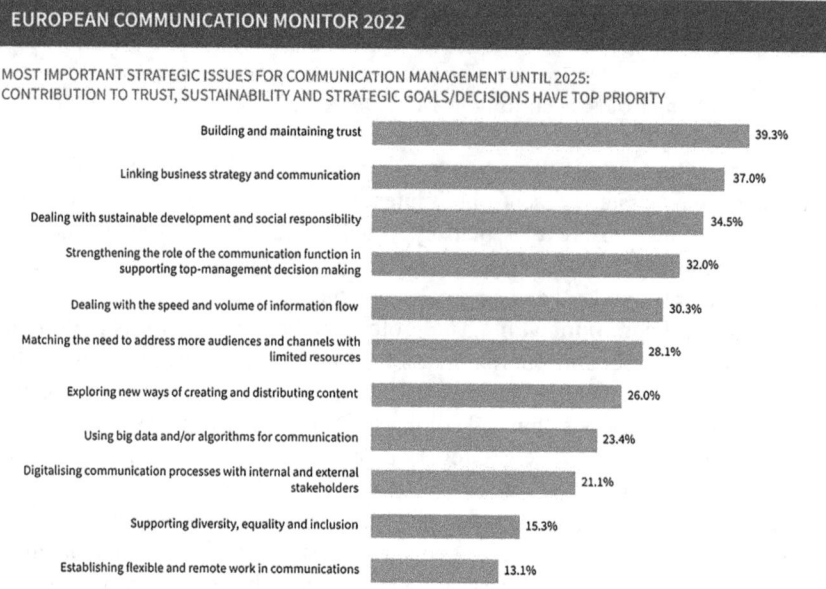

Fig. 2.4 Key strategic challenges for European communication leaders. Source: European Communication Monitor 2022

If you ask the communicators themselves, creating and maintaining trust with all stakeholders is the most important issue. In second place is the link between communication and business strategy—creating and ensuring coherence is challenging and has been for a long time. As the European Communication Monitor 2022 report concludes: 'This topic, after dominating the strategic debate for a whole decade since the inception of the ECM studies in 2007, started a noticeable decline to the bottom of the list between 2016 and 2019. It has regained its position as a top strategic issue over the past three years—especially in corporations (38.8%) as well as for consultancies and agencies (39.4%). As forecast in last year's report (Zerfass et al., 2021), the economic turbulences related to the pandemic have indeed seemingly perpetuated this trend, as evidenced in a 7-point jump from last year—the steepest incline among all strategic issues between 2021 and 2022' (Brockhaus et al., 2022).

In third place is the work on environment, social and governance (ESG), although this has dropped from first place the previous year.

The challenges from the communicators' point of view are in some ways a reflection of the practical work: managing pace (5), reaching audiences with limited resources (6), developing new ways of getting content across (7), big data (8) and digitalisation (9). It is clear what is being mulled over. Namely, the challenges of reaching out and getting through.

The many challenges and roles show how nuanced the communicator's roles are—and it may be difficult to keep track of it all. In practice, the roles are good tools for regularly reviewing whether the communications function covers a wide range of functions, and they can inspire us to bring many facets into play in our work as professional communicators when aiming to make an organisational difference. However, they must always be brought into play with a deep understanding of what the specific situation requires.

2.3 Organisational Anchoring

No matter how strategically clever a communication effort may be, the professional communicator will only succeed in creating an impact if all efforts are planned on the basis of a great deal of organisational and psychological understanding. This includes incorporating cultural and psychological analyses in any preparation.

As early as 1986, the organisational psychologist Edgar Schein pointed out that internal counsellors should never be misled into looking only at the surface of an organisation when designing an intervention. His ideas have often been illustrated with an organisational iceberg to show that, as with icebergs, we can only see the surface of the mountain, named 'artefacts' by Schein, but that most of the mountain is in fact below the water's surface and thus not visible to the observer. Schein referred to these invisible elements as 'values' and 'basic assumptions'.

Professional communicators need to be aware of all three levels: artefacts, values and basic assumptions. Artefacts are all the things that can be seen and heard in the organisation. The visible artefacts can literally be observed and can act as important signposts. Examples include symbols in the organisation's interior design, from the way offices are laid out to posters with values or screen savers with sales figures.

But as important for signalling and nudging change as artefacts may be, it is equally important to not only look at the tip of the iceberg, but to get below the surface when orchestrating communication.

At the next level, Schein places (espoused) values. Of course, to be effective, values must not just be wishful thinking, but lived values. The professional communicator must be able to recognise this and relate to it. It is not necessarily problematic to want to communicate something that you are not yet delivering on, but communicators must be aware of it in order to be able to organise efforts that hit the mark. If, for example there is an espoused value of being customer-oriented, it may be a communicator's task to help turn the image into reality by example, by ensuring customer-oriented communication, making sure that customers are visible at major events etc.

Essential for the professional communicator is also getting below the organisational surface and to have an eye for what Schein calls the basic assumptions. With an analytical eye, the communicator must be able to act on what can be spotted here. It is not necessarily a communicator's responsibility to develop or change a culture, but it is a necessary context to understand in order to succeed in communication. An example could be the organisation of an executive meeting where management wants to set a new course for an area of the organisation. It might be tempting to simply help by making engaging slides and an explanatory film that unfolds the rationale for the change. But the professional communicator can make a quick analysis using Schein's organisational iceberg to find out if there is anything else that needs attention. At the artefact level, you can work to show the change visually in a clear manner and spot what needs to be changed. At the (espoused) value level, you can work on what needs to be articulated verbally. A look at basic assumptions can also help to understand what can hinder or promote the actual realisation of the ambitions. Is there, for example resistance towards the new ambitions, are there everyday practices that will now become more difficult, do employees already feel pressurised, do they feel competent to do this? There may be a lot at stake and by taking an interest in this level as a professional communicator, you ensure that you organise communication that does not just operate on the surface but can help to bring about real change. Organisational analysis can also help the professional communicator identify which role is most needed for communicators to make the right difference.

2.4 Situational Anchoring

The professional communicator must not only be strategically and organisationally anchored, but always situationally anchored as well. Quality communication or advice is situationally bound and must work and function in the current situation. The fundamental rhetorical sense of the situation is thus crucial. The professional communicator must be able to read what is at stake, what affects a situation and make wise choices that can be acted upon. This applies to all types of tasks, from the facilitation of large-scale processes to a simple posting on an internal channel. The professional communicator must thus have a work process that ensures situational anchoring. In addition, it is no good being unilaterally focused on, for example a specific communication product or a fixed role. The professional communicator works with a focus on creating value for the organisation with all key stakeholders. It is not about one message, one channel or one process, but always about ensuring the reputational impact that you are tasked with maintaining. That is why there must be both horizon and depth in the work process, even in the often very busy workflows of organisations.

The workflow must ensure that the professional communicator starts from the needs of the situation, anchors all efforts strategically and organisationally, assumes the relevant roles, carries out the right communication work and monitors its success. Often, the professional communicator must orchestrate organisational voices rather than communicate themselves, and tasks can range from setting up the right team of organisational spokespersons for a task, training them, ensuring sustainability in resource use and taking responsibility for framework, quality and impact.

In simple terms, four steps can help to ensure an effective work process, as shown in Fig. 2.5. The four steps of the model are described below.

The first step of the model is the strategic analysis. Here, ambitions, challenges and opportunities are analysed in relation to all relevant stakeholders. An almost rhetorical situational analysis of possibilities and challenges and identification of

2.4 Situational Anchoring

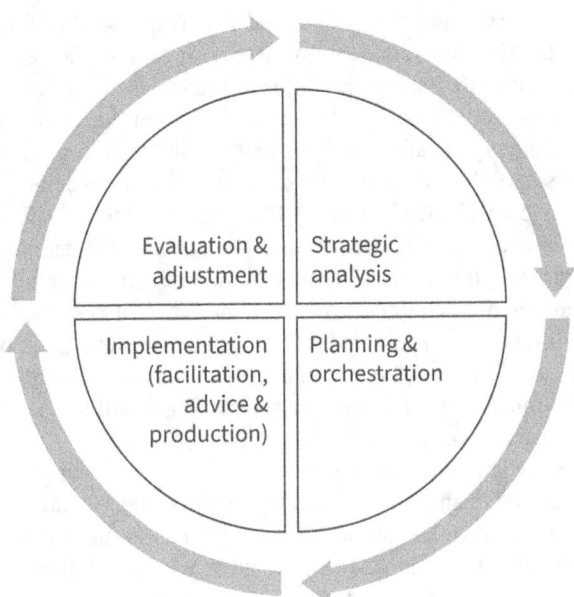

Fig. 2.5 A systematic work process focusing on strategic analysis, planning, implementation and evaluation. Source: Lund and Refshauge (2023)

what communication may contribute with and how. This initial analysis ensures that the communication task is carried out with a both strategic, organisational and situational approach in mind. By analysing what is desired and what the challenges are, the professional communicator can decide on an analytical foundation what the right thing to do is in a given situation. After conducting the strategic analysis, the professional communicator thus knows what the goal is for a given action and what could hinder the achievement of the goal.

The second step, the planning and orchestration phase, is about planning so the professional communicator does not immediately implement an action but ensures that it is orchestrated wisely. Who will do what, when and how? And why? This is where not only senders and content are chosen but also the necessary formats for both implementation and channel mix. It is also at this stage that the professional communicator decides what roles this situation calls for. Is this, for example a process where the professional communicator is mainly a counsellor, bringing others into play, or do they also need to prepare playbooks and talking points that make it easier for others to succeed, meaning there are both facilitator roles and trainer elements in the task solution?

Some of the considerations about orchestration are also relational. The professional communicator can only create support for his or her recommendations by ensuring that the necessary authorisation is in place (Lund & Petersen, 2018). Part of the authorisation comes from above. That is, from the mandate that the communications function holds in the specific organisation. Is this a task that communicators are expected to step into and take responsibility for, and that they are trusted to fulfil? However, one cannot simply sit back in the department's mandate. The individual professional communicator must also be able to establish their authorisation in the situation itself. For example, when the communicator is in a remote corner of the organisation, perhaps in the middle of a crisis situation and has to stand up to a senior director, the individual must be able to demonstrate concrete decisiveness or agency (Hoff-Clausen, 2018). The work takes place in actual situations where the organisational licence must be translated into action and a concrete mandate in a trust-based relationship between the individual communicator and the manager they are helping communicate. A point that is also supported by Moreno et al. (2021), whose studies show that: 'Trust in the communication professional as a person is perceived as being higher than trust in the communication departments and in the communication professional in general. These differences are significant; personal trust versus departmental trust' (15).

This requires the individual communicator to be assertive but also to have an eye for both building relationships and being able to assess their strength. Schein (2018) has introduced a useful relational perspective that can be used to actively analyse which communication tasks may be carried out in various relationships.

To begin with you have the professional, transactional relationship. After that, you may develop a more trusting and open relationship, until you have worked your way towards a very close relationship. According to Schein, advising professionally is possible at all steps, but in the framework of the relationship. In the initial transactional relationship, professional communicators can help to fulfil the specific tasks desired or requested. The level of trust is not high enough to allow for proper insight into various underlying conditions that could hamper or hinder successful communication. This could be the case, for example when providing communication training to a manager who does not feel confident enough to say that he/she suffers from stage fright. A knowledge that could change the whole training programme and ensure a greater impact. This does not mean that the professional communicator cannot be of help, but the effect could have been greater if the relationship was characterised by more trust. These relationships can usefully be built up so that it gradually becomes possible to help better. If you already know in your planning that it is this type of relationship, you may also consider whether something could be done to strengthen the relationship from the start or, for example through research or organisational lifelines, thereby gaining insight into other ways.

The open and trustful relationship is, namely, characterised by trust, which means that you can explore and recognise *together* what would be the right thing to do in various situations and co-create solutions. This is of course preferable for professional communicators who want to ensure that they are contributing to the creation of the right and most effective solutions. At this level of relationship, the communicator can best bring their expertise to bear in a way that is listened to and the advice given is acted upon.

Subsequently, once you have obtained a very close relationship, you would think that everything is even better, as you are very familiar with your advice taker in a close, transparent and collaborative relationship. But Schein warns that new challenges can arise in such a relationship. The relationship may become so close that it is difficult to see challenges from a professionally neutral perspective. It is part of the communicator's professionalism to be able to put themselves in the shoes of others without letting personal biases or relationships obscure their professionalism, so of course it is possible to provide professional advice in such a close and confidential relationship. It just requires a special attention to one's own preferences, e.g. emotionally, because one may share the counsellor's feelings, or factually, because one shares the same perspective and forgets that other stakeholders may have a different level of knowledge.

The character of the relationship is thus crucial to focus on when planning and orchestrating the work of a professional communicator, as it may have a major impact on the plans to be made and the preparatory work to be carried out.

When a professional communicator has completed the second planning step in Fig. 2.5, he or she will thus have a plan for how to solve the given challenge in order to create following and impact. This may, for example, be a plan for an interview with specific media, where you have not only analysed and strategically ensured that the right messages are ready to be conveyed but have also assessed how the spokesperson may best succeed in creating the right impression. In addition, it has been assessed which roles are most appropriate to take on, such as producer of the message platform, media trainer of the spokesperson, coordinator of press contacts and writer of postings for the internal media at the same time as the external message. All decisions are translated into a plan for a solution that will only rarely match an often unpredictable reality on a one-to-one basis, but which is a good starting point for dealing with this particular situation.

In the third work step in Fig. 2.5, the implementation phase, the professional communicator must act on the plan. This means that ambitions must be translated into effective initiatives. This often requires the mobilisation of all the specific functional and communicative skills. Perhaps the film needs to be shot with a manager and processed, the script for the town hall meeting needs to be implemented with the communicator as moderator, or the change needs to be facilitated with management advice, communication material in the form of 'slide decks' and internal articles. The actual implementation takes place when all the plans are realised with high-quality initiatives. As a professional communicator, one extra communicative burden often needs to be lifted in this phase of work. It is the communicator's job to be a good communicative role model.

The fourth work step in Fig. 2.5, the evaluation and adjustment phase, is about evaluating and adjusting, because an intervention can always be developed further. That is why a good communicator has an evaluative mindset. Constructive evaluation can not only help the organisation in the long term and ensure, for example more appropriate workflows. It can also often enhance the impact of an endeavour by learning new things along the way. Many communication channels can now be updated and edited, so it is often possible to react immediately to responses to an intervention, and many processes offer the opportunity to learn something new that may be incorporated into the next planned communication. Technological possibilities make it much easier to collect input and use the insights gained from data for continuous improvement. An evaluative mindset creates learning that can be used actively and constructively to prepare both short- and longer-term actions. This is illustrated in Fig. 2.5 by the arrow in the fourth phase of the model leading on to the next challenge for the professional communicator, where the strategic analysis is the starting point once more. The work phases thus follow a circular movement and illustrate how a systematic approach to your own work processes is a way of ensuring that as a professional communicator you take responsibility in a complex reality.

2.5 Case 1. In Maersk's Communicative Engine Room

In this case, we open the doors to Maersk's communication engine room to share examples of considerations and dilemmas, ambitions and challenges, solutions and effects. The aim is not to highlight Maersk's way of communicating as an ideal but to inspire and concretise the theory through cases, interviews and examples from the day-to-day work of a communications function.

In order to understand the reality from which the examples are drawn, this case is initiated by a brief description of A. P. Møller—Maersk. Maersk is a global container and logistics company with over 100,000 employees in more than 130 countries. Maersk's strategy is to uphold, digitise and decarbonise its global supply chains, supporting its more than 100,000 customers with integrated logistics solutions at sea, on land and in the air.

Since 2016, the more than 100-year-old company has been undergoing a profound transformation from a conglomerate focused on transport, logistics, energy and energy-related businesses to an integrated container logistics company. The transport part of Maersk is typically associated with the giant blue container ships, but the strategic transformation has made Maersk much more than that, as there has been significant growth in land-based logistics to support customers' door-to-door transport needs. The strategy has fundamentally changed the company's business model, focus and skills mix. The organisation is in constant movement and development, so check out the current key figures here: https://www.maersk.com/about, or read more about Maersk's history here: https://www.maersk.com/about/our-history

The communications function has been an active part of this transformation and has itself changed significantly in recent years—both because of the internal transformation in the organisation in order to best support the process and because of changes in the mediatised melting pot of the outside world that a communications function must navigate. The following sections provide insight into the role the communications function at Maersk plays in making a difference and give examples of what they are working on in concrete terms.

Maersk's global communications function has around 70 employees located both at the head office in Copenhagen and around the world, for example in Singapore, Panama, China, India and the USA. The communications function has actively chosen not to formulate a specific communication strategy. Instead, they insist that Maersk as a company has only one strategy—the business strategy—and the communications department's task is to communicate and support it. This is a managerial move to help ensure that everyone in the department is committed to knowing and understanding the business strategy, and that everything the department does is aimed at supporting the same priorities and direction. The strategy is, of course, translated into positions and messages that can be communicated, and each communicator performs the role taking into account both the strategic direction and the current situation and part of the organisation he/she supports.

Overall, the department's external role is to protect and enhance the reputation of the organisation so that there is trust in the company and its ability to deliver on its strategy, live up to its purpose and be a responsible workplace and corporate citizen. Internally, it is particularly about creating an understanding of the business, priorities, customers and ensuring culture-bearing, engaging and relevant content through effective and skilful management communication and internal mass media. Communicators must provide the right infrastructure for top-down, dialogue-based and community-based communication and consult with leaders on how they and their messages are best understood and received. Looking at the communicator's function in the context of the theory from this chapter, the areas of responsibility cover all four strategic perspectives from Falkheimer and Heide (2018) with organisational effectiveness, transparency, image and organisational identity. The four flows (Feldner & Fyke, 2018) with institutional positioning, activity coordination, member negotiation and self-structuring are also in focus, although with the HR function as the central, responsible actor in relation to some of the self-structuring, e.g. feedback systems, where the communications function is more advisory.

As a communicator at Maersk, you are thus in play both in the personal one-on-one sparring and in the grand narrative of the company when the strategy is to be translated into effective communication. That is why the development of the business must also be constantly reflected in the organisation and work of the communications function, and this requires constant adaptation.

'A communications function must be a mirror of the organisation so it facilitates the development that has been decided for the business. But it must also be a mirror of the demands and opportunities of the outside world, so it requires a constant readiness to change the organisation and ways of working and living', stresses Mette Refshauge, who has been Director of Communications at Maersk since 2017.

In concrete terms, this has meant very significant changes in recent years, because Maersk as a business has changed significantly. From a diverse conglomerate, the business has undergone a strategic transformation into an integrated transport and logistics company that supports customers' global supply chains from factory to consumer. As part of this, all parts of the business have become even more aware of how they contribute to helping customers get their goods smoothly from a to b. This requires, amongst other things, an efficient network and IT solutions that make things as simple as possible and provide customers with insight into their supply chains. At the same time, Maersk has taken responsibility for the green transition in the industry and has stepped up significantly on the climate agenda. These transformations require a colossal change on many fronts, and Maersk must both *find* and *lead* the way in an industry that is neither particularly digital nor climate-friendly. The digital and green ambitions have required some changes both in the core processes of the business and in the company's positioning. At the same time, this transition has taken place at a time when the global supply chains that Maersk helps to keep going have climbed higher and higher up the strategic agenda of customers, politicians and in the public debate, partly as a result of the pandemic, macroeconomic and geopolitical changes. The other cases in the book provide examples of how Maersk has worked specifically to build trust in the strategy and give the company a credible voice on the business-critical agendas, whilst this chapter focuses on what this has meant for the organisation of the communications function and the way communicators work.

2.5.1 A Changing Communications Function

As Maersk was a conglomerate of many independent business areas, communication work was also organised in local departments. Each unit had its own skilled team that ensured competent communication in the individual areas.

'One of the first major tasks when Maersk decided to become a more collaborative global integrator was a necessary change in the whole way we worked and organised ourselves.' This was true for all staff areas: the business was in the process of transforming itself from large stand-alone units focused solely on, for example, ports, container shipping or land-based logistics, to an integrated company focused on supporting customers' supply chains across various transport and logistics needs. This meant that the staff areas also needed to have a cross-functional perspective and support the transformation towards—and the narrative of—the new Maersk. 'In the communications function, we thus brought together a number of independent departments into one global function and defined a direction that was directly dictated by the strategy of becoming 'The Global Integrator of Container Logistics',' says Mette Refshauge.

At the same time, the rapid transformation of media, communication, channels and audiences had to be taken into account: 'The pace of change in the organisation and the demands for speed from the world at large made it essential to make another very big change. It became increasingly important to be able to deliver with a minimum of production time and across formats, channels and stakeholders. This was difficult because we were organised in a number of specialist functions, some in an advisory role and others primarily in a production role. Initially, we talked a lot about how we could all practise taking a 360-degree perspective on our work, so our content was published in more than one format and to all relevant audiences with a minimum of hand-offs, without compromising on pace or quality. The massive changes internally and the rapid evolution of communication formats and channels as such called for a new way of working', Mette Refshauge explains.

After a while, it became clear that this also required organisational changes, so both the entirely advisory function and the production unit were closed down. The new communications function was set up to deliver solutions and advice in one singular effort. At the same time, the last analogue formats were phased out and replaced by digital and social formats. This is exemplified in Fig. 2.6.

2.5 Case 1. In Maersk's Communicative Engine Room

Fig. 2.6 A former analogue product—Maersk Post—and a screenshot from the One Maersk intranet

Covid-19 meant a virtual quantum leap for all organisations, including Maersk, and accelerated the evolution of the communications function. Everyone became more self-reliant on digital channels, and the ability to position oneself and build relationships virtually became even more crucial in relation to employees, customers, talent and society at large. In the first lockdown, it was mostly about getting by with the art of the possible, whilst later it became important to develop and refine the skills and formats and raise the standard of virtual positioning, communication and collaboration.

The next major organisational change was closely linked to the demands for a new and different organisational presence. The world's demands on organisations have changed, just as trust in the media has changed. The possibilities for stepping out yourself have multiplied, and naturally this has also meant changes for the communicators at Maersk.

'To drive the change in our organisation, we need to, for example, step up as thought leaders, also on a technological agenda that has not necessarily been traditionally associated with a shipping company. This means that we as communicators have had to facilitate more organisational voices in the public sphere', says Mette Refshauge. This change has meant a conscious effort to take co-responsibility for orchestrating all organisational voices across platforms. It has also meant that communicators have had to take on many new roles, such as hosting internal or external events, where they have had to moderate profound conversations, or they have been sparring partners and coaches for spokespersons who have had to learn to present themselves in completely new ways in a new public sphere. Communicative tasks have placed entirely new demands on the communicators at Maersk.

At the same time, the changing media landscape, with less trust in the media and the increasing emergence of own channels, has made entirely new ways of working possible. 'Roughly speaking, today anyone with a mobile phone is their own channel—and so are companies. At Maersk, we have more followers than most media, e.g. 1.5 million people follow us on LinkedIn right now', says Mette Refshauge.

Maersk actively considers all channels and evaluates and experiments with what works. The multiplicity of channels and the move towards developing their own channels meant another reorganisation of the work, where the boundaries between strategy, consulting and production had to be further broken down, whilst traditional channel responsibilities had to be rethought.

'We had already been working for a long time with a so-called 'newsroom approach', where we published across channels. One example is the mention of our rainbow containers, which travel around the world across all channels from social media to pitching press reviews and internal news on our internal social media. But it also applies when we publish financial statements, announce acquisitions or other news. Cross-channel collaboration is natural and useful for both impact and efficiency. We were still to some extent organised around channels, but a future-proof set-up had to be channel-independent. Simply because the pace at which communication channels come and go will only accelerate in the future', Mette Refshauge elaborates.

Maersk's messages of diversity and inclusion have been symbolised by a rainbow container that has travelled the world. The content has been used across all platforms, as shown in the collage in Fig. 2.7.

The recent organisational change in the communications function is a consequence of the desire for even more interaction across all platforms and channels, so the traditional disciplines such as internal communication and branding have changed to form a more cross-cutting and process-oriented organisation. This transition is an attempt to move even closer to the organisation's need to position itself as a thought leader and emerge as its own channel with a connection to all key stakeholders.

The evolution of the communications function can be summarised as a move from local to global, from classic production processes to real-time solutions and towards an integrated newsroom approach, as shown in the model here:

Figure 2.8 shows that the communications function was initially organised into local units supporting each business area. It then followed the evolution of the organisation and supported the ambitions of a global logistics integrator by forming one global function. Next, the speed of change and channel development meant a greater focus on 'instant production' in a shared newsroom, and most recently, the

Fig. 2.7 Examples of Maersk's 'newsroom approach' across channels and platforms in relation to rainbow containers

2.5 Case 1. In Maersk's Communicative Engine Room

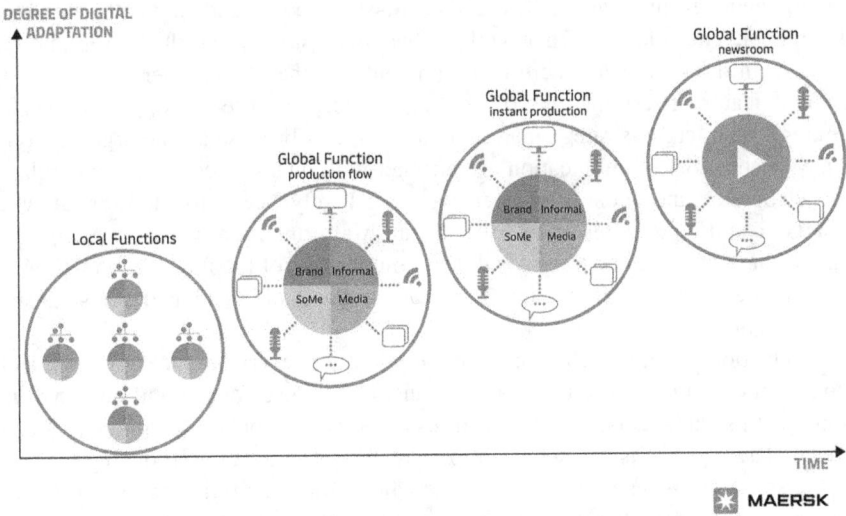

Fig. 2.8 Visualisation of the transformation of Maersk's communication function

virtual quantum leap with a fully integrated view of communication across internal and external channels and a focus on Maersk as a channel has brought new changes.

2.5.2 The DNA of a Communicator at Maersk

The rapid development of communication as a field of competence and education is evident in the way communication departments organise themselves and in the profiles emerging from the various communication programmes. A couple of decades ago, communication started to climb up the strategic agenda and many higher education institutions started to include different types of academic communication programmes in their curricula. Until then, it had mainly been more practically orientated journalism schools that trained communicators. 'In my experience, the practical and theoretical skills have been drifting apart for a number of years. Many departments have even organised the two skills into separate teams. But for the communicators of the future, mastering both is a must', emphasises Mette Refshauge.

'In my view, as communicators, we simply risk making ourselves irrelevant if we don't take pride in mastering the craftsmanship side of things', emphasises Mette Refshauge. 'It is very easy to read whether a communicator is trained in the craftsmanship when it comes to production. A too one-sided focus on the strategic advisor role entails a potential lack of concrete solutions, which imposes a risk that the solution is neither really helpful nor fast enough for the pace at which the organisation works today. A deep, theoretical foundation underpinning the advisor role is important, but if you can't simultaneously turn around and put together your recommended solution yourself, you'll be too slow, too dependent on others and too theoretical. The role of advisor without backbone skills in production is just not enough. In the same way, there is an inherent risk that the unilaterally producing communicator undermines his or her importance, because the opportunities for linking to the larger, strategic narrative are lost, and because all the organisation's many wishes for communication are not met with qualified co- and counterplay', she elaborates and adds: 'And then we have barely begun to think about what ChatGPT and other AI assistants will mean. Mastering AI at work is certainly an independent competence track for the communicators of the future, who will soon have no idea what we mean when we talk about good, old-fashioned craftsmanship in production'.

Production is not detached but integrated into the everyday maelstrom of decisions and executions. The organisation must be in close contact and ongoing dialogue with stakeholders, and this requires a communicator who is not only able to create classic products, but who can to a greater extent act as a producing function in the sense of orchestrating. A producer who ensures the right production by, for example, supporting the communication of others, facilitating a meaningful dialogue or delivering a classic communicative product such as a presentation, a video or an article. That is why Maersk has chosen to call their communicators' approach to the task solution the '**strategic producer**' to emphasise the connection between strategic anchoring and good communicative solutions. This fusion is described as a merged DNA, where production and advice meet in the role of strategic producer, as illustrated in Fig. 2.9.

Figure 2.9 emphasises that a strategic producer takes responsibility for the entire communicative process and switches between advisory and productive roles on an ongoing basis. This does not mean that communicators always do everything themselves, but they take responsibility—sometimes on their own and sometimes through collaboration—for all the various steps in the value chain. The following sections illustrate with a few examples how the strategic producer can work at Maersk.

MIND THE GAP BETWEEN STRATEGY AND EXECUTION

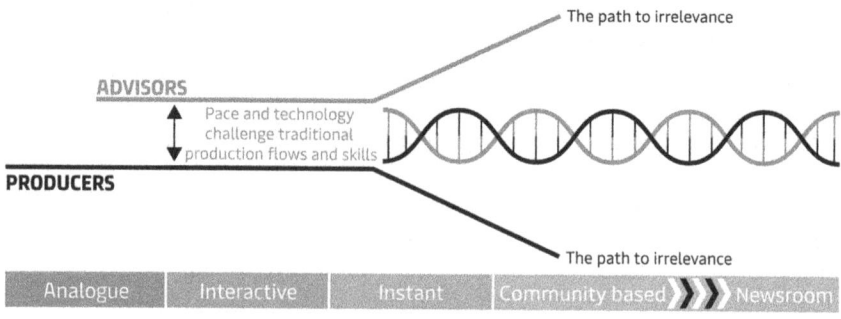

Fig. 2.9 DNA of the strategic producer

2.5.3 The Viral Maersk Shoes

An example of how the strategic producers at Maersk work is the story of a pair of shoes: the customer's shoes (Fig. 2.10). Here, the communicators at Maersk were not just acting as producers or as advisors. They were both and more: Strategic producers who, with courage and creativity, tried to concretise Maersk's new strategy very literally.

Maersk's work on culture and strategy means placing the customer centre stage. That is why the organisation thought creatively about how they could raise internal awareness of this in a special way. The idea for the specific proposal came from a slightly unusual angle. 'Puma is one of Maersk's major customers—and at a meeting with our then CEO of Ocean & Logistics, Vincent Clerc, their CEO had jokingly made a slide with a picture of a pair of Maersk-blue Puma shoes with the Maersk seven-pointed star logo on them. Vincent was quick to ask if they could supply 150,000 pairs so the whole organisation could literally walk in the customer's shoes', says Sam Poulter, Head of Corporate Branding & Channel Development. The Maersk Blue shoes were secretly put into production in the run-up to a major conference for Maersk's top 1200 executives in 2022, where the company's updated purpose would be launched. The participants would be the first to be presented with the shoes. 'It was a new type of task to get them designed so they lived up to our brand and are, for example, produced in our own blue colour', says Anja Andersen, who suddenly, in addition to her work as Head of Brand Management, can now also add shoe designer to her CV. 'The aim was for the shoe to be a tongue-in-cheek literal concretisation of our ambitions', says Sam Poulter, who explains that one of the reasons they thought it was an idea that would work at Maersk was that employees are generally very proud to work there. 'We have a very strong culture, and we can see that as employees we generally value corporate merchandise, so we were hoping that we could hit on something with the shoe that would be really appreciated and used, but we honestly had no idea that it was going to be as successful as we can now see externally', emphasises Sam Poulter. This is an example of how the starting point for a communication task is anchored organisationally with a cultural

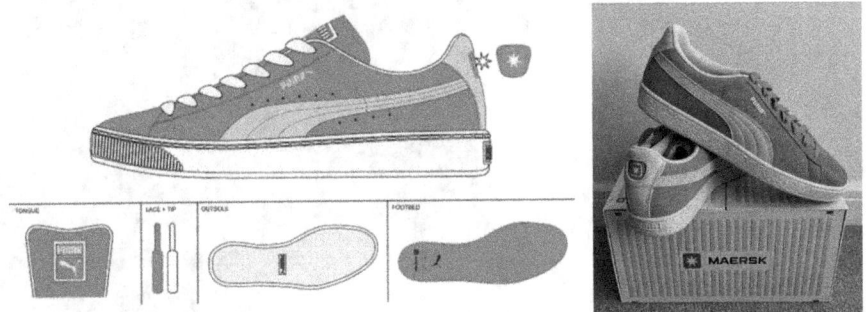

Fig. 2.10 The viral Maersk shoes

understanding of what can inhibit or promote an ambition by having insight into employees' views on artefacts, values and basic assumptions. Three organisational levels, which are described in more detail in the chapter's theoretical introduction.

The launch was by no means left to chance. It wasn't just a pair of shoes for each leader. The shoes had to be presented in conjunction with the strategically important messages from the stage. 'Vincent Clerc was to launch it in his speech in front of the 1,200 managers (see Figs. 2.11, 2.12 and 2.13). He has been the driving force in the transformation to make the whole of Maersk more customer-centric. The launch had to happen with a bang, so that it got the focus—and yet also be sneaked in with a little communication cunning. We didn't want it to take the focus away from the big launch of our updated purpose', says Sam Poulter. The right combination of spokesperson, timing and staging ensures both weight and impact for the individual message, and the communicator helps to facilitate that the message gets across more effectively. 'The solution was a carefully considered launch, with Vincent Clerc wearing the shoes as he began his big speech. In the auditorium, people started to notice his footwear, but it wasn't pointed out.'

Poulter continues: 'When the shoes were finally presented in the presentation—with a nice 360-degree film of the shoes shown on the many screens behind and around the entire stage—the response was overwhelming. People laughed and cheered at the same time, and many pulled out their phones and took pictures that were immediately shared on social media. It was exactly the shared ownership and celebration we had hoped for, and when most of the senior managers turned up later

Fig. 2.11 Maersk's CEO, Vincent Clerc, wearing Maersk shoes

Fig. 2.12 Maersk's CEO, Vincent Clerc, wearing Maersk shoes

Fig. 2.13 Top managers at Maersk wearing Maersk shoes

that evening in their new shoes, it gave a sense of shared identity that we honestly hadn't anticipated or planned for. Imagine more than 1000 colleagues heading to dinner in the same blue shoes', laughs Sam Poulter. That was the day the Maersk shoe went viral, but that was just the beginning.

The viral journey for the shoes was kicked off with the leaders' photos from the hall. Many posted, and it was seen by a lot of people in the first few days alone. 'It went better than we had dared to hope', says Sam Poulter, who was particularly pleased that so many of the posts reflected the joy and pride the managers have in being part of Maersk. 'The shoes became an opportunity for very authentic posts that do everything we want to do on social media. Not just claiming something clever but showing authentic Maersk DNA'. The strategic producers kept an eye on what was happening and tracked whether any adjustments or additions needed to be made.

The shoe was also launched on internal channels to the rest of the 100,000-plus employees (Fig. 2.14). 'It was important that we declared right away that this was not a management favour, but something for all of us', says Sam Poulter. 'So Maersk's communications functions made sure that there was a clear message that

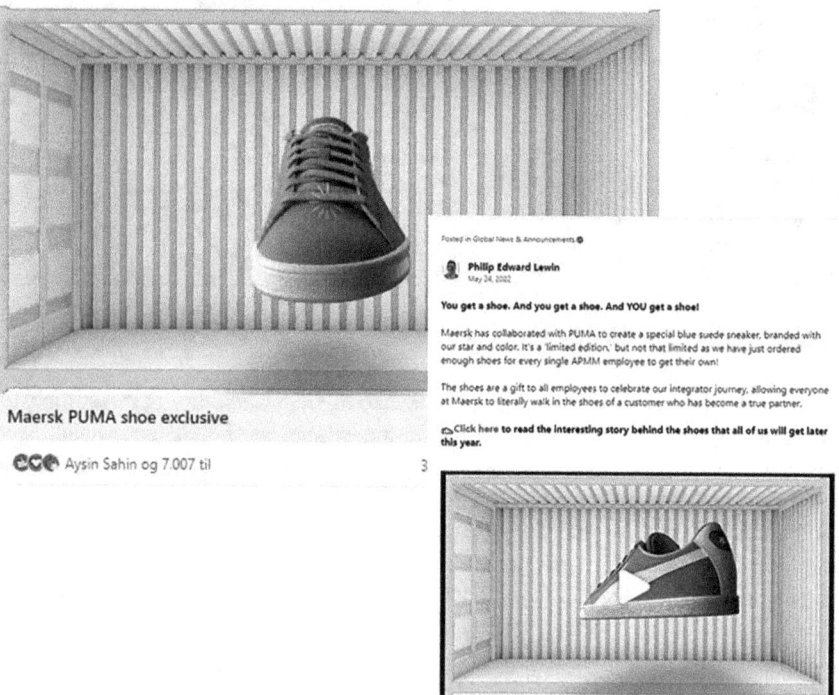

Fig. 2.14 Extracts from internal publicity

they would also come, in the right size, for all of us'. The article became one of the most widely read and the film was seen by many internally. The shoes became very popular. So popular, in fact, that Sam Poulter has been surprised by how time-consuming the effort has been. 'Almost a year went by where we were still almost acting as the customer service in a shoe shop, and we spent a lot of time on the administrative side. Still, it's quite a task to fit over 150,000 people in over 130 countries with the right size of Maersk shoes'.

The press also picked up the story because it was a funny story (Fig. 2.15). 'Again, it was something we might have thought but not taken for granted', says Sam Poulter, 'but it's an echo chamber effect that can sometimes happen. Our social media are also followed by a lot of journalists, so it's not surprising that they come across this funny story'. It was not just in the Danish press.

The shoes are travelling far and wide. When the shoe boxes arrive at our colleagues' homes, many choose to share posts of themselves wearing the shoes. 'So far, we have actually reached much further with this story than we had thought. We have countless posts of Maersk shoes being unwrapped and photographed all over the world: Maersk shoes in front of the Arc de Triomphe, Maersk shoes on their way up mountainsides, Maersk teams at work in their shoes, even colleagues' dogs and cats wearing the blue shoes. It's a great example of going all the way with a single good idea, but there's also a lot of luck involved. Will you strike a shared sense of pride and a desire to share it or not? It wasn't just a clever idea, it was an idea rooted in our senior management, our strategy and our culture, but we were also lucky that it became almost cult', concludes Sam Poulter, who is himself regularly seen wearing the blue shoes at the head office at Esplanaden in Copenhagen.

As an artefact, the shoe has also become the starting point for the strategic producers' launch of the latest update of the business strategy (Fig. 2.16). This has built on the ownership and popularity of the blue shoe to spread the messages of the updated strategy and emphasise that it is a continuation of the journey Maersk is already on.

2.5.4 Relational Work of Strategic Producers

Advising managers is a central part of the work of Maersk's communicators. The communication advisors are ready as soon as there are changes and challenges. But it is not only when the organisation is under external or internal pressure that the advisors are needed. 'We are keen that there are also strong advisor relationships in everyday life, so we help managers succeed in communicating with all stakeholders, both when they ask for it and when we think it is needed', says Jesper Løv, Head of Media Relations & Leadership, whose team of communicators includes press officers, change specialists and internal communicators. In other words, Maersk's communicators must work to create open and trusting relationships, which corresponds to level 2 in Schein's description of relationship levels, so that the relationships are not just transactional in nature at Schein's level 1. They must be able to help both proactively and reactively.

A good example of the importance of open and trusting relationships in communication work might be reporting to the Maersk Executive Board. Here, there is plenty of daily sparring and assistance, but monthly planning and reporting are also

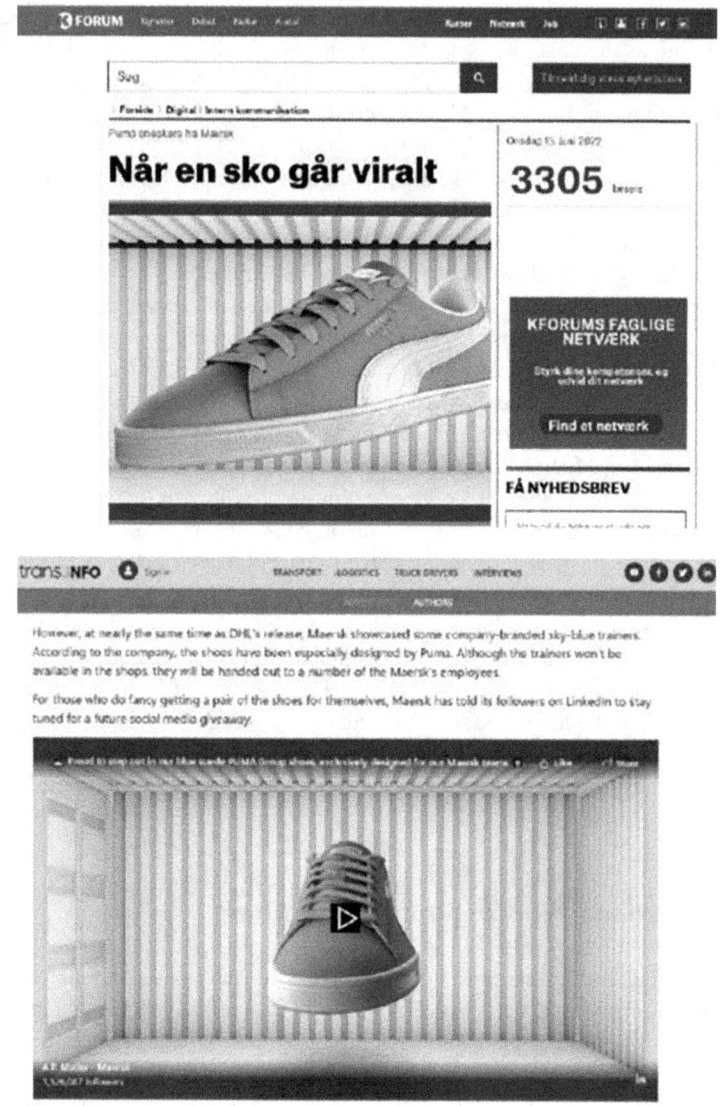

Fig. 2.15 Press coverage of the Maersk shoe

in focus. 'It's a good way to be accountable for the impact of our efforts and take a joint look at what's in store for the coming month. It also helps to ensure that we don't get so caught up in ad hoc tasks that we forget to focus on the longer-term perspective. We need to make sure we systematically evaluate and talk about our long-term ambitions', says Jesper Løv.

Thus, monthly reports look both forwards and backwards: what is going to happen? What are the risks, for example in the media context? What does the data show

2.5 Case 1. In Maersk's Communicative Engine Room

Fig. 2.16 The Maersk shoes as an artefact in updating the business strategy

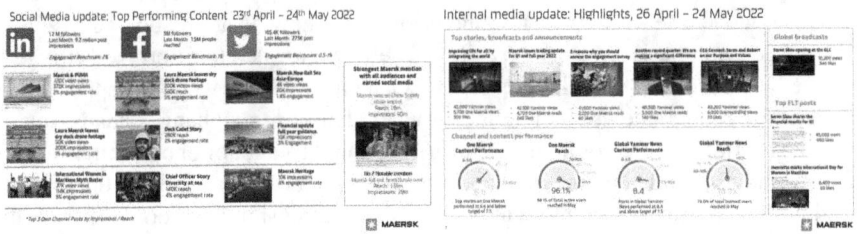

Fig. 2.17 An example of reporting from social and internal media that forms part of the data basis for communication decisions at Maersk

about how things are going and what may need preparation (Fig. 2.17)? 'It is as much a discussion of risks and potentials for the coming period, so we have aligned expectations in the short, medium and long term. It's important so the Executive Board knows what we might need to involve them in, and they are not unnecessarily surprised by anything that happens'.

Communicators must use both their professionalism and their professional judgement to anticipate stakeholder responses. 'It's clearly part of our job to bring those perspectives to the table. It can be difficult for colleagues elsewhere in the organisation to assess what is relevant to, for example, the public. An issue may be of critical importance within the walls, but if it doesn't have a news hook or speaks to a larger, current agenda, for example, it's not something we can position Maersk on externally. The opposite may certainly also be the case—that something that is seen as almost a trifle internally can have great external potential. These conversations are important to have as an advisor, so you do your part in creating the necessary awareness among internal stakeholders of how the world looks through the eyes of external stakeholders', elaborates Jesper Løv, who bases his forecasts on hard data from e.g. social media activity, press clippings and internal statistics but also on his professional judgement from many years of experience with organisational interaction in a large organisation.

When advising, the relational aspect is essential. Maersk prioritises that the communicators build good relationships with the internal advisors by thoroughly familiarising themselves with the specialist areas, regularly evaluating the collaboration and participating in external presentations and other such specific initiatives. This is partly because it is important that communication advisors build up the necessary knowledge of the individual business areas in order to be able to help in the best possible way, and partly because following advice requires trust between advisor and advisee. Especially the unexpected advice, such as when someone just pokes their head into your office, or those who comment on the personal execution of the communication. 'It's important for me to always emphasise to my staff that it's not just about being excellent professionally. You have to be that too. But you also have to be good at building trusting relationships and remember to prioritise that. This is the part of the job that is the hardest to put into a formula and has a lot to do with personality and the ability to put yourself in someone else's shoes, see the situation from someone else's point of view and be aware of how what you do or say will be perceived', emphasises Jesper Løv. He himself has just had to prioritise getting off to the best possible start with the new CEO, Vincent Clerc, who was appointed at Maersk in 2023. 'The good thing is that when that position changes hands, lots of good opportunities for communication arise—and thus a lot of opportunities to step in as an advisor and build the relationship. So it's important to seize that opportunity and put some extra effort into making sure the relationship is a good one from the start. And it will only be good if you really invest in it'.

'The change of director was to some extent a surprise externally, certainly the timing. We knew that the outside world had speculated from time to time about when it would happen. So it was important, for example, for us to show that it was a unified management team, with the chairman of the board, former and current CEO standing shoulder-to-shoulder and conveying a coherent story (Fig. 2.18). Here, as communicators, we need to be able to predict what signal value we can achieve in the organisation itself, so there are no myths or grounds for speculation about the motives or reasons other than the actual ones behind an event, such as a

Fig. 2.18 Press conference on the occasion of the change of CEO in Maersk with the chairman of the board, the outgoing and the incoming CEO

change of CEO. In our case, it was crucial that this 'breaking news' became an undramatic story about a change of CEO well planned by the board, about new times but also about continuity, and that both the outgoing and the new CEO were seen as the 'right man at the right time", says Jesper Løv.

In addition to orchestrating the overall communication, a communicator must also be able to find and improve the individual expression of each person. That is why a change of CEO often means a new focus for some of the personalised advice. Exactly what kind of support is needed? What are the work methods, and how and when is the best way to help? 'As an advisor, you always have to focus on the person, so when we get a new person in at the top, we have to find out how best to support them. Now Vincent Clerc was not new to us, he has been with Maersk for over 20 years, but the role is new, and as advisors we thus have to focus on how we can best help him'. It can be very specific things that need to be communicated. For example, a Swiss CEO may need a deeper introduction to the Danish media landscape, the individual media or the journalist prior to an interview. It may also be about the communication style. Vincent Clerc would like to be a bit more informal in internal communication, signalling both a change of gear and continuity. Specifically, for example, speed was more important to him than long, elaborate planning when he changed the organisation shortly after taking office. There were still many open questions that he was still working to clarify. That's why, for example, he addressed the organisation directly from his own desk rather than from a staged studio. 'It's often a matter of minor nuances, but it makes a difference that you are aware of them and hit the mark in your briefings and recommendations from the start', emphasises Jesper Løv.

2.5.5 A Communicative Quantum Leap in Progress

'We have called our own change process in communication nothing less than a quantum leap, driven by the ambitions of the business strategy and by the accelerated development of new channels, technologies and a changing media landscape. All this has accelerated the need to develop communication skills and a shared understanding of how we—and Maersk—meet future expectations of a communicating organisation', Mette Refshauge emphasises. This is not something Maersk has demanded that all communicators should be able to do straight away. The development into a strategic producer has been part of an ambitious skills development programme, where communicators have gained a shared approach and have been able to tailor elements to improve themselves where it was most relevant individually. The task has been approached from several angles. First through individual skill development, then through collaboration processes, channels and formats, and finally by changing the organisation. The whole development towards mastering the role of the strategic producer is neither simple nor done. It is ongoing, and every single communicator in Maersk is on their toes to live up to and execute the shared ambitions by looking at their own habits, skills and behaviour in the everyday routines of a busy, global organisation.

2.6 Interview. With Symmetry as a Goal

Few have influenced both research and practice in communication for a lifetime the way theorist James Grunig has. From his armchair in Maryland, he is looking back and ahead and maintains that, whilst the world is spinning and digital media are changing, communicators still need to focus on behaviour, relationships and symmetry. He has proven that in his research.

'I was in the classroom in a public relations course at the University of Wisconsin taught by Scott Cutlip, who wrote one of the first textbooks on public relations and is widely recognised as the father of public relations education in the United States. Professor Cutlip passionately drew an arrow at one end of a communication model, by the sender in the model, and wrote "one-way". Then he drew one more "one-way" by the receiver, and then he looked at us with a fixed gaze and said: But PR has to be a two-way practice'. Grunig smiles at the thought, but it was right there, as a young PhD student in mass communication, that he saw the light: Symmetry in communication between stakeholders became the focus of all his subsequent, world-famous work. Communication is not from and to someone but between someone. It sounds simple, but it is not, and even in an age where digital communication has turned receivers into co-producers, the communication guru believes that we are far from achieving true symmetry.

'Unfortunately, too many people still have an asymmetric focus on communication. Too many senders see receivers as targets to be targeted and influenced. But my research has clearly shown that it is neither useful nor effective', the professor stresses.

In general, James Grunig gets annoyed when he sees examples of an overly narrow definition of creating necessary, strong relationships with all stakeholders. 'It's not about convincing—not by raising awareness, changing attitudes or behaviour. This gets far too much attention in research and practice. Great public relations are based on thorough research and knowledge both ways. It is symmetrical and requires organisational support; otherwise they often go back to thinking asymmetrically, prioritising what they themselves want to promote. But that is not good enough. Just as relationships can only be built if we base contact on genuine interpersonal communication mediated by the situation'.

2.6.1 Organisational Positioning Needed

A lifetime of research took him from acknowledging the need for symmetry that day in the classroom to, for example major studies of aspects that create excellence in communication. In collaboration with the International Association of Business Communicators (IABC) Research Foundation, he and fellow researchers spent 15 years analysing the characteristics of effective public relations work in organisations.

'We found many key findings in the extensive research, but without doubt the most powerful prerequisite for effective PR work was rooting it in a strategic leadership role within the organisation', James Grunig says emphatically. 'It's crucial that it's not about sending out a lot of messages but rather about working strategically to cultivate relationships. The work can therefore not be rooted peripherally in the organisation but close to the senior management'. We may take that knowledge for granted today, but back in the early 1990s it was a very uncommon insistence from a field like communications and was far from recognised as strategically vital.

'Stakeholder work is really about joint problem solving', James Grunig stresses, 'not about sending a lot of messages back and forth but about working strategically to cultivate relations. Those problems usually have to be solved at the senior management desk'. He knows the practice well enough to know that this is easier said than done and reminds us that there is nothing like a crisis to create the necessary understanding of stakeholder work in senior management. Crises can make room at the right tables. It is about seizing the opportunities.

2.6.2 It Took a War

James Grunig's passion is evident. Not only does he have a lot of opinions, but he has done a lot of research. With the tenacity of a scientist, he has analysed, hypothesised, investigated and learned. He has enriched us with hundreds of publications based on that knowledge. But he laughs a little when we naively ask if he always knew that he was meant to do this very thing. He grew up on a farm in the countryside and, together with his older brother, was the first in the family to get a higher education. His focus was a bit random in terms of proximity to home and heart. Agriculture, economics, journalism. And then he was supposed to be done with 'that education stuff' and had settled into a nice communications job in the food industry in Chicago.

But then the Vietnam War began; a war he opposed. Nevertheless, he was 2 days away from being drafted and could only get out if he was in the process of training. So, with the drive that has always characterised him, he immediately explored all opportunities, and in no time, he was back in academia and had an agreement for a research career with PhD studies at the University of Wisconsin. For his dissertation, he conducted research on the communication behaviours of both large landowners and peasant farmers in the South American country of Colombia. Here, he examined, amongst other things, the communication attempts to disseminate knowledge about new agricultural techniques to farmers. This was something that succeeded to only a very limited extent, precisely because communication was asymmetric and sender-oriented. The way had been paved for his fundamental focus on symmetrical communication and a long research career.

2.6.3 Essential Receptiveness

James Grunig is very well aware that he has been criticised by other researchers over the years for being too organisation-focused, even though he insists that his theories are focused on publics. So there is extra keenness in his eyes when he stresses that you cannot have too much focus on the organisation: You just cannot have *only* that. A symmetrical perspective goes both ways, so the interest must never be one-sided.

> Listening to your stakeholders is crucial. We must always conduct research that can be carried into the organisation and ensure the right basis for decision-making. Decisions must always be based on a genuine understanding of stakeholders.

'All things being equal, listening should be somewhat easier in modern times, considering all the big data that is available', the professor says with a smile. He believes that listening is not being prioritised enough in research and practice, even though it has been documented as a gap in research since Jim Macnamara of Australia demonstrated it in a book written in 2016.

'We need to have a better understanding of listening properly. That issue has not become less important in the polarised world we live in', the professor stresses. He is pleased that several of his former research students have set out to gain an understanding of how conspiracy theory communities are created. 'We have to insist on understanding relationships, understanding trust, understanding the challenges of communicating symmetrically with each other. It takes for us to listen—and to be aware of the best way of listening'. This also underlines James Grunig's fundamental awareness that PR can contribute not only to interaction between organisations and media but between people in democracies.

2.6.4 Be Curious and Inquiring

The field is broad when it comes to the discussion of where to get knowledge and skills when developing stakeholder work in the attentive organisation. James Grunig himself has always made sure that his own expertise is complemented by others, and he has not just looked narrowly at his own field of research. 'For example, I was very much inspired to understand stakeholders better by taking an interest in cognitive psychology', he says.

Another field that has always interested James Grunig a lot is problem solving: What is it based on, what does it require, how is it facilitated? He has also naturally drawn a lot of knowledge, tools and awareness from management theory: 'It made me much wiser about a lot of things to which the other competencies can contribute but also much wiser about ways in which we can contribute, ways that they don't see. After all, it's that curiosity about each other that drives genuine understanding and develops something that can make a difference'.

James Grunig fundamentally believes that education must ensure that we master the ever-increasing research-based knowledge within the field: 'In my view, the most important characteristics of today's and tomorrow's professionals are that they familiarise themselves with all this knowledge. The subject has been misunderstood at a time when we may not have had the necessary professional knowledge on which to base our work and recommendations. But we now have that knowledge. We must not let a few practitioners who forget ethics and only look at efficiency discredit the high professionalism and usefulness of good public relations'.

If we are to succeed in communicating on the basis of Grunig's symmetrical model, our mindset must be open, curious, systematically investigative and problem-solving. 'We must dare to be open and investigative in our approach to all stakeholders in order to ensure the right knowledge on which to base our communicative solutions, just as we must always be progressive in our search for solutions so that we make specific contributions as communicators. This combination will also strengthen the understanding and recognition of the communication profession—especially if, along the way, we remember to act responsibly and to explain the value of our work to both the organisation and the outside world. Respect for our professionalism should preferably increase. Good communication is very much needed'.

It is easy to see that he himself has practised curiosity, thoroughness and orderliness for more than 50 years, during which he has been a leading researcher—and that it remains his focus, albeit a little more from his armchair as emeritus. Grunig is keeping an eye on whether we continue to keep symmetry in focus.

James Grunig

James Grunig, Professor Emeritus, Communication, University of Maryland

James Grunig is an award-winning academic who has pioneered theoretical and practical work within public relations. He is the author of more than 250 articles, books, chapters and reports. His works are cited worldwide, and he has lectured and shared his knowledge in more than 50 countries. His work has contributed with fundamental models to the understanding of PR, and his research has documented the importance of that very professionalism.

James Grunig has been awarded several prizes, including the Public Relations Society of America Outstanding Educator Award (1989), the Institute for Public Relations' Pathfinder Award (1984), Lifetime Award of the Association for Education in Journalism and Mass Communication (2000) and Paul J. Deutschmann Award for Excellence in Research (2000). He has received honorary doctorates from universities in Peru, Romania, Turkey and Canada.

References

Berger, K., Volk, S. C., Zerfass, A., & Koehler, K. (2017). How to play the game. Strategic tools for managing corporate communications. *Communication Insights*, Issue 3.

Brockhaus, J., Buhmann, A., & Zerfass, A. (2022). Digitalization in corporate communications: Understanding the emergence and consequences of CommTech and digital infrastructure. *Corporate Communications: An International Journal*. https://doi.org/10.1108/CCIJ-03-2022-0035

Cornelissen, J. P. (2020). *Corporate communication: A guide to theory & practice* (6th ed.). Sage.

Dozier, D. M. (1984). *Program evaluation and the roles of practitioners. Public relations review, 1984*.

Falkheimer, J., Heide, M., Simonsson, C., Zerfass, A., & Verhoeven, P. (2016). *Doing the right things or doing things right? Corporate Communications: An International Journal, 21*, 142–159. https://doi.org/10.1108/CCIJ-06-2015-0037

Falkheimer, J., & Heide, M. (2018). *Strategic communication: An introduction*. Routledge.

Feldner, S. B., & Fyke, J. P. (2018). Organisational communication. In R. L. Heath & W. Johansen (Eds.), *The international encyclopedia of strategic communication* (pp. 1–14). Wiley.

Gravengaard, G., Rendtorff, A. M., & Eiberg, K. (2022). *The communications advisor*. Samfundslitteratur.

Gregory, A., & Willis, P. (2013). *Strategic public relations leadership*. Routledge.

Grunig, J. E. (2018). Strategic behavioural paradigm. In R. L. Heath & W. Johansen (Eds.), *The international encyclopedia of strategic communication* (pp. 1–6). Wiley.

Heath, R. L., Cheney, G., & Ihlen, Ø. (2018). Identification, connection and division. In O. Ihlen & R. L. Heath (Eds.), *The handbook of organisational rhetoric and communication* (Handbooks in communication and media). Wiley.

Hoff-Clausen, E. (2018). Rhetorical agency: What enables and restrains the power of speech? In O. Ihlen & R. L. Heath (Eds.), *The handbook of organisational rhetoric and communication* (Handbooks in communication and media) (pp. 287–299). Wiley.

Lund, A. K., & Petersen, H. (2018). Advisor with impact: *The DNA of the effective advisor* (1st ed.). Gyldendal Business.

Lund, A. K., & Refshauge, M. (2023). *Strategisk kommunikation ipraksis*. Samfundslitteratur.

Macnamara, J., Lwin, M. O., Adi, A., & Zerfass, A. (2015). *Asia-Pacific Communication Monitor 2015/16. The state of strategic communication and public relations in a region of rapid growth. Survey results from 23 countries*. APACD.

Moreno, Á., Tench, R., & Verhoeven, P. (2021). Trust in public relations in the age of mistrusted media: A European perspective. *Publications (Basel), 9*(1), 7.

References

Moss, D. A., & Green, R. (2002). Re-examining the manager's role in public relations: What management and public relations research teaches us. *Journal of Communication Management, 6*, 118–132.

Mykkänen, M., & Vos, M. (2015). Contribution of public relations to organisizational decision making: Insights from the literature. *Public Relations Journal, 9*(2).

Robichaud, D., & Cooren, F. (2013). *Organization and organizing: Materiality, agency and discourse*. Routledge.

Schein, P. A. (2018). *Humble leadership: The power of relationships, openness, and trust*. Berrett-Koehler Publishers. ISBN 978-1523095384.

Steyn, B., & Everett, T. (2009). International comparative study indicates different PR roles in South Africa and the UK, using the same measuring instrument. *Trípodos, 24*, 95–105.

van Riel, C. B. M. (2012). *The alignment factor. Leveraging the power of total stakeholder support*. Routledge.

Zerfass, A., & Franke, N. (2013). Enabling, advising, supporting, executing: A theoretical framework for internal communication consulting within organisations. *International Journal of Strategic Communication, 7*(2), 118–135.

Zerfass, A., Stieglitz, S., Clausen, S., Ziegele, D., & Berger, K. (2021). *Communications trend radar 2021: Denialism, virtual corporate communications, sustainable communications, digital nudging & voice interaction* (IDEAS Working Paper Series from RePEc).

Credibility and Trust as a Field of Work 3

Credibility and trust are fundamental for us to listen to each other. But how do you work with this in practice as a professional communicator? In this chapter, we take a closer look at the elements of credibility and the points to bear in mind when working to build and protect the organisation's credibility in a transparent reality.

The case study in this chapter provides an insight into the complexity of managing a crisis that risks undermining the trust of key stakeholders.

The chapter's international reflections come from the world-renowned Professor Emeritus Robert L. Heath, who has a keen eye for and many good tips on how professional communicators work constructively with credibility in their relations with all stakeholders.

When trust and credibility are the foundation of all effective communication work, you might think that there would be a simple, well-documented approach to the work. Theoretically, however, trust and credibility are approached from many different perspectives. That is why this chapter contains some of the most important approaches from various disciplines, as the professional communicator must have a nuanced approach to both what strengthens the organisation's credibility and what risks undermining or may increase trust from stakeholders.

Credibility and trust are closely related but are nevertheless different concepts. Trust is something that a receiver has towards a sender. It is an 'attitude of positive expectations towards the behaviour of other people and is directed towards the future' (Hoff-Clausen, 2010: 55). Credibility, on the other hand, is a quality we attribute to and judge the sender to have 'based on impressions of past actions and current appearance' (ibid.: 55). This means that the professional communicator must work both to understand current trust and to develop the quality that establishes credibility so the organisation can gain future trust. We talk about gaining trust by presenting yourself as credible and about extending that trust by showing trust in others, thereby increasing mutual trust.

Credibility and trust support one another and both will thus in this chapter be integrated into the description of points of attention for the professional communicator.

Economic and social science approaches to trust distinguish between three types of trust:

1. Calculated trust based on a rational analysis in relation to utility (Lane, 1998): in other words, that it pays to trust.
2. Value- or norm-based trust based on a fundamental community and solidarity approach (Fukuyama, 1995): i.e. people share the same values and stand together in solidarity in a community.
3. Cognitive trust, where common cognitions are the foundation and common frameworks for understanding are embedded in expectations (Moreno et al., 2021): i.e. a similar view of the world means that you encounter it with the same expectations.

All three forms of trust can be constructive tools for the professional communicator, both when analysing trust and credibility in order to know whether there is, roughly speaking, an opportunity, a tailwind or a headwind for communication, and when organising practical communication. The professional communicator must be aware whether trust is present with the stakeholder before any communication—and what kind of trust is likely to be present. This will make it possible to identify what the communicator needs to maintain or expand in order to increase awareness, responsiveness and followership amongst stakeholders.

Communication work is much easier to carry out when trust is present, because there is responsiveness and the possibility of effective interaction with the stakeholder, as emphasised for example by Moreno: 'Where trust is present, possibilities for action and experience increase, bringing more complexity to the social system but also multiplying the number of possibilities to be reconciled with its structure. Thus, trust for a sociologist is the most effective way of reducing complexity' (Moreno et al., 2021: 3).

Research on organisational credibility from a public relations point of view thus views trust and credibility as a complex responsibility and field of work for professional communicators. From an organisational perspective, this is because nowadays an organisation is not only published on a few top-down channels, but every employee almost constitutes their own channel with the rise of social media. At the same time, media developments have also meant that more internal voices are speaking out on behalf of organisations. That is why there is a whole polyphony of internal voices that the communicator seeks to orchestrate. At the same time, external voices have also become far more numerous, because organisations today meet stakeholders on many different platforms, so external voices must be vigilantly watched, listened to and responded to on all channels and platforms.

So, when professional communicators have to take co-responsibility for the credibility of the organisation and the trust created with all stakeholders, it is increasingly a question of getting the orchestration of communication right. It is an impossible task to professionally manage and quality assure all communication. So, the communicator needs to look at how to better orchestrate an organisation's expression by, for example training managers and key employees to be skilled representatives of the organisation when they communicate. It is also an increasingly important task to ensure that it is easy for all internal stakeholders to communicate well and correctly, for example by making knowledge, arguments and infographics available to the organisation's potential ambassadors when communicating with external stakeholders.

Verhoeven and Madsen (2022) have defined eight roles that employees take on and which the strategic communicator can usefully work specifically to understand, inform, activate and manage:

The typology in Fig. 3.1 provides a nuanced image of the counter- and co-play of the internal stakeholders, who may help to work specifically to mobilise the internal archetypes in a wise manner. One example could be the critic. Sceptical internal voices are often a problem in external communication as well because they can directly undermine communication and act as external truth witnesses. Of course, muzzling employees is not an option in a country with freedom of speech, but the strategic communicator can be aware of the potential grounds for criticism and whether it could be prevented by communicating in a more nuanced way internally. For example, a sceptical employee will often be provoked by communication that can be perceived as assertive, salesy and justified in a superficial way. A communication style can easily arise when things are moving fast, and a management team may be more concerned with arguments for a decision, thus making the strategic space in the organisation too narrow. If the professional communicator helps to unfold the nuances and justifications internally and create space for discussion, the critical employees will gain a deeper understanding and perhaps a more nuanced expression of themselves.

Similarly, all kinds of employees can be identified as stakeholders for the professional communicator to ensure that internal communication includes what different employees need, so that they have the most nuanced basis on which to stand as ambassadors for the organisation.

In other words, the professional communicator must activate key internal stakeholders as voices for the organisation by ensuring that they have the knowledge and skills to communicate. A role that calls for the professional communicator's overview and ability to bring others into play rather than solely communicating on behalf of the organisation.

3.1 Trust Can Be (Re)Won

Trust is an expectation of stakeholders towards the communicator. An expectation is based on the experience that stakeholders have with the organisation/sender (McCroskey, 1982). In other words, trust is directed towards the future but based on the past. That is why we can talk about circular trust, which can be positive or negative. If we have positive expectations of senders, we listen willingly, but if we are

Communication role	Definition	Example of roles and concepts from literature
The embodier	Displaying organisational characteristics and values by embodying organisational traits through their communication and behaviour while doing their job	Brand ambassador, brand builder, organisational citizen behaviour, 'living the brand', responsible corporate citizen
The promotor	Strengthening corporate reputation by communicating positive messages about the organisation	Brand ambassador, brand builder, employee advocate
The defender	Defending the organisation against bad news or criticism from external stakeholders	Faith-holder, brand defender, crisis communicator
The relationship builder	Initiating, maintaining and improving shareholder relations	Boundary spanner, employer branding, CSR communicator, corporate employee volunteer
The scout	Gathering environmental information about organisational, societal and technological developments	Scouting organisational listening, knowledge sharer, knowledge broker
The sensemaker	Organising organisational and environmental information into comprehensible meanings/frames	Sense maker, narrator, storyteller, change agent
The innovator	Proactively coming up with new ideas and initiating organisational change	Entrepreneur, idea developer, innovator, co-creator, decision maker
The critic	Addressing shortcomings in the organisation (either internally or externally), by raising their voice to upper management, colleagues, social media or the press	Whistleblowing, employee voice, dissenter, hate holder, moral work climate

Fig. 3.1 A typology of employees' communicative roles. Madsen and Verhoeven (2019, 2022)

distrustful, we may not listen at all, or we may be prejudiced by bad experiences and thus treat every word with scepticism. Trust is 'given' to or placed in either a person (micro level), an organisation (meso level) or more broadly, for example in the structures of society (macro level) (Moreno et al., 2021).

Trust and credibility are essential for the cohesion of society and for the interaction between all stakeholders (Rawlins, 2007). Recent studies on trust show that this trust is increasingly challenged, resulting in distrust and increased polarisation on a global scale (Edelman, 2023). However, from an organisational perspective, the professional communicator should not perceive a trust challenge as an impossible headwind in communication work but instead, look at what can be done to work towards changing that expectation. In their book *The Power of Trust*, Sucher and Gupta (2021) dispel some of the myths that prevail in relation to trust work and indicate some ways of working constructively to (re)gain trust. This is shown in Table 3.1.

In debunking the myths, Sucher and Gupta help to define some areas of work for the professional communicator. They emphasise, for example that trust is not boundless but is created in defined relationships. So trust can be worked on within the relationship itself. Since trust is not objective but subjective and thus lies with the individual stakeholders, the communicator can work on how the organisation can earn more positive expectations by working on credibility. However, working on trust is not something that can be spun or marketed. It is about creating coherence between words and actions. In short: 'Be trustworthy and you will be trusted' (ibid.: 20).

Furthermore, in myth four, Sucher and Gupta dispel the notion that trust is something that can be earned by an organisation by having the right ambitions in, for example the organisational purpose. Stakeholders assess not only the organisation's ambitions but the difference they make—both intended and unintended.

The last myth that is challenged is precisely the core of communication work, namely that trust cannot be restored. It requires constant work to safeguard trust in words and actions: 'Building trust depends not on good PR but rather on clear purpose, smart strategy and definitive action. It takes courage and common sense. It requires recognising all the people and groups your company affects and focusing on serving their interests, not just your firm's. It means being competent, playing

Table 3.1 Overview of myths and reality

Myth	Reality
1. Trust has no boundaries	Trust is limited
2. Trust is objective	Trust is subjective
3. Trust is managed from the outside in—by controlling a firm's external image	Trust is managed from the inside out—by running a good business
4. Companies are judged for their purpose	Companies are judged for their purpose and their impact
5. Trust is fragile. Once lost, it can never be regained	Trust waxes and wanes

Source: Sucher and Gupta (2021)

fair and most of all, acknowledging and, if necessary, remediating, all the impact your company has, whether intended or not' (ibid.: 22).

3.2   Elements of Credibility

In the research on organisational trust, there are many operationalisations of the credibility that professional communicators can demonstrate in order to build trust with stakeholders. Key elements are openness and transparency, dialogue, corporate citizenship, credibility, reliability and goodwill (Moreno et al., 2021: 7).

An important characteristic of trust is that it is reciprocal. It is not only something the stakeholder meets the communicator with, but it is also something the communicator invites. Trust thus implies a reciprocity that arises relationally. Trust requires not only that the communicator seeks to ensure that words and actions are coherent, transparent and credible. The professional communicator must also ensure that the communication signals that they themselves meet all stakeholders with trust and thus invite reciprocity. As Rawlins emphasises: 'To gain this trust, one must trust others, because trust is reciprocal. One must also be trustworthy, which seems to be best measured by whether one is perceived as having competence, integrity, goodwill, reliability and is open. Caring about the needs of others, telling the truth and being dependable all increase trustworthiness. Trying to exert influence or pressure on others for the sake of meeting self-serving interests appears to damage trust' (2007: 11).

In short, the self-interested, know-it-all organisation is not capable of meeting its stakeholders with open trust and it is thus more difficult for them to trust it. So, it is also about mobilising responsiveness and contact in the communication itself, from content to form.

A key factor is transparency, which is defined as 'the perceived quality of the information a sender intentionally provides' (Schnackenberg & Tomlinson, 2016: 1789). The definition clarifies that it is the sender who chooses what is intentionally shared, but that it is the recipient who determines the 'perceived quality'. Information can be shared through many different channels, e.g. in financial statements, annual reports, official presentations and in contact with the press. This means that in assessing transparency, the stakeholder must look at many channels and be able to assess any distortion of the truth. Christensen and Cheney clarify the sharp focus on transparency: 'As organisational activity, transparency involves a host of practices such as disclosing, presenting, explaining, accounting, reporting and auditing. Investigating these practices as manifestations or mechanisms of the transparency pursuit helps us maintain a focus on the perils as well as on the promises of increased transparency. Potential perils relate to practices such as selecting, displaying, posing, framing, hiding and distorting, as well as observing, checking, (self)-controlling and monitoring. These practices are not accidental side-effects of an otherwise "pure" quest for knowledge and insight but inexorable dimensions of the transparency enterprise' (2015: 75).

The work of ensuring an organisation's transparency is thus not simple for the professional communicator. It is important to have a nuanced view of both

3.2 Elements of Credibility

verifiability and actions (Albu & Flyverbom, 2019) and of how to work on organisational transparency. For example, is transparency understood solely as sharing relevant information, or is there also a view of all the processes that must be linked to what is said in order to create credibility? Is transparency only viewed from a sender's perspective as a question of information quality, quantity and relevance of what is shared, or is there a focus on the experience itself and the negotiation process that is part of the interaction with the stakeholder? And are the possible consequences considered? Because being transparent can often mean potentially surprising complications (Albu & Flyverbom, 2019). So, the professional communicator must not only be able to figure out what is to be shared through which channels but also have an eye for how it will be perceived by stakeholders and in the context of the organisation's other actions. To put it somewhat plainly, you can claim, however, eloquently, that you are working with a focus on, for example employee well-being, but if examples of critical employee stories flourish on social media at the same time, then your credibility is threatened, and trust is at risk of being undermined.

It can be easy to get lost in the many parameters and divisions of the concept of credibility, but common to them all is that they must be viewed through a stakeholder prism: Trust is based on stakeholders' perception of credibility. That is why Sucher and Gupta (2019) suggest that the professional communicator looks at the concrete promises that you as a communicator make to your stakeholders. By looking at the promises, the professional communicator can gain insight into what expectations and obligations the promises create—and what it takes to fulfil them in words and actions. Table 3.2 summarises the fundamental promises.

The practical translation of a perhaps somewhat airy ambition to safeguard trust into a concrete look at the promises that the communicator may have made is a

Table 3.2 Fundamental business promises

Stakeholder	Economic promise	Legal promise	Ethical promise
Customers	To provide products and services that enhance their lives	To follow consumer protection laws and industry regulation	To make good on commitments To disclose risks To remediate mistakes made or harm done
Employees	To provide a livelihood (pay, benefits, training, opportunity)	To follow labour, antidiscrimination and workplace safety laws	To provide safe work conditions and job security To treat everyone fairly
Investors	To provide returns To manage risk	To fulfil fiduciary duties To disclose material information	To oversee employees' conduct To abstain from trading and self-dealing
Society	To offer employment and economic development To fulfil important needs	To follow local and federal laws To work with regulators	To protect public health, the environment and the local community To set industry standards

Source: Sucher and Gupta (2019)

fairly simple approach to work with as a professional communicator. What do stakeholders expect? Is there some kind of psychological contract with unwritten but concrete expectations (Schein, 1993)? The written or unwritten psychological contracts can become self-fulfilling prophecies (Rousseau, 1995), whether they are fair, just or something else entirely. If there is an expectation amongst stakeholders, the professional communicator must relate to it. It is in relation to this expectation that credibility is assessed and trust may be generated. This sometimes requires analyses of the stakeholders' experience, and it always requires conversations in which the communicator clarifies the expectations at stake and the implicit or explicit promises that the communication must address. This is the kind of knowledge and perspectives that the communicator must bring into a decision-making space, because many other disciplines may tend not to recognise it—not out of malice, but because the perspective is different.

3.3 Trust Is Challenged

International population surveys suggest that trust is generally declining in a wide range of areas. For 20 years, the global consultancy Edelman has been measuring trust in society with their 'Trust Barometer'. The survey is conducted in 28 countries, amongst over 36,000 respondents and with at least 1150 respondents from each country. The results in 2022 led to the title *The Circle of Mistrust* (Edelman, 2022). Edelman was able to document a growing distrust of media, which have lost both reputation and trust over many years due to 'fake news' and what is seen as a battle for attention and money with 'clickbait' and exaggerations. The data also showed that concern about fake news has never been higher. As many as 76% are concerned about fake news or false information being used as a weapon. Trust in social media, which has become an increasingly important source of information, is the lowest. But distrust in governments and public institutions has also grown. This trend continued in the Trust Barometer 2023 figures, where an increasing polarisation is evident due to increased economic uncertainty and institutional imbalances, amongst other factors. For the professional communicator, this data on trust is, of course, interesting in terms of media presence, for example but also because the data suggests that in a global society characterised by distrust and polarisation, there is a greater need for organisations to be clear voices in the world. Indeed, Edelman's Trust Barometer shows that in 2023, companies—compared to interest organisations, governments and media—are rated as the most trustworthy institutions.

Edelman calls the survey results a call from the public for businesses to step up: 'The Trust Barometer shows that, by an average five-to-one margin, respondents want business to play a bigger, not smaller, role on climate change, economic inequality, workforce reskilling and racial injustice. Every stakeholder group expects businesses to lean in—nearly 60 per cent of consumers now buy brands based on beliefs while 6 in 10 employees choose a workplace based on shared values and expect their CEO to take a stand on societal issues' (Edelman, 2022). The increasingly polarised political landscape also calls for businesses to address issues such as gender equality, inclusion and climate and take the lead in working with governments to raise living standards, develop skills and create security (Edelman, 2023).

This development has, amongst other things, contributed to creating a completely new role and a new focus for organisations in society, which has put pressure on the development of corporate citizenship (see Chap. 4). For the professional communicator, this new role also means an increased focus on credibility and trust, and how the organisation should be positioned in the world.

The professional communicator must guard the credibility of organisations and make every effort to create and maintain trust. This is crucial not only for the organisation's mandate and position externally but also for its internal direction, well-being and commitment. At the same time, it is also a fundamental prerequisite for any organisation's communication to have any effect at all. If the stakeholder does not trust the communicator, they are unlikely to read, listen or look long or favourably on the communication product, no matter how high the quality may be. Establishing credibility and trust is thus crucial for the communicator, and it requires the use of all skills from analysis to production and orchestration to manoeuvre in the relational field of work. It also often involves co-responsibility for areas that are not the communicator's primary responsibility, because coherence between words and actions is paramount. So the professional communicator needs to take an interest in and potentially influence many of the actions of the organisation to ensure coherence of expression and impression.

3.4   Case 2. When Credibility Is Challenged

What do you do as a professional communicator when serious violations are reported that go against everything the organisation stands for? That was the challenge Maersk faced in September 2021. In this case study, Maersk provides insight into a violation case that had huge internal and external consequences, and where strategic producers played a key role in fighting to maintain and regain the company's credibility by working both internally and in external communication.

'I still remember clearly how horrible I felt when I heard about it', is how then Head of Media Relations Signe Wagner describes the situation when a serious case of harassment came to light on 27 September 2021. In an anonymous post on an American blog, a young woman published a post describing how, as a 19-year-old new cadet, she had been plied with drink and sexually assaulted by an older and higher-ranking colleague on board a ship from one of Maersk's US subsidiaries, Maersk Line Limited. In such a situation, what do you do as a professional communicator? Massive external pressures and the fear of scandalous headlines can easily lead to a communicator's focus becoming too external when quick action is needed. But not only do you need to act quickly, you also need to act wisely when the organisation's credibility is at stake.

3.4.1 The Ethical Commitment Was Clear

Maersk is a value-driven organisation where integrity has always been and continues to be important. So there was no doubt about how to position themselves when the assault case came to light: There had to be no doubt about what Maersk thought and whose side they were on, and that they took the anonymous blog post at face value. Maersk had also previously made its position on such offences very clear in the public debate. In Sucher and Gupta's (2019) terminology of fundamental corporate promises, clear promises had been made to stakeholders. The ethical promises were indisputable and formulated by then CEO Søren Skou. 'As an organisation, with our CEO at the helm, we had chosen to take an active stance before there had been a single mention of MeToo cases in our own industry', says Signe Wagner. Søren Skou chose to make his position very clear when the cases were breaking out in other industries and organisations. He wanted to make it very clear that no one should go to work and feel harassed at Maersk. So he took the rather unusual step of sending a letter to all employees with a clear message (Fig. 3.2). Amongst other things, he wrote:

> I personally feel very strongly about this. We all have a responsibility to create an inclusive culture that is free of discrimination, harassment and bullying. Let's use this moment in history to reflect, listen to each other and together ensure that we take care of ourselves and our colleagues by standing united against harassment.

At the same time, he made himself available to any Maersk employee who might have experienced anything:

> If you have experienced or witnessed inappropriate workplace behaviour, harassment or discrimination, I encourage you to report it. You can either go to your immediate manager or to one of our Executive Leadership Team members. You can go to HR or anonymously through the whistleblower system. Also, you are welcome to come directly to me.

'We were well aware that a letter to so many employees does not remain a secret, even if it is internal communication', says Signe Wagner. At the time, Søren Skou was one of the most prominent CEOs to declare the message so directly—knowing that it could also bring up potential cases. The letter immediately generated interest and headlines externally as well, which meant that Maersk had already made its mark on this agenda internally and in the public eye when the serious assault case from the USA came to light. The ethical promises were made to Maersk's employees and to society at large.

When the story broke, the work of the strategic producers was far from being concerned only with external communicative management but rather a co-facilitation of the entire organisation's work on creating coherence between values and actions. It was important to work with transparency so it became clear that there was a connection between the company's words and actions, which at a theoretical level corresponds to Albu and Flyverbom's (2019) focus on both verifiability and actions in connection with achieving transparency. First and foremost, concrete internal actions had to be taken to ensure that the terrible case gave rise to concrete changes

3.4 Case 2. When Credibility Is Challenged

This email is sent to all employees in Denmark

Dear colleagues,

The ongoing debate in Denmark on sexual harassment in the media and entertainment industry as well as the political stage reminds me of the importance of this topic for all of us, and I wanted to take this opportunity to share my view.

The people of A.P. Moller - Maersk are the foundation for our success. This is why one of our Core Values is "Our Employees - the right environment for the right people". I personally believe that the *right environment* is an environment where harassment does not happen, and the *right people* do not harass, bully or discriminate their colleagues. At Maersk, we treat our colleagues with respect and dignity, and we do not tolerate discrimination or harassment of any kind. It is as simple as that.

To protect this high standard and safeguard our employees from any unwanted conduct, our Code of Conduct emphasizes what we stand for as a company, and our Maersk Behaviours as well as the Commit Rule on Global Employee Relations all aim to ensure that these standards are embedded in everything we do. This framework states our commitment as a company and outlines our expectations to every employee at Maersk.

I personally feel very strongly about this. We all have a responsibility to create an inclusive culture that is free of discrimination, harassment and bullying. Let's use this moment in history to reflect, listen to each other, and together make sure that we take care of ourselves and our colleagues by standing united against harassment.

If you have experienced or witnessed inappropriate workplace behavior, harassment or discrimination, I encourage you to report it. You can either go to your immediate manager or any of our Executive Leadership Team members. You can go to HR or anonymously through the Whistleblower system. Also, you are welcome to come directly to me. Please take some time to use the resources below to learn more about how we all have a role to play in creating a positive environment.

Our values remain constant. They are deeply ingrained in our behaviors and the way we do business. It is by living them every day that we continue to thrive as individuals, and collectively as Maersk.

Stand united and stay safe,

Søren Skou
CEO of A.P. Moller - Maersk

Fig. 3.2 Former CEO Søren Skou's letter to all Maersk employees in connection with the MeToo debates

that could drive cultural change throughout the industry. The only way to preserve trust was to ensure a safe working environment for everyone on board the ships. The entire starting point for the professional communicators was a belief in the reality that Sucher and Gupta (2019) dispel in Myth 3 of trust work in organisations, see Table 3.1, namely that trust should not be managed from the outside in, but from the inside out. In practice, this meant that a lot of communicative measures had to be taken internally. It was important that the anonymous woman who had reported the harassment case was not seen as a disloyal critic, but that all employee profiles were addressed. For example, using Verhoeven and Madsen's (2022) terminology—i.e.

the eight employee roles that professional communicators must relate to in their communication work—it was important to activate the 'innovator' to find solutions, communicate meaningful explanations to the 'meaning maker', give nuanced points to the 'scout' and show the 'critic' that you were listening.

3.4.2 The First Communicative Handling

Transparency was a keyword for the credible handling of this case. That is why the first external communication was to step out in the open (Fig. 3.3)—even before Danish media had picked up the story. A decision that would only work if the strategic producers and management were in full agreement on the necessary courage and transparency.

'When we first learnt about the blog post, the case had not yet been picked up by Danish media. An anonymous source had been quoted in the Washington Post, so we realised that it was a matter of a very short time before it moved across the Atlantic. We spent a couple of days setting up our own investigations and planning how to deal with it, but then we decided to go public ourselves', says Signe Wagner. 'When you are employed to protect a reputation, you have to think twice before you actively decide to go public with a story that inevitably puts the words 'Maersk' and 'rape' in the same headline. But it was nonetheless our recommendation, and we got support for it without hesitation all the way through management. After a deep breath, we sent the anonymous blog post to a journalist at the national newspaper Berlingske, and the then head of Maersk's fleet, Palle Laursen, gave a major interview in the newspaper, where he himself spoke about the case and expressed exactly how we felt, so no one could be in any doubt. We wanted to be the first to both express dismay and at the same time take responsibility for cultural change on board our ships'.

By raising the issue in the media yourself, an organisation can have a little more influence on the perception that stakeholders have from the outset, because you avoid being put on the defensive by actively stepping forward and helping to shape the coverage. A crisis management technique called 'stealing thunder' (see also Chap. 9).

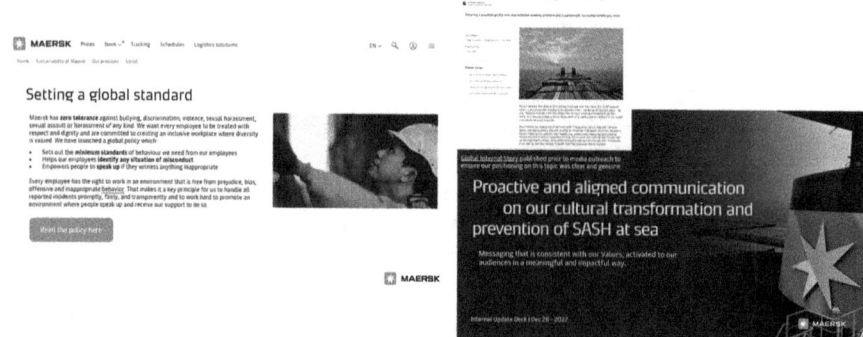

Fig. 3.3 Examples of the internal communication in connection with the Maersk assault case in 2021

3.4 Case 2. When Credibility Is Challenged

In other cases, it might have been a difficult task to get a top manager to face such an unpleasant case as this in the media and to emotionally reflect the seriousness of the case without becoming too technical, legal or otherwise distanced, but Signe Wagner says that they were all so shaken that this part of the preparation was not at all complex: 'Palle Laursen himself was so affected by reading the blog post that he was very explicit about how serious it was and how much it was against everything Maersk stands for. He communicated this very clearly both internally and externally; there was no doubt about the human aspect, that he himself and the entire Maersk management with him were deeply concerned and stood behind an unequivocal ambition and a concrete plan to investigate the case and the entire field to ensure that this kind of thing cannot happen'.

Palle Laursen was quoted in Berlingske (Fig. 3.4) as saying: 'We are deeply shocked by this. The way in which the incident is described is not only contrary to common decency but also in particular to our values and what we stand for at Maersk. Under no circumstances should this be allowed to happen, neither on board our ships nor anywhere else in the company', says Palle Laursen. He emphasises that the company takes the anonymous blog post at face value. '[...] Maersk has now launched an independent investigation involving, among others, trade unions, the woman's school and the maritime organisation in the United States' (Berlingske Tidende 7/10 2021).

When a case like this happens in a large organisation spanning several continents and with local management in subsidiaries, many legal advisors etc., the strategic producer must not only relate to external communication but also address the many internal stakeholders. It was complex to balance the local US approach, which was largely characterised by the legal aspects of the case, possible future litigation and a political consideration for the US authorities, with the more value-driven approach, which emphasised the consideration of Maersk's self-understanding, employees, reputation and credibility that characterised the management at headquarters. 'As communicators, we worked hard to ensure long-term credibility and good

Fig. 3.4 Articles on assault case in Maersk in Berlingske Tidende, 7 October 2021 (Translated, the headlines read *'Alarming rape case shocks Maersk: "We are deeply shocked by this"'* and *'Maersk after numerous #MeToo cases: We have a problem'*.)

interaction with all stakeholders and all parts of the organisation, because there had to be no doubt about where Maersk stood. For example, we did not want it to appear in any way that we were questioning whether the incident had happened because the post was anonymous. No matter what that might mean for a potential future legal action. We wanted to be on the same side as the victim', emphasises Signe Wagner.

It was also important not to be perceived as being too preoccupied with technicalities or not showing trust in stakeholders in the communication itself, which is in line with Rawlins' (2007) view that trust and credibility are crucial in the interaction between all stakeholders. This was a danger that Maersk's professional communicators were very aware of in the process because there were also many lawyers involved in the case internally. 'We were careful not to get bogged down in details or formalities that might be important internally but would not make sense externally. For example, it may well be that it had happened in a subsidiary where it was the American unions and not Maersk themselves that were responsible for manning the ships, but in those moments it doesn't matter. Maersk was responsible. Cases like this simply must not happen, and no one could be in any doubt about what we mean. Facts and details about the company's structure, Maersk's mandate in the situation, employment contracts, etc. must give way to the bigger picture of Maersk's values and responsibilities', says Signe Wagner, who advised all managers who were to speak out on the matter. The response was carefully considered, as it was important that the spokespersons not only expressed their unreserved dismay and apology but were also able to take the consequences of the case and show decisiveness by, for example suspending the people involved in the incident. At the same time, concrete initiatives had to be followed up to effectively identify whether there were any more cases and to ensure that the incident would not be repeated. In this way, the internal work on the case was ongoing, with the external communication task reflecting the organisational work.

In February 2022, Maersk was able to conclude its own internal investigations into the specific case, but without having had the opportunity, for legal reasons, to speak to either the perpetrator or the anonymous victim. As a result of the investigations, five employees were dismissed in February 2022 for not acting in accordance with Maersk's values and rules. 'It was of course unsatisfactory not to be able to act on the offence itself, but it was not legally possible. We thus made this clear in our background talks with the journalists who followed the case, so they did not get the impression that Maersk was trying to minimise the seriousness of the situation', says Signe Wagner.

The cases rolled on. From the same website where the first blog post was published, other cases began to emerge. Another woman who had felt harassed via text messages chose to give interviews to both a Danish and an American media outlet. 'Again, it was important for us to get our position out there from the beginning to protect trust in the fact that we as a company take care of our employees', says Signe Wagner. Several media outlets followed the surveys on an ongoing basis, and Maersk agreed to talk about the cultural change underway in interviews with two media outlets.

'Again, it felt a bit counter-intuitive to present the negative stories to the media ourselves. But in the long run, it was important for the trust in the company that we didn't try to hide anything and that we weren't put on the defensive by others who could choose to take up the matter themselves. That would only have made the media story even bigger. We had to be clear that we did our utmost to solve these problems', says Signe Wagner.

The interaction with the press was close: 'We talked a lot with our stakeholders, including the journalists, and also provided them with background knowledge about what we were doing, what was delaying the process, what legal challenges there were—or whatever could create the basic understanding of the complexity that was necessary to be able to cover the cases adequately and influence the industry to do something about this. It is not enough for Maersk to change their behaviour. It must be safe to be a woman anywhere. At the same time, of course, we also had to navigate the fact that more cases could still come to light that we did not yet know about'.

When, a few weeks later, then CEO Søren Skou had a strategy interview scheduled with the Danish business newspaper Børsen (Fig. 3.5), it was also an opportunity to once again make it clear both to the outside world and internally in the organisation how high on his agenda the harassment cases were. 'It turned out to be a pretty strong interview that was really noticed and—I think—built some trust that Maersk meant and did the right things', emphasises Signe Wagner.

Whilst the crisis was being handled by professional communicators at Maersk, the case was of course handled legally. The anonymous woman had come forward as Hope Hicks, providing an active, personal and credible voice in discussions about improving the industry—work and discussions that Maersk also takes an active role in. 'While the litigation is going on, we are always very bound legally to not say much, but we have been working behind the scenes to do something about this, so the case does not become just one of many, but an opportunity to do something about it', says Head of International Media, Mikkel Linnet, who took over the area at the time when the long-term preventive organisational work was about to begin. A phase in crisis management that requires even more active stakeholder work.

Fig. 3.5 Former CEO Søren Skou in an interview with Børsen on harassment cases in Maersk (Translated, the headlines read: '*A breakdown in leadership*' and '*Søren Skou wishes to eradicate culture of abuse at Maersk: "That is in no way the kind of company we want to be"* '.)

'It's a very complex stakeholder scenario, because if we want to change something, we can't just act on our own, we also need to involve other actors. For example, it is the trade unions in the United States that man all the ships that service the US government, and all employees are trained at the same American academy. So we need to talk to them about how we can change the culture going forward', says Mikkel Linnet. The long-term work is also very important to Hope Hicks, who still works in the industry herself.

3.4.3 Long-Term Preventive Organisational Work

The communications department worked in close collaboration with a wide range of internal actors, and several internal activities were launched, such as anonymous surveys and listening sessions, where management made sure they learned as much as possible about what might be going on in the organisation and what they could do. Maersk was well aware that the cases could point to more serious problems, so the perspective of the investigations was much broader. How big was the problem? 'Even more investigations were launched, for example, all female employees across Maersk's entire fleet of ships were interviewed so we could hear their perceptions of the reality on board. A dedicated team was hired to lead a culture change. Among other things, a new practice was introduced that if there are women on board the ships, there are always at least two'.

Those who live quietly do not live well when there are problems of this kind, so one of the areas of work was to create a better 'speak-up culture': 'Yes, it was about getting the issues out there, because this was not an exercise in reputation. It's a question of creating safety and security and long-term change, so we are working hard to create a more open culture at sea. Employees must speak up if they experience something and managers must react promptly. This is the only way to change the culture. We know it's a long haul, but we also know it's necessary. We have more than 12,500 employees at sea—350 of whom are women—and they should not feel that they are alone with any problems', Mikkel Linnet emphasises.

In future work on changing the culture, there are three main tracks involving communication work: (1) internal communication, (2) external media and (3) public affairs.

1. In the internal communication track, communicators help facilitate cultural change by maintaining focus, driving activities and taking up agendas across all internal media. For example, emergency hotlines have been established, internal campaigns have been prepared, and a management training programme has been developed and communicated. In the wake of the harassment cases, all new employees at sea must go through an onboarding programme to ensure that they feel safe and know where to go if they experience harassing behaviour. In this way, you work actively to articulate and fulfil the internal promises to employees legally and ethically (Sucher & Gupta, 2019).

2. Communication work involving external media also has a sharp focus and clear basic messages: 'We are ready to go out ourselves and not wait for a new case to come up, but always stay ahead of the agenda. We also media train our managers to be able to handle such cases, so we are ready to do it in a respectful manner', emphasises Mikkel Linnet.

> The key messages from Maersk are unequivocal:
>
> - Maersk has zero-tolerance against sexual assault and sexual harassment (SASH).
> - It is deeply rooted in our values that no matter who or where you are, you should always feel safe as an employee at Maersk.
> - The recent SASH cases (Sexual Assault Sexual Harassment) in the fleet of our US operator Maersk Line, Limited, are horrific and unacceptable. They go against everything we believe in as a company.
> - We reacted immediately when learning about cases. Apart from investigating and dealing with specific cases, we decided to broadly examine the work environment across our global Maersk container fleet.
> - We were reaffirmed that the vast majority of our colleagues working at sea are highly honourable, respectful, hardworking women and men. Also, it was evident that we have not had a safe and trusted environment across all social settings on our vessels.
> - That is why we have set out to create a cultural change.

3. At the same time, public affairs is also an important communication effort, because Maersk wants to change the industry in order to have more women on board, and so they are treated with respect. 'We are doing everything we can, for example in the US market, to get good dialogues going with all the relevant stakeholders from Congress to the unions, the naval academies and the public, so this can become a better industry for women. And we of course do the same internationally—and with the recruitment we ourselves are responsible for, which is for the vast, vast majority of our ships, we can also do even more in our campaigns and selection', Mikkel Linnet elaborates.

The work ahead is extensive, and the change is facilitated by broad cross-functional collaboration, which is testimony to the fact that cases like this are not about media management of a scandal but about a long-term effort for a healthy culture at sea. The communications department contributes to the change with active communication across all channels internally and externally, supporting internal activities, training and continued management of media attention globally. In short, there are no easy shortcuts to safeguarding credibility and trust.

3.5 Interview. Watch Closely!

There is a need for skilled communicators who keep a watchful eye on the link between words and action. Professor Robert L. Heath has followed the credibility and communication of organisations for a lifetime, and he has no doubts. Communicators are in demand—and must safeguard the credibility and trust of society. Heath is one of the world's leading researchers within rhetoric, public relations and strategic communication—and he shares his most important advice with us.

'Do you know Picasso's painting Guernica?' Robert Heath's dynamic energy is infectious throughout the virtual crackle of the Team meeting. 'I saw it once in Madrid, and it struck me as an insanely good example of discreet and effective crisis communication'. Picasso's famous painting depicts a bombing in the then-current Spanish Civil War of the town of Guernica in the Basque country, in which probably more than 1000 people died. 'Picasso artistically documents the Germans bombing and entering the Spanish Civil War on 26 April 1937. That's what he chose to paint in great haste to tell the world at the World's Fair in Paris that the situation was very bad, and it was in fact very important communication and helped to get the world's attention. It's a good example of the existence of many ways to communicate, something that all communicators need to be aware of'.

It is also a good example of the professor always having his eyes on the prize. He simply cannot help himself—and that is the everyday practice he recommends to all communicators.

'One of the most important things for all communication is credibility, and we have to protect that', he stresses. 'Incidentally, it's also our best defence against all the negative energy that the communications field encounters; being "spinners" who can twist everything to their own benefit. We need to show that we are standing up for trust and credibility by creating coherence, and this is a very important task for communicators'.

Few have influenced international communication research the way Robert Heath has done for a lifetime as a researcher—and he has travelled the world with a keen eye and his evidence in place.

3.5.1 Be the Credibility Sheriff in Your Organisation

Management may say the right thing, but communicators need to make sure that it is translated into action in all the organisation's multivocal voices and behaviours. This sums up one of Professor Heath's key messages to communicators. 'We can't trust management completely', he says with a slightly indulgent smile, 'They can't help it. Management is all about being in control, so they find it really hard to let go. And real communication is about the opposite: about being in touch with your stakeholders and preferring dialogue to monologue. We must not fall into the trap of simply helping management obtain controlled 'window dressing' of beautiful messages, but must help them be in real contact', he stresses—and with the wall behind him full of cowboy hats at his home office in Texas, one cannot help but imagine the dedicated professor as a kind of credibility sheriff, getting managers to notice when they are violating the 'credibility law' of the connection between words and action.

Heath has oceans of examples of large companies calling him to fix their credibility with new values, a new purpose or a new vision. But he is not a fan of having external people help fix their problems. 'I think one of the first ones was Shell in the 70s. They were setting up their US headquarters here in Texas. They called and asked if I could write about their "corporate soul"'. He shakes his head a little. 'I said "no", of course, but "yes" to helping them with real soul-searching, because it makes sense not to write out an identity but to analyse what you actually are and make that the basis for identity management', he explains.

3.5.2 A Historical View of the World

Robert Heath stumbled into the world of communications by accident. He studied history and liked it. But then he got caught up in rhetoric and historical activism, and suddenly it was 'issues management' that captured his attention. Back then, it wasn't something you could focus your research on, so he had to put it into a public relations framework, and the rest is history. He is one of the key fathers of public relations research, focusing also on the ethical dimensions, and he has by no means lost his historical perspective: 'We should never look at the world, nor at our organisations, without a historical perspective. History comes along, and there is never a fresh start—we cannot be afraid of bringing the past with us, and we should never communicate without history', he stresses.

This often means that communicators have to speak against the management, if they just want to sell new messages without actively addressing the context of past or current behaviour that is not in sync with the message. Being communicators, we must help them work actively with the organisational history, both as a co-player and an adversary to current wishes and ambitions.

3.5.3 Create Joint Action

Robert Heath is a declared constitutionalist. 'I firmly believe that we must communicate in order to organise. That our role is thus not just to communicate to get messages out. We need to take action with our communication. Not only joint action in our organisations but in our entire contact with the outside world. We need to create communities of shared agency', he stresses.

Amongst many other things, he has worked with the stakeholder concept in his research. In his view, it is a matter of organisational 'stakeseekers' understanding that we only get real interaction by actually understanding our stakeholders and finding the common basic interests that make us not fake a relationship but find a real common interest or ambition. 'We shouldn't go out and dominate or manipulate, but we should go out and listen and talk to our stakeholders', he stresses. 'This is also how organisations earn their voice, so to speak—get their 'Social License to Operate'", he stresses.

The point is quickly backed up with an example from his work with the chemical industry. After all, in American culture, lawsuits are often the way to go in case of problems. And that is exactly what the lawyers at a major Houston chemicals company recommended when the press found a story in a soil contamination case. It was the soil of an elementary school playground, where children suddenly found themselves playing on dangerous, contaminated soil. Images were strong. Black goo below the sandpit and swing set. 'The case is a good example to illustrate that a reactive communicator simply could have stepped forward to help contain the damaging publicity and handle the press side of a long, expensive lawsuit. But fortunately, the solution was different, and the communicator took on more responsibility', says the professor. Instead of fighting costly and futile battles over sections and dollars, the company stepped forward in an accommodating manner. They took responsibility and sought cooperation to find good solutions. The messages from the company were very clear: We obviously do not want children to play on contaminated soil. We inherited the land, and the problem, through acquisitions. In a community such as Houston, Texas, now we cannot always know what mistakes companies made in the past. So let us hurry; let us solve the problem and get the soil cleaned up. We agree to pay, and we help the school district find the best people to solve it in a way that makes everyone happy. 'In my view, this was genuine stakeholder work where the goal was to solve a shared problem together, and true shared agency was created. I'm sure it was also much better, and probably more cost effective, for long-term confidence in the company', Heath says.

3.5.4 Train Your Observation Skills

In Heath's view, being a good communicator is thus very much about being aware of the context in order to maintain credibility. 'We need to use our eyes and ears and constantly look at behaviours to ensure that we can create genuine consistency. It's something we have to practice all the time'. He himself still does this every day. He cannot help it in his encounter with the world.

For example, the day before our interview, the GPS in his car suddenly malfunctioned, and as he was heading to a destination, he was getting the wrong instructions. He pulled over at a large Walmart. Here, as in most places today, no textual framing has been spared—for example you are not a customer but a client when you enter, and assistants, not cashiers, are employed. But when Professor Heath asked for advice at the checkout, he noticed that, although the assistant was itching to help, she was looking over her shoulder first. If she spent time giving advice, rather than just entering the item and closing a sale, she might risk trouble with the boss.

'Of course, I wouldn't have asked if there was already a long queue at the checkout', the friendly professor stresses in his story, unconsciously illustrating how he, as a stakeholder, had already shown care and respect in the situation.

The story ends happily. He was given the right advice and was able to drive on with a GPS that helped him reach his destination. But to Heath, it was a good example of minor observations of the 'say-do gap' that occurs on any normal day; the nice words about clients were being challenged by a management practice with a one-sided focus on sales and efficiency. Communicators need to keep an eye on these gaps and constantly train their eyes so that gaps are spotted even in their own organisation, and adjustments are made to either assure that smart words support helpful behaviour, leaving credibility intact.

3.5.5 Mind Your Own Ethics

Heath is not blind to the fact that being a credibility guard is a difficult role for the communicator. Especially because management does not always really understand. 'It may seem quite tempting for management to simply use communication for nice messages without any regard for history or reality, and some battles are bound to arise along the way'.

Therefore, the most important advice from the professor is to stand up for your own credibility: 'I always recommend my students to sit down with a piece of paper before starting a new job and write down specifically: What is important to me? What do I not want to be a part of? Where are my ethical boundaries? What will it take for me to quit? They need to look at that piece of paper every now and then to make sure their ideals are not quietly crumbling away ethically, suddenly not being able to recognise themselves and their own boundaries'.

The voice is serious. You can sense that this particular advice comes from many experiences with communicators who have regretted their participation in certain situations, unloading their frustrations on the professor afterwards. Situations where the power and power struggles in the organisation have made them act contrary to their own ethics. 'We must not lose ourselves. It's better to keep your ethics and then update your CV in search of a new job with a better identity match', Professor Heath concludes.

Robert Heath

Robert Heath is Professor Emeritus of Communication at the University of Houston. He is an internationally recognised researcher within public relations, crisis communication, issues management and business-to-business communication. Trained in history and rhetoric before shifting his focus to corporate communication, he has remained true to his educational roots in all of his research, focusing on historical perspective, credibility and a keen eye for textuality. He is the author of many award-winning books, such as 'The SAGE Handbook of Public Relations' (2010); 'Strategic Issues Management' (2009); 'Rhetorical and Critical Approaches to Public Relations II' (2009); and 'Terrorism: Communication and Rhetorical Perspectives' (2008). In addition, he has authored numerous articles, chapters and reports—and still does. In his long professional life, he has also received numerous awards for his academic work. His greatest satisfaction is seeing his students have successful, rewarding careers.

References

Albu, O. B., & Flyverbom, M. (2019). Organizational transparency: Conceptualisations, conditions and consequences. *Business & Society, 58*(2), 268–297.

Christensen, L. T., & Cheney, G. (2015). Peering into transparency: Challenging ideals, proxies and organisational practices. *Communication Theory, 25*(1), 70–90.

Edelman. (2022). https://www.edelman.co.uk/2022-edelman-uk-trust-barometer

Edelman. (2023). https://www.edelman.co.uk/2023-edelman-uk-trust-barometer

Fukuyama, F. (1995). *Trust: The social virtues and the creation of prosperity*. Hamish Hamilton.

Hoff-Clausen, E. (2010). *Retorisk handlekraft hviler på tillid, Rhetorica, June 2010*. Retorikförlaget.

Lane, C. (1998). Introduction: Theories and issues in the study of trust. In C. Lan & R. Bachman (Eds.), *Trust within and between organizations, conceptual issues and empirical applications* (pp. 1–30). Oxford University Press.

Madsen, V. T., & Verhoeven, J. W. M. (2019). The big idea of employees as strategic communicators in public relation. In *Big ideas in public relations research and practice (Advances in Public Relations and Communication Management)* (Vol. 4, pp. 143–162). Emerald Publishing Limited.

Mccroskey, J. C. (1982). Oral communication apprehension: A reconceptualization. *Annals of the International Communication Association, 6*(1), 136–170.

Moreno, Á., Tench, R., & Verhoeven, P. (2021). Trust in public relations in the age of mistrusted media: A European perspective. *Publications (Basel), 9*(1), 7.

Rawlins, B. L. (2007). *Trust and PR practice*. Institute for Public Relations. Available online: http://bit.ly/ecm2019ref10

Rousseau, D. M. (1995). *Psychological contracts in organisations: Understanding written and unwritten agreements*. Sage.

Schein, E. H. (1993). *Organisational psychology*. Systime.

Schnackenberg, A. K., & Tomlinson, E. C. (2016). Organizational transparency: A new perspective on managing trust in organisation stakeholder relationships. *Journal of Management, 42*, 1784–1810.

Sucher, S. J., & Gupta, S. (2019, July 16). The trust crisis. *HBR*.

Sucher, S. J., & Gupta, S. (2021). *The power of trust: How companies build it, lose it, regain it* (1st ed.). PublicAffairs, Hachette Book Group.

Verhoeven, J. W. M., & Madsen, V. T. (2022). Active employee communication roles in organisations: A framework for understanding and discussing communication role expectations. *International Journal of Strategic Communication, 16*(1), 91–110.

4. Corporate Citizenship in a Changing World

That organisations have a responsibility not only for their own products but also for society and our planet, is a new norm called 'corporate citizenship'. As (co-)responsible citizens, organisations must act differently and communicate on an increasing number of agendas, making it crucial that the professional communicator helps to position the organisation wisely. CEO activism is an important communicative task in corporate citizenship.

In the chapter's case study, Maersk provides insight into how the company has taken greater social responsibility in the field of climate change and what role communicators have played in supporting this, including through CEO activism.

The chapter's international expert is Rupert Younger, co-founder of the Centre for Corporate Reputation at the University of Oxford. He gives his take on the challenges of the future and stresses the importance of the professional communicator bringing knowledge into the organisation, not only to satisfy shareholders but to satisfy all stakeholders. This requires listening and communicating.

The world is constantly changing and the role of organisations is changing. This also means changes for the professional communicator who is to support the positioning and reputation of the organisation. Since the beginning of this millennium, many societal developments have meant that organisations have had to become more visible. Whereas it used to be enough—to put it bluntly—to be competent and run an efficient business that made customers, owners or shareholders happy, today the requirement is a different one. Since 2007, researchers have been talking about 'shareholder capitalism' being replaced by 'stakeholder capitalism' (Freeman et al., 2007). This basically means that it is not only the bank book but also reputation and agency that are crucial to success. At the same time, awareness of the state of the planet and the widespread global endorsement of the UN Sustainable Development Goals (SDGs) have meant that organisations have been held more (co-)accountable and have chosen to step forward themselves as co-responsible (Rendtorff, 2020).

The expectations for organisations come from everywhere: (Potential) employees want to work in organisations that make a difference to society and the planet. Shareholders want to be sure that the organisation not only makes money but contributes to society. Customers want sustainable products from organisations they can vouch for. The public wants organisations that take responsibility. This movement towards taking their place as 'corporate citizens' has meant many new areas of work for the professional communicator. This includes communicating on multiple agendas, working more on transparency, orchestrating more organisational voices in entirely new channels and listening even more to stakeholders. Organisations must thus step forward and engage with society in a new and more active way. As Ihlen et al. summarise: 'Corporate activities are increasingly scrutinised for their effect on society and the environment. It is unthinkable that a corporation today will declare publicly that its only goal is to make money for its shareholders. Instead, corporations typically claim to balance the needs of society and the environment against the need to make a profit' (2011: 21).

4.1 Build Social Licence to Operate

As stakeholder capitalism gains momentum, the role of the professional communicator changes significantly, as the success of the organisation becomes even more dependent on being supported by good communication. The ambition is to succeed in the eyes of stakeholders, and you might say that organisations must earn their so-called 'social licence to operate'. There is no single recipe for how to achieve this licence, and quite often different stakeholders may have decidedly conflicting expectations of an organisation. However, in simple terms, an organisation must take co-responsibility and act as a corporate citizen:

> Organizations in community need social licences to operate (SLO) that are derived from their ability to engage to serve communities of individuals (identities and identifications) in agonistic association. Engagement that does not resolve issues needed to make communities more fully functioning is not true engagement (Dhanesh, 2017; Heath, 2018a, 2018b; Koya et al., 2021). (Heath, 2022: 1)

In other words, it is not enough for an organisation to have good intentions and a desire to behave in a certain way. You have to be genuinely engaged in actions that demonstrate your commitment. When you meet your stakeholders, you should not only have a selfish desire to influence but also find shared problems, interests and ambitions through open dialogue. In this way, you can try to create a shared agency (Bratman, 2014) that addresses the challenge that has been identified. This means that the professional communicator should not only help communicate the organisation's solutions but even more so facilitate dialogue with the outside world. It also means that co-creation is an increasingly important key to organisational positioning, as highlighted by Ihlen and Raknes: 'An organisation's social license to operate depends on how it acts according to social norms, engages with stakeholders and meets some kind of public interest' (2022: 1).

When you want to step forward as a corporate citizen and carry out what is also called 'corporate social advocacy' (O'Connor 2023), the licence must be in order, and it must be clear that you are looking for a shared solution to a perceived problem. Again, it is crucial to focus on the wishes and experiences of stakeholders, as emphasised by Miller and Austin, for example 'Corporate social advocacy is initiated on behalf of stakeholders (both in and outside the company) despite the potential negative fallout for the company resulting from a negative public response' (O'Connor 2023: 179).

In the context of stakeholder capitalism, the professional communicator must help understand and listen to the complex societal trends and stakeholder demands. This knowledge needs to be communicated, for example in the form of recommendations, to the right decision makers in the organisation. On this basis, the most appropriate agendas and positions can be chosen. The communicator has an important role in ensuring that the legitimacy of the organisation is built so that the organisation obtains its social licence to operate according to its values, even in today's increasingly polarised society (Capizzo, 2020).

Stakeholders must feel met and be able to identify with the sender and their ambitions before it is perceived as legitimate: 'In the end, the social license to operate will hinge on whether or not important stakeholders believe an organisation to be a legitimate social actor that is beneficial for society' (Ihlen & Raknes, 2020: 7). 'The same is true for the discipline of public relations which can assist the search for order by defining and achieving public interest as place' (Heath, 2022: 12).

That is why it is necessary for communication to be organisationally anchored in real ambitions and concrete actions in order to be credible. This also requires the professional communicator not to run ahead with good stories but to ensure that they are properly anchored—and conversely, sometimes to return to the organisation with concrete demands for action based on input from stakeholders obtained through, for example so-called 'social listening'.

4.2 A Strong Purpose as a Starting Point

One place where professional communicators can often help to ensure a well-considered starting point for corporate citizenship work is by helping organisations to find their overall and socially beneficial purpose. This is an area of strategic development that has been in focus in recent years in both public and private organisations. Traditionally, strategic work in organisations has been about defining visions for the future of the organisation and missions that clarify how that vision is to be achieved. A purpose, on the other hand, is characterised by explicitly placing an organisation in its societal context. It defines why the organisation exists and what it contributes to the bigger picture. In this way, purpose becomes a concrete starting point for stepping forward as a corporate citizen. A concrete purpose can be the organisation's own bid for its 'social licence to operate', and the positioning work is a question of making this purpose credible in the eyes of stakeholders.

There is no single way of defining purpose, but there are three typical categories that frequently form part of the positioning work, all closely related. The first one is **competence**, understood as the function our product serves. The second one is **culture** which may loosely be translated as the intent with which we run our business. Third and last, the positioning work may also revolve around the **cause**, that is the social good to which we aspire in our work.

The three types of purpose place different organisational emphasis on competence, culture and cause, which will be described in turn below.

The 'competence-based purpose' is where the organisation wants to clarify its specific competence and place it in a societal context. One example is the car manufacturer Mercedes, whose purpose emphasises the company's competences to create value for its customers by using them to create concrete movement. This movement is transferred to society as such in a purpose that reads: 'First Move the World'.

The 'culture-based purpose' is where the organisation wants to clarify who they are and how that driving force creates value for others. An example is the online clothing, shoes and accessories platform Zappos, who define their culture-based purpose as: 'To Live and Deliver WOW'. Here, the direction is less clearly societal but more directly aimed at the specific stakeholders: The employees, who are given a direction for their work, and the customers, who are to experience the value that a WOW can create for them.

The last type is 'cause-purpose', which focuses on the meaning of the organisation. One of the most famous worldwide is the outdoor clothing manufacturer Patagonia, whose purpose is defined as: 'We're in business to save our home planet'. A type chosen by many organisations to define their purpose with a stakeholder-oriented direction, where ambitions are set in a larger context. A few other examples are the electric car manufacturer Tesla's purpose, which is 'to accelerate the world's transition to sustainable energy', or the supermarket chain Whole Foods Market, which defines its purpose as: 'Our purpose is to nourish people and the planet'.

All three types can create a meaningful *why*. A clear purpose can both unite the organisation and the organisational positioning around a clear aim and act as a strategic driver, just as ways of demonstrating a positive impact on the financial bottom line are gaining ground (Carucci & Ridge, 2022).

The role of the professional communicator in shaping corporate purpose varies widely from organisation to organisation. The work typically involves bringing all facets of the professional communicator into play in close interaction with senior management and other key organisational stakeholders, from strategic analysis of the stakeholder scenario to planning and orchestrating the development process. This is followed by a more creative process of shaping the concrete purpose, which will then be brought to life internally and externally through quality communication.

Since 2020, the Enacting Purpose Initiative has brought together global researchers and leading practitioners in a joint partnership to inspire best practices in developing and managing an effective purpose. The partners behind the initiative include the University of Oxford, the University of California Berkeley, BCG BrightHouse,

Federated Hermes EOS and the British Academy (see more at https://enactingpurpose.org/). Their recommendations include developing a purpose that fulfils a number of quality criteria to make it effective. It must:

- Be simple
- Provide opportunities to connect to the world
- Be within reach of something the organisation can do
- Can be exemplified
- Can be directly recognised by the stakeholder

Whether the professional communicator is directly involved in devising it or not, a formulated purpose is an important tool in positioning the organisation and building the role of a corporate citizen with a social licence to operate. All communication must be anchored in supporting the credibility of a purpose so that it does not risk becoming an organisational showpiece (Schein, 1983). Ensuring this is a crucial part of the professional communicator's strategic and organisational anchoring of the positioning work.

4.3 Positioning Potentials in a Changing Media Landscape

But where should this positioning of the organisation as a corporate citizen take place? Traditionally, positioning has been about marketing, branding and press coverage, but the media landscape has changed, and the professional communicator must now work across multiple channels and platforms.

The media landscape is becoming increasingly complex to navigate for the professional communicator, because how big a part should the classic editorial media actually play in the work of positioning the organisation? For years, studies have shown that trust and especially support for editorial media has been declining. The Reuters Institute for the Study of Journalism follows the development closely, and a look at their figures can show the declining importance of traditional media. In 2017, more people found their news via an algorithm than via a human editor. In 2019, only 11% paid for their news. In 2021, there was a slight increase due to the coronavirus pandemic, but this does not change the fundamental decline in the use of traditional media and the necessary re-calibration and consolidation is in full swing. The analysis tracks an increased polarisation, with some people remaining engaged with news coverage, whilst others are starting to avoid it altogether. In the USA, in particular, interest is declining sharply. New generations have new media habits (Klopčič et al., 2020), and the rapid pace of change is illustrated by the evolution of the media landscape in the USA: 'More than 100 newspapers have shifted from daily to weekly issues and between 2004 and 2014, at least 664 newspapers shut down. Newspapers reduced employment by 47 per cent between 2008 and 2018' (Minow, 2021: 11).

Not only are there fewer newspaper readers, they also have less trust in what they read (Reuter, 2021). For the professional communicator, this means that traditional media are fewer central channels and platforms for positioning than in the past, when press coverage was the primary goal of most media teams.

However, positioning in traditional media still plays a key role, as the editorial lens and third-party coverage adds a level of credibility to news that money cannot buy. At the same time, there are many highly skilled journalists who put stories into perspective in an entirely different way from how you would do it in your own channels. Research also shows that it is often of great importance internally to see your organisation mentioned in traditional media—also known as 'autocommunication' (Christensen, 2003). What an employee sees about his or her own organisation in external media is also of great importance for the internal creation of meaning and is part of identity creation as a 'discoursive amplifier between management and employees in their ongoing identity construction' (Kjærgaard & Morsing, 2010: 108). Finally, it may be added that most executive boards and boards of directors still belong to a generation that still reads newspapers and pays heed to what the big TV stations bring.

However, classic media can no longer stand alone as channels and platforms for positioning the organisation's corporate citizenship. One way of illustrating the possibilities is the division into 'paid', 'owned', 'shared' and 'earned' media, which will be described below.

'Owned media' means that the organisation owns the channel and shares information directly and unfiltered to stakeholders without direct interaction. These are typically print channels, websites and social media accounts.

There is an overlap from all media types to the so-called 'shared media', where everything can be shared and where both your own and other people's mentions of the organisation are mixed together. These are the typical social media from LinkedIn and Instagram to Facebook.

'Paid media' means that the organisation pays for publicity. This can be in the form of sponsored content or direct adverts, supplements etc. Paid media can come in all formats, from large, expensive adverts in the street or traditional media to a small payment to ensure that social media content is promoted.

Last but not least, the three media types provide input to stakeholders that can result in 'earned media', where others choose to mention organisations and thus create visibility in editorial media or on social media.

As Fig. 4.1 shows, there is a great deal of overlap between the different categories of media. New hybrids and models are constantly being developed, and there is an explosive development in the grey areas between 'earned', 'owned' and 'paid', to which media houses, influencers, companies and social media platforms are actively contributing.

For the professional communicator, a major task lies in orienting yourself and working consciously in this new media landscape and using every opportunity to position the organisation. If you compare these opportunities with the increasing trust in companies as an institution, as documented by the previously mentioned study, Edelman's Trust Barometer 2023, there is probably no doubt that this is also part of the communication professional's current and future resort: To develop and

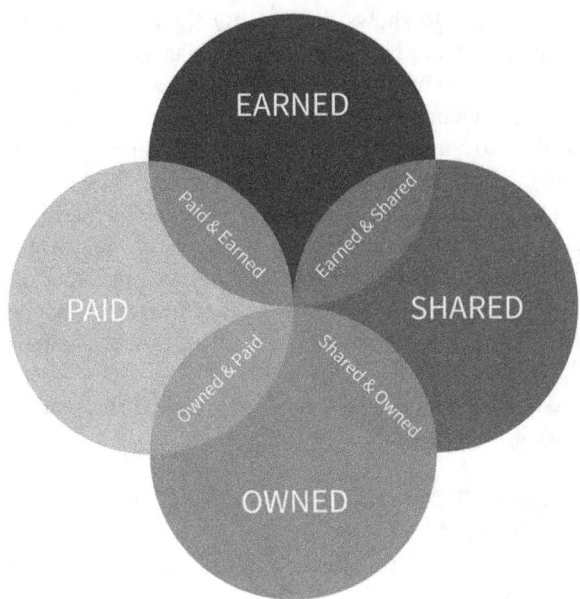

Fig. 4.1 Overview of the four channel types. Source: Dietrich in Travis and Lordan (2021)

establish the organisation as its own credible channel that can become an independent and strong voice to go to as a stakeholder, even without classic media as an intermediary.

4.4 With the CEO as a Cross-Platform Channel

One of the crucial channels for positioning an organisation as a corporate citizen is the CEO. As early as 1973, Mintzberg defined the role of the CEO as, amongst other things, 'interacting with internal and external parties' (Mintzberg, 1973) and this interaction on climate and societal issues, where a top leader actively reaches for and obtains influence on the public agenda, has since 2015 been defined as 'CEO activism' (Chatterji & Toffel, 2018). CEO activism is becoming increasingly prevalent in the public debate (Olkkonen & Morsing, 2022). As a communication professional, it is thus a task to help ensure that this activism is used wisely to position the organisation as a corporate citizen and to advise and help managers in this regard.

CEO activism is not only a desire from organisations but has also become an expectation from stakeholders. Edelman's Trust Barometer (2023) shows that there is a clear expectation in society that a CEO will step forward on important agendas. Specifically, data shows that this is expected in relation to employee well-being, climate change, discrimination, inequality and immigration, the first one clearly topping the list with 89% expecting a CEO to take a public stand on issues concerning the treatment of employees.

However, the survey also shows that a CEO should not become *too* political. Respondents believe that the best way for an organisation to protect itself from becoming too political is to maintain being a credible source of information (46%), to base its actions on science (43%), not to associate itself with only one specific political party (39%), to consistently act on the same values (36%) and to constantly link its actions to the Trust Barometer to be competitive (33%).

The voices of top organisational leaders have become increasingly vocal, and the issues they raise have increasingly become potentially controversial: 'Although controversy and conflict are not new to research areas focusing on businesses as societal actors, it has been unusual for top management to deliberately seek public positions where they create controversy on their own accounts' (Olkkonen & Morsing, 2022: 2).

Rumstadt and Kanbach (2022) have taken stock of what research on CEO activism has shown so far, summarising it as follows:

1. The public expects CEOs to take a stand in public debate, whether or not it is related to their business.
2. CEO activism appears to have a direct impact on customers' willingness to buy a company's products.
3. CEOs run a real risk of annoying stakeholders with consequences for reputation and sales (Rumstadt & Kanbach, 2022: 308).

CEO activism is indisputably one of the professional communicator's fields of work, as the impact can be significant for the reputation of the organisation as a whole (Gregory, 2020), for the customer experience (Rumstadt & Kanbach, 2022) and for potential and existing employees (Branicki et al., 2021). The internal importance in relation to existing employees has been shown to be not only about engagement but also about innovation and efficiency. Here, research shows that it is crucial for the internal stakeholder that there is a correlation between the external CEO activism and how competent (Melloni et al., 2019) he or she is considered internally, just as the perception of humanity, morality and authenticity (Yim, 2019) is crucial.

However, as point 3 above clarifies, CEO activism is not without risk, because stakeholders may be annoyed by specific positions or perceive leaders' activist expressions as untrustworthy schemes to look good or even as morally offensive (Branicki et al., 2021). This can lead to accusations of so-called 'woke washing'—also often concretised in, for example 'green washing' in relation to climate change, 'pink washing' in relation to LGBTQI+ rights or 'blue washing' in relation to social responsibility. The professional communicator can only protect the organisation from such undermining accusations by ensuring that there is a credible and transparent link between what is said and what is done.

When the CEO suddenly functions as a communication channel, the professional communicator's field of work also becomes the leader as an individual, which is rarely simple because it can be a complex power space to work in. However, there is no doubt that the individual is part of the message and can both inhibit and promote the desired effect of CEO activism. Researchers have documented, amongst other things, that it can inhibit the effect if stakeholders sense narcissism, just as stakeholders assess the individual CEO's underlying values and perceived authenticity (Chatterji & Toffel, 2018). At the same time, studies show that the impact is enhanced if CEOs are able to inspire and communicate with emotion and clear language. It is also clear that individual stardom has an impact on the effectiveness of CEO activism (Hambrick & Wowak, 2021).

In other words, it is not entirely safe to go public if you have not assessed the sender's authenticity and communicative skills. An important part of the professional communicator's work is thus also to work with the individual CEO's authenticity and communicative abilities, so that topics are chosen where the commitment is genuine, and so work is also being done on being inspiring. This means that part of the work as a communication advisor involves getting very close to the CEO's abilities and potentials, which calls for roles such as communicative sparring partner and coach.

The active use of knowledge and data on inhibiting and enabling factors can help to ensure the necessary impact of CEO activism, whilst ensuring that sticking one's neck out does not backfire. However, the positive impact of CEO activism can be documented across the entire stakeholder landscape from suppliers (Gregory, 2020) to investors (Afego and Alagidede, 2021), politicians (Chatterji & Toffel, 2018) and the general public (Chatterji & Toffel, 2018; Hambrick & Wowak, 2021). However, it has not yet been documented what influence activism has on boards—only that support from boards is important for the individual CEO's activism (Rumstadt & Kanbach, 2022). CEO activism is thus a natural part of the field of work for the professional communicator in the age of stakeholder capitalism.

4.5 The Practical Work of CEO Activism

The professional communicator can benefit from working very systematically with the practical management of the work with CEO activism. Olkkonen and Morsing (2022) have, on the basis of a close analysis of specific CEO activism, identified and developed a process model that can ensure that your work with CEO activism is constructive. They recommend dividing the work into three overall phases and working continuously to increase credibility and impact, as shown in Fig. 4.2.

The three phases are, respectively:

1. Pre-phase: The pre-phase is the initial phase before deciding to take a position. It is a decision and analysis phase where the CEO anchors the position in his or her own values too in order to provide a personal voice and ensuring also that the viewpoint can be meaningfully anchored in the organisation's values and purpose.
2. During-phase: The during-phase begins when an organisation takes on the point of view, the CEO steps forward with his/her own voice, and the organisation

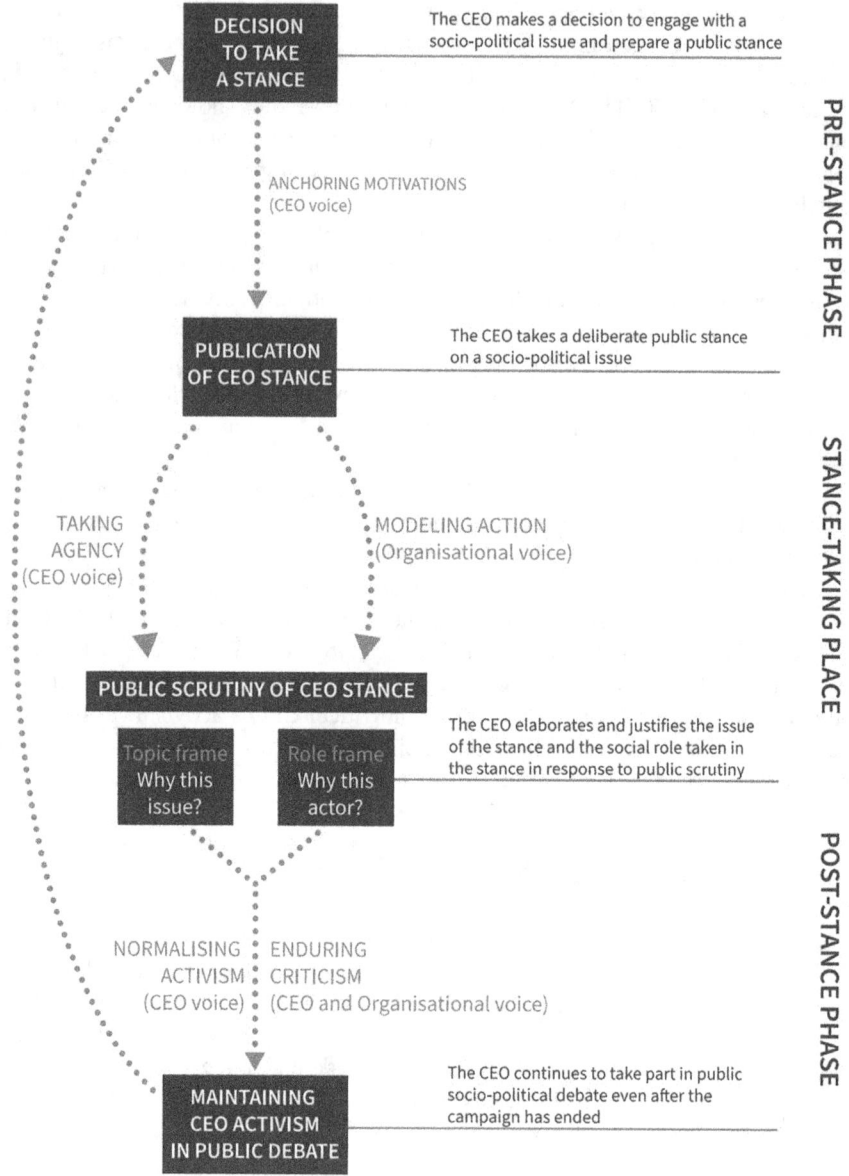

Fig. 4.2 Process model for CEO activism over an extended period of time. Source: Olkkonen and Morsing (2022)

simultaneously does the same. Here, recipients also start scrutinising the issue and the role of the CEO.

3. Post-phase: The post-phase refers to both the CEO and the organisation remaining visible in the current debate on the issue and possibly refining the position or

4.5 The Practical Work of CEO Activism

supporting it with arguments as to why it is relevant for the CEO/organisation to take this position.

The coherence of the process is shown in the model below:

The model was developed after following a Finnish company and their CEO for 6 years in order to shed light not only on a single announcement but to look at continuous CEO activism. One of the points is that CEO activism will rarely consist of a single announcement, but rather a stream of external activities that are modelled and orchestrated from within. Olkkonen and Morsing (2022) thus highlight the orchestrating part of the work, which is one of the communicator's central tasks: not only to produce announcements but to orchestrate the organisational execution of a decision by both facilitating and producing actions.

In addition, they emphasise the importance of paying attention to the role of the active CEO. This is because it is a role that is actively pursued, whilst the subject matter can change from time to time. The Finnish CEO they follow takes positions on issues such as sexuality, the refugee crisis and women's rights over the course of 6 years. In other words: The position changes, but the role of the CEO activist remains the same.

Olkkonen & Morsing point to five specific activities that appear to be crucial across campaigns, as shown in Fig. 4.2. These are anchoring motivation (1), which is part of the preparation phase. The planning of the actions themselves and modelling of messages heading into the during-phase (2) and mobilising the necessary agency in the situation (3). This is followed by the management of criticism, which is an ongoing process of the CEO inviting and responding to criticism (4) and followed by the normalisation of activism (5) in the post-phase, where the position is backed up by continued action.

In this approach, the link between the individual voice of the CEO and the voice of the organisation becomes clear. A CEO can both anchor something in his or her own values in statements such as 'I personally think that ...', whilst at the same time referencing a common voice in the organisational value chain by saying: 'In NN organisation we have no doubt that ...'

For professional communicators, this requires orchestrating a good interaction with the CEO and other key stakeholders, for example in the field targeted by the activism. But most of all, it requires a CEO who is willing, able and daring to step forward, as summarised by former General Electric communications director Gary Sheffer:

> The new reality requires a strong sense of self and a willingness to make a decision that may be detrimental to your financial performance. Business character is being judged by a wider range of stakeholders on a wider range of issues than ever before and all of this is happening in full view. This is new and this is where the CCO must take the point (Page, 2019).

Positioning your organisation as a corporate citizen is an important and complex task as a professional communicator. It requires active use of the professional communicator's entire field of work, from analysing external challenges, trends and the stakeholder scenario to facilitating specific decision-making processes on where and what to position across platforms and often direct instructional work, for example in preparing a CEO or other spokespersons for activist communication. It requires strong communicative skills to sharpen messages, positions and the spokesperson's communicative skills in a way that suits both a broad, relevant debate and a single person who has to position an entire company and inspire confidence amongst all stakeholders.

4.6   Case 3. With New Fuel in Sight

'If Maersk can do it, everyone can become climate neutral'. This was the reaction of many when Maersk announced in December 2018 a goal to make its shipping business climate neutral by 2050. It was something to get started on, as the global group emits as much CO_2 as the whole of Denmark, where their headquarters are located. They decided to take the lead for the entire industry and share responsibility for the green transition, which meant developing new types of ships and fuels. These were challenges that, at the time, were very far from having concrete solutions. Maersk stepped forward as a 'corporate citizen' in the climate area, and CEO activism was a key tool in the positioning of Maersk's climate ambition, which took place on all platforms and channels and was intended for all stakeholders.

'We knew that many people would be surprised and that we would probably also be met with some natural scepticism', says Head of International Media Relations Mikkel Linnet, who has been in charge of the communication side of the work. So the preparations were also complex in terms of communication: 'We wondered how we could come forward and engage in a conversation where we didn't have all the answers but a lot of sincere ambitions'.

Maersk's then CEO Søren Skou was a very important channel in the communication work. He took the lead with personalised, committed CEO activism. 'He really stepped up in this work together with the rest of our senior management, even more than many might have expected', says Mikkel Linnet.

The first announcement was seen as a 'moon shot'. And so it was for Maersk themselves, as they did not yet have the answers *how to* become climate neutral. That is why it was really what researchers call 'aspirational talk' (Christensen et al., 2013). It is daring as an organisation to talk about something you want to achieve but do not yet know how to make a reality. By putting the ambitions into words in this way, they hoped to create movement and followership to make it possible to fulfil the ambitions. The communication department was a very active part of the preparation, with ambitious positioning across all media and platforms, and specific coaching and training of the top management and other organisational voices to deliver the new messages. But the plan could not be a detailed script, because much was unknown, both about what, how and when it would all begin to manifest itself.

4.6 Case 3. With New Fuel in Sight

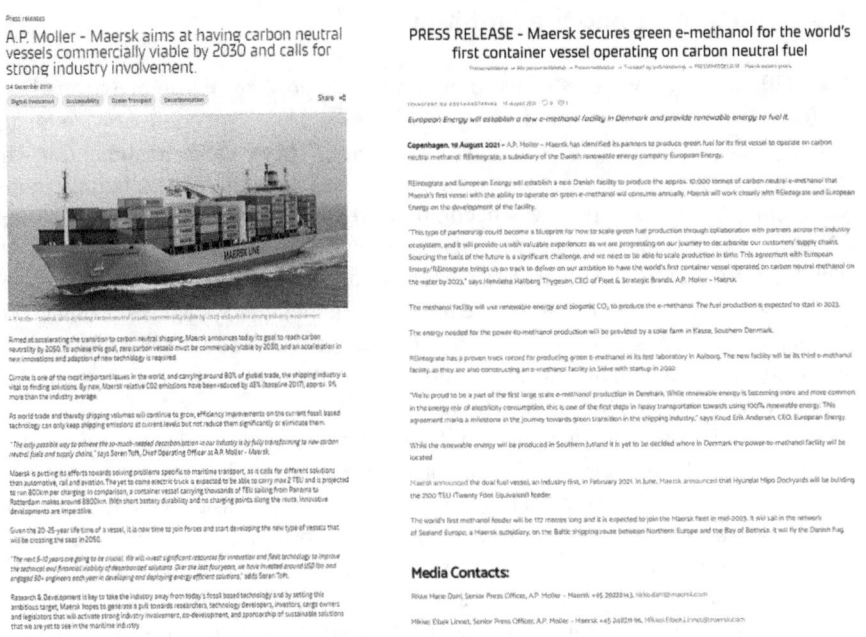

Fig. 4.3 Examples of press releases related to Maersk's ambition of being climate neutral by 2050

So the communicative decision was to be transparent about the work and engage in open dialogues with stakeholders.

The ambition to significantly change emissions was so concrete that it was announced in a press release at COP24 in Poland in 2018 (Fig. 4.3): 'Aimed at accelerating the transition to carbon neutral shipping, Maersk announces today its goal to reach carbon neutrality by 2050. To achieve this goal, zero carbon vessels must be commercially viable by 2030, and an acceleration in new innovations and adaption of new technology is required'. A clear indication on 'owned media', i.e. their own media platforms, aimed directly at the classic news media, who did immediately take up the ambitions.

An ambition no one yet knew how to deliver on but by saying it out loud, Maersk put pressure on themselves and initiated dialogues with stakeholders who wanted to join in and start finding solutions together. Because Maersk cannot initiate the transformation alone. It requires, amongst other things, ships that can run on other fuels, and more importantly, it requires a huge scale-up of the production of new green fuel at an affordable price. In the years around 2019, the world's major companies committed to climate neutrality in various forms and at various paces, depending on the industry to which they belonged. This meant that most of Maersk's large clients soon had ambitious plans for climate neutrality themselves and thus became deeply dependent on green logistics solutions—and Maersk's climate ambition—to achieve their goals.

4.6.1 Action Behind the Ambitions

By 2020, the first few years of the programme had gone further than expected and various viable pathways towards the goal of climate neutrality could now be identified. A collaboration began with, amongst others, a ship engine manufacturer who could make an engine that could run on the new fuel methanol. Initially only with a small ship, but the solution was becoming a reality. In terms of communication, Maersk was constantly and persistently reporting on all the efforts, trying to create a dialogue with all stakeholders and making sure the agenda was clear. 'At the same time, it was also a challenge to not be too sanctimonious', says Mikkel Linnet. 'We are one of the largest players in the world, and we want the whole industry to be involved in this development, so we don't want them to withdraw because they think we have become holier-than-thou'.

So a lot of work was also put into, for example the tone of the announcements and on always being very specific about what was being done, so it was not just lofty ideals. A concreteness that also became easier and easier as solutions were found and various initiatives were launched. It has been an ambition to be able to document all points in action. 'By focusing on concrete facts, we have succeeded in keeping the narrative together. For example, when the ship engine was ready for the very large ships, of which we subsequently ordered 18—a billion-dollar investment in US dollars—there was something concrete to tell, and this prompted several of our primary competitors on the seas to follow suit. I would venture to say that the communication effort has been a crucial driver in accelerating the development and in the decisions made by a number of key stakeholders in a complex stakeholder landscape', he elaborates. Communication efforts have been cross-platform, partly by making announcements on owned media channels and partly by sharing news on social media ('shared media'). Both with many organisational voices in play from internal experts to the CEO and using everything from press releases to newspaper interviews, films on social media, LinkedIn Live with stakeholders etc. This also meant that Maersk's climate efforts were increasingly shared and discussed by others ('earned media').

The efforts went so well that in January 2022 Maersk was able to cut a full 10 years off the plan. Now it was not 2050, but as early as 2040. The new and even more ambitious plan was announced, with Executive Board member Henriette Hallberg Thygesen (Fig. 4.4) as spokesperson: 'Our updated targets and accelerated timelines reflect a very challenging, yet viable pathway to net zero which is driven by advances in technology and solutions. What is needed is a rapid scale-up which we will strive to achieve in close collaboration with customers and suppliers across the entire supply chain'. The style is still the ambitious, nuanced and collaborative organisation that does not meet the ambition of climate neutrality but helps facilitate an important change as a corporate citizen.

The communication work in connection with Maersk's position as a corporate citizen has also been very much about collaborating with other stakeholders such as NGOs and other opinion leaders: 'We have always had an ambition to speak openly, but also to ask and listen. This is not something we can do alone, so we have worked

4.6 Case 3. With New Fuel in Sight

Fig. 4.4 Henriette Hallberg Thygesen in dialogue with, amongst others, US President Joe Biden and President of the European Commission Ursula von der Leyen at the Climate Summit in Glasgow 2021

closely with NGOs and all sorts of other parties with whom we discuss opportunities and challenges along the way'.

It has also been necessary to develop entirely new communication formats for the process. For example, Maersk organised open discussion meetings with internal and external experts. These were held as webinars that were filmed live so the media could also listen in. The format was a short one: 12–18 min of dialogue between experts, followed by an often lengthy Q&A session where the media could ask questions. 'The new format made it possible to include far more nuances than classic statements such as in press releases and also to use our platform to give others the floor, so it became a completely different kind of conversation', says Mikkel Linnet, who admits that they were a bit apprehensive the first time, but that the format has essentially worked very well. 'Afterwards, we edited the film version so we could, for example, share the main points on our social media. In this way, Maersk also stepped in as an independent channel, rather than just relying on the hope that the press would cover the process with the necessary nuances'. The ambition was to give the press good working conditions but also to be a clear sender on their own platforms: 'We have a lot on our website, we write about it on our social media, it is included in our investor events. There is so much communication about this that we cannot possibly write or ensure the quality of everything. So it is increasingly about drawing the lines and ensuring that everyone internally knows where to get our core narrative and core facts, for example, so that the many efforts (roughly) work together. There is a huge amount of communication from all parts of the organisation—insurance, public affairs, investor relations, finance, operations both on land, at sea and in the air'.

Maersk's climate ambitions have grown throughout the process, often with the CEO leading the way in making significant announcements. Maersk has stepped forward where few expected it. In May 2021, for example then CEO Søren Skou

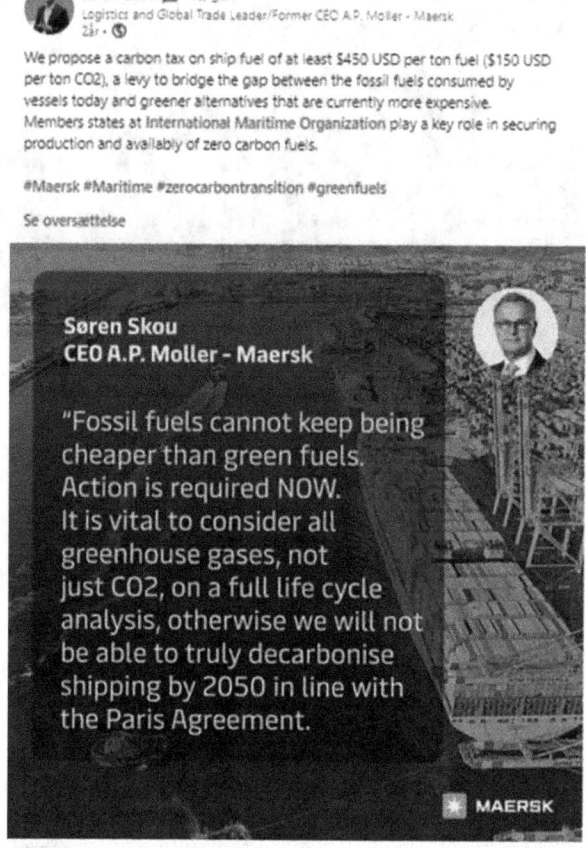

Fig. 4.5 An example of CEO activism on LinkedIn

was the first to recommend an ambitious 'carbon tax' for shipping (Figs. 4.5 and 4.6), and a few months later, at an important meeting of the shipping industry, he proposed a specific end date for fossil fuels.

The work on CEO activism was based on a sincere commitment and a clear decision to take a stance—'a decision to take a stance anchored in motivation' cf. Olkkonen and Morsing (2022)—and an ongoing and active dialogue on the interplay between the organisational voice and the CEO's ('during-phase'). The agenda was set across all channels, and the CEO had specific opportunities to step forward and set the direction. At the same time, the entire communication effort was closely monitored ('post-phase'), so that knowledge of input and reactions from stakeholders could be integrated, possibly resulting in adjustments to the choice of channels, spokespersons, tone, explanations or examples.

However, working on external communication alone is not enough—internal communication has also received a lot of attention. For example, work has been done

4.6 Case 3. With New Fuel in Sight

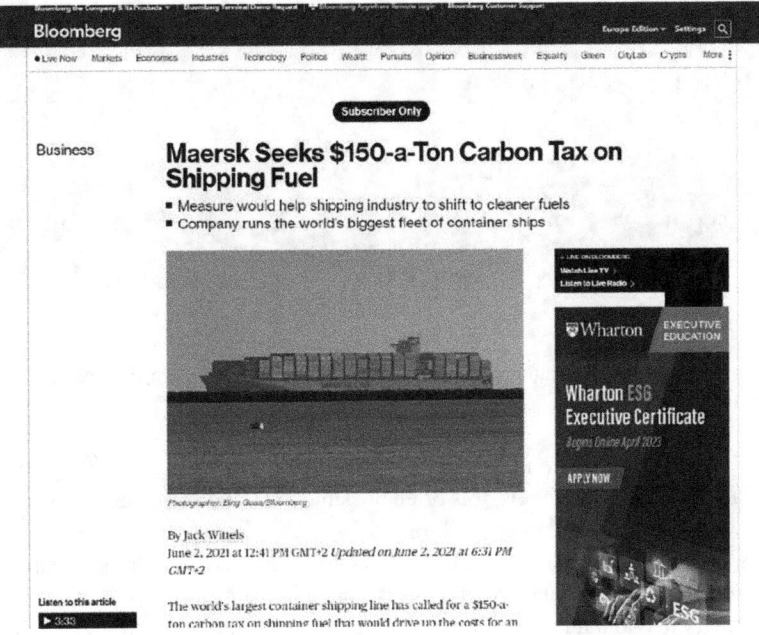

Fig. 4.6 The press, in this case American Bloomberg, has continuously covered the work closely

on very specific 'message maps' that could help all managers to put Maersk's climate ambitions into words. Not as a toast speech, but as a blueprint for concrete action, because it affects the entire organisation when ambitions are to become reality.

The work has also been closely monitored on all internal communication channels, so that staff have been able to contribute to solutions and dialogues with all the stakeholders they are in contact with (Fig. 4.7). Employees themselves have also been actively involved in communicating with the outside world. For example, a film for social media closely follows the employees on the first large ship with the new engine and fossil-free fuel. Because what is it really like to be a pioneer?

4.6.2 'Maersk Channel'

As the example of Maersk's climate neutrality ambitions has clearly shown, the organisation has increasingly embraced being a channel in their own right. 'It's a natural consequence of the fact that we've seen a decline in trust in the media, and we've also seen an increasing number of followers on all our external social media channels', says Sam Poulter, Head of Corporate Branding and Channel Development. This awareness has meant that Maersk is increasingly recognising a new balance between 'owned', 'paid', 'shared' and 'earned media', where it is clear that on their own channels they are trusted by the outside world and reach a wider audience than through single large editorial media outlets.

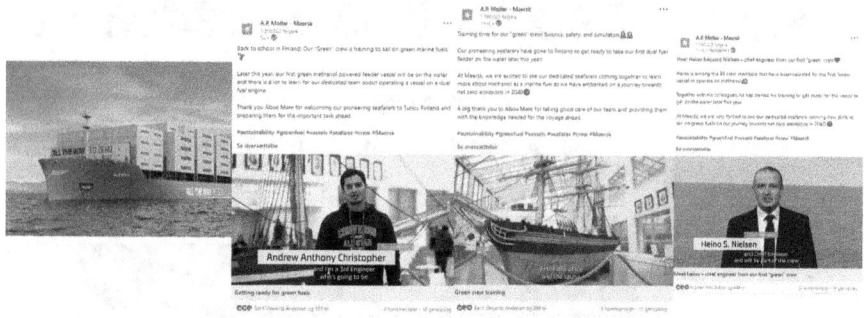

Fig. 4.7 Internal communication about Maersk's work process to reach the goal of becoming climate neutral

'This means that we consider our own channels very actively in any communication plan. In our own channels, it is often possible to include other and more nuances than if we are edited by external editors', he says.

The move towards their own channel has made Maersk even more conscious of building trust by being balanced and introspective in their approach to the world. 'It's a trust we try to maintain by earning it every time with an open, concrete and fact-based approach to our content', he emphasises, 'and it also requires something of us as communicators. We need to be even more critical of our own internal sources so that we get the right nuances across and don't just communicate glossy images'.

The communications department has developed a concept they call 'Maersk Studio' (Fig. 4.8). It is both a physical studio and a mindset of the strategic producers. The physical studio exists both as a stationary set-up in the head office and as a mobile studio in a glass container that can be set up anywhere to broadcast from various events around the world.

The mobile studio was, for example in Gothenburg for Maersk's global leadership meeting in 2022, allowing live interviews with leaders and guest speakers to be broadcast to the rest of the organisation's many employees.

'The glass container was in itself a symbol that we want to be open, because it is a container that is very much associated with us and all the goods we ship around the world with the starred containers—and it is entirely transparent. That's why it has a great effect to put it up. It was a wow effect, but it's also a very practical framework for a lot of communication formats', says Sam Poulter, 'such as interviews, when we present our financial statements, or when we have special events that the whole organisation needs to be aware of'.

> Technically it was not an easy exercise, as a container is fundamentally not the most suitable for a studio with multiple camera angles and quality sound. But the container is an important symbol for and of us at Maersk, so we found some creative solutions to make it work.

As mentioned, Maersk Studio is also an expression of the mindset of the strategic producers. This means, amongst other things, that Maersk also works very actively to make the studio a watermark of trust. A mental stamp of trust on productions that

4.6 Case 3. With New Fuel in Sight

Fig. 4.8 Maersk Studio in the Maersk headquarters

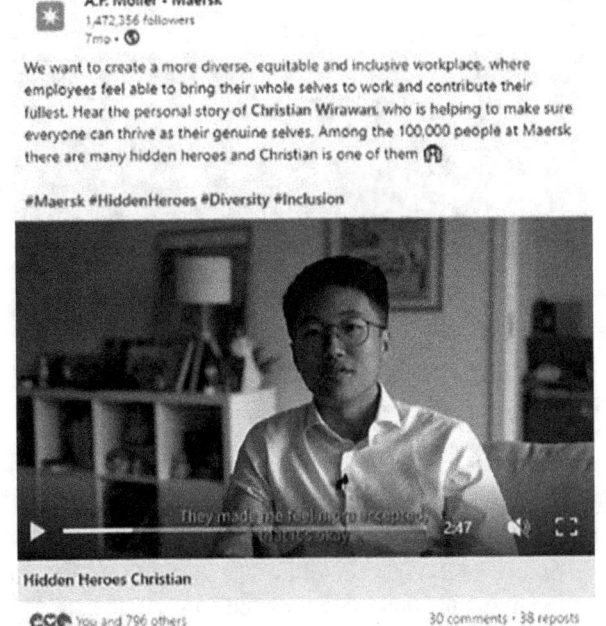

Fig. 4.9 The 'Hidden Heroes' series produced as part of Maersk Studio

become credible with a clear, recognisable Maersk sender. That's why time was put into creating a recognisable setting and visual style. 'It has been important for us to show approachability and openness'.

All staff in the Communications Department are trained to incorporate studio productions into their internal and external communication solutions. In the coming years, new formats will increasingly emerge from the programme, which everyone has been involved in developing. 'We have simply involved all our skilled communicators in a long, creative process of developing a lot of new concepts that we are now preparing for use both internally and externally', says Sam Poulter.

One example is the 'Hidden Heroes' series (Fig. 4.9), where Maersk shines a light on people who are making a difference in all sorts of ways, such as an episode

Fig. 4.10 The 'What's cooking' series produced by the strategic producers

on the chairman of their LGBTQI+ activities. The short films are produced in-house and are used both in internal communication and on social media. 'The intention is to be incredibly present here and probably also to surprise by showing things that people don't imagine Maersk doing. We want to take a step forward and show a little more nuance', he emphasises.

Another series is 'What's cooking' (Fig. 4.10), where a chef and a Maersk executive cook together and talk about, for example the surprising similarities between running a professional kitchen and managing a supply chain, as Maersk does. The idea of the series is to create new kinds of conversations and engage different stakeholders than they might have traditionally done by daring to play with the formats.

'We also have a 'Tech Head2Head' series, where we focus on digital developments and put our senior tech people together with industry experts. We're busy developing, testing and inventing', says Sam Poulter.

For Maersk, this part of the channel work is a natural consequence of developments in the media landscape, in trust in the world and in the ability of recipients to concentrate, which requires new formats. 'Of course, it's not easy nor free to work with all these productions, but if we compare it to the cost of purchased exposure, we really get a long way by investing a little in technology and skills here. We are working hard to find good formats that also have a broad application across all our platforms, and I also have the impression that all our communicators think it's a lot of fun to have been let loose a little more and be able to work with completely new possibilities and new creativity', concludes Sam Poulter.

4.7 Interview. Be a Stakeholder Capitalist

'Stakeholders must be in focus now. Organisations need to migrate from the shareholder capitalism model to one that embraces stakeholder capitalism' stresses Rupert Younger, co-founder of Oxford University's Centre for Corporate Reputation. The shift may seem a big one, but let's not forget that the one-sided focus on shareholders has only been around for 50 years: and 50 years is nothing in world history, so it's about time to give your entire attention to all stakeholders and focus on direction and relationships, making strategic communicators important as the intelligentsia of that shift.

Rupert Younger has one foot firmly planted in organisational reality as a co-founder of strategic consulting firm Finsbury, which is now called FGS Global and today has offices in 27 countries. The other foot is firmly planted in academia as founder and inaugural director of the Centre for Corporate Reputation at the University of Oxford, an academic research centre studying the dynamics and value of legitimacy, status, stigma, reputation and trust. He includes experience from both worlds in our conversation about how organisations build positive social evaluations in today's stakeholder economy.

4.7.1 The Meaning of It All

In Younger's view, an organisation's reputation rests best on a clear purpose that answers the question: Why does the organisation exist in the first place? Preferably, it should point out towards the world. 'We have traditionally worked with visions that tell us what happens when we succeed and with missions that put into words how we should do it. But an ambitious organisation today must be able to justify the meaning of their existence with a clear purpose', Younger stresses. The first of several reports issued by the Enacting Purpose Initiative, which Younger chairs, set out how leaders could anchor their pursuit of purpose using five clear priorities: simplicity, connectivity, ownership, rewards and examples. The report, which emerged after a year-long consultation with business leaders from across Europe, formalised this insight in its SCORE framework, which was published separately in the Harvard Business Review in September 2020.

Younger is convinced that this is necessary for any organisation today. 'Times are changing. Succeeding in terms of shareholders or the bottom line is no longer enough. If we are to succeed as an organisation and enjoy a reputation that attracts shareholders, retains employees and recruits the customers and employees of the future, we must have a greater purpose. As organisations, we need to help make a difference in a bigger picture than our own little pond'.

Rupert Younger believes that organisations often have too narrow a view. Senior management teams mostly want to do more of the right thing, but instead of thinking deeply about their purpose they can become seduced into a short-term focus on tactical work. They look at sustainability strategies, social engagement, initiatives and collaborations. That work is important, but if management teams are to make a difference to the organisation's reputation and to all stakeholders, the thinking has to be bigger and must be embedded in the raison d'etre of the entire organisation. They have to answer the questions 'why are we here, and what difference can we make to society?' How can a pharmaceutical company, for example improve the health of the world in a systemic way? Answering this allows the overall strategic orientation to shift, enhancing the meaning of what they do with a variety of different groups. The focus at Oxford has been encapsulated by Professor Colin Mayer's assertion that 'businesses should profit from providing solutions for people and for the planet'.

4.7.2 Credibility Is the Core

A reputation has to be based on a credible claim—so it is about being sure that the organisation is ambitious enough on the one hand and not too far-fetched on the other when it comes to its reality and raison d'etre. 'Today we see many organisations suffer serious reputational consequences because they have claimed something that has no basis in reality. These could be accusations of green, blue or pink washing, all of which can be very serious for an organisation's reputation'.

For Younger, the central *why* in a good purpose is a guide to what you should do—and what you should not do. 'Making an active decision, for example at board level, about what to opt out of when committing to a purpose is equally important. It's the first protection against all kinds of potential boomerang effects'.

From Younger's perspective, this requires some deep discussions and delimitations: 'You have to understand how you as an organisation are part of a larger ecosystem and make an active decision about what roles you play and do not play in that ecosystem'.

4.7.3 From Shareholders to Stakeholders

In Rupert Younger's view, shareholder capitalism has dominated economic thinking for the last 50 years. Slightly caricatured, companies were driven by what it took to make shareholders happy with a good bottom line results and solid returns. But that's no longer enough: 'There's a lively, global debate going on about the shift from a focus on shareholders to stakeholders in order to be a globally accepted organisation', he emphasises, adding that Europe is the most advanced, with many organisations having come very far in this shift, whilst the USA, for example is still lagging behind, with some organisations still thinking mainly about the bottom line.

But the movement is happening. 'Organisations need to change their understanding, because stakeholders today are making demands in a completely different way than they did before. We are not just talking about shareholders but also customers, potential customers and internal stakeholders, such as employees. Organisations today do not operate in a vacuum but in a close relationship with all their stakeholders. That's why I'm a dedicated stakeholder capitalist myself—and that's the direction I'm convinced we should take'.

Rupert Younger believes that in time even the most reluctant boards will switch to stakeholder capitalism, because the demands are inevitable, be it employees suddenly 'silent quitting' in large numbers or vocal NGOs or politicians. 'Tomorrow's winners are organisations with a clear purpose on which they actively act', Rupert Younger stresses, but obviously, it rests on a fundamental belief in the conscientiousness of man, as the philosopher Rousseau would put it.

'Modern shareholder capitalism has only dominated economic thought since the 1950s, but the history of economic thought has embraced stakeholder capitalism for a lot longer', Younger says with a smile.

4.7.4 Communication in a Changed World

In the new reality, it is important to look at the role of communication with fresh eyes, says the Oxford thinker. 'It is increasingly important to collect much more knowledge of stakeholders. Communicators must be an intelligentsia that collects relevant knowledge'.

At the same time, he believes that we should distinguish between three types of communicative contact: The classic one is what one might call **direct → direct**, meaning communication from the organisation directly to the individual stakeholders whether they are customers, employees, shareholders or society.

The other type is: **Direct → indirect**, which are all situations where communication from the organisation must go through a filter. This may, for example be communication via the media, where the media has the direct stakeholder contact. Here, the credibility of the gatekeeper also becomes essential—for example, does carrying it forward with their reputation reinforce the message? Or the opposite?

The third and last type is the slightly more complicated but important **indirect → indirect**. Here, the organisation communicates indirectly, for example through an employee who may be active in an NGO. That NGO then brings up the agenda and discusses it with the media. This is a form of communication that has become increasingly common with the easy shareability of social media.

The third form of contact is often not cultivated enough, says Rupert Younger: 'There is a huge potential here in many places. Managers can influence the way others talk about and share communications materials. They just need to be aware of the poor effect that will often be the result. This is where we see the effects, for example on social media'.

4.7.5 Communication Drives the Work

'Communication shouldn't just be an afterthought, it's an absolutely central part of the architecture of creating purpose, strategy and action. We live in an age that calls for strong strategic communicators', he stresses. 'If you think about it, there aren't that many functions in an organisation that entail outside-in thinking. Done well, this is a very valuable resource and critical if you are to succeed in a stakeholder capitalist world'.

Knowledge of the world around the organisation, of stakeholders, trends and perspectives, is crucial for communicators to collect and bring into the organisation. Only that knowledge can ensure that the right ambitions are identified—and the right actions are put into motion. This is why communicators are much more necessary in the future: 'Excellent strategic communicators no longer see themselves simply as media or communications experts, but as a strategic decision-making part of the management of an organisation'.

Rupert Younger concludes with a call to all communicators: 'Read widely and read wisely'. In an information rich world, identifying, distilling and translating knowledge and different perspectives are critical pre-conditions to becoming the strategic resource for leaders that is required for business success today.

Rupert Younger

Rupert Younger is the founder and director of the Oxford University Centre for Corporate Reputation. He is the co-author of two books—'*The Reputation Game*' (with David Waller) and '*The Activist Manifesto*' (with Frank Partnoy). He chairs the Enacting Purpose Initiative, a collaboration between the University of Oxford, the University of California at Berkeley, investment manager Federated Hermes and the British Academy focused on how organisations can successfully translate purpose intent into action. He teaches on the University of Oxford's MBA programme at the Said Business School and is the Academic Director of the University of Oxford's Corporate Affairs Academy.

> He is a co-founder of the consultancy business FGS Global, which has 27 offices and 1200 employees and is a global advisor in stakeholder economics with a focus on insight and communication.

References

Afego, P. N., & Alagidede, I. P. (2021). What does corporate social advocacy signal? Evidence from boycott participation decisions. *Journal of capital markets studies, 5*(1), 49–68.

Branicki, L., Brammer, S., Pullen, A., & Rhodes, C. (2021). The morality of 'new' CEO activism. *Journal of Business Ethics, 170*(2), 269–285.

Bratman, M. (2014). *Shared agency: A planning theory of acting together*. Oxford University Press.

Capizzo, L. (2020). The Right Side of History, Inc.: Social issues management, social licence to operate and the Obergefell V. Hodges Decision. *Public Relations Review, 46*(5), 101957.

Carucci, & Ridge. (2022). How executive teams shape a company's purpose. *Harvard Business Review*.

Chatterji, A. K., & Toffel, M. W. (2018). The new CEO activists: A playbook for polarised political times. *Harvard Business Review, 96*(1), 78.

Christensen, L. T. (2003). Corporate identity as seduction and self-seduction. In J. Helder & B. Kragh (Eds.), *When the company opens its window—A corporate perspective* (pp. 87–100).

Christensen, L. T., Morsing, M., & Thyssen, O. (2013). CSR as aspirational talk. *Organisation (London, England), 20.3)*, 372–393.

Dhanesh, G. (2017). Putting engagement in its proper place: State of the field, definition and model of engagement in public relations. *Public Relations Review., 43*, 925–933. https://doi.org/10.1016/j.pubrev.2017.04.001

Freeman, R. E., Martin, K., & Parmar, B. (2007). Stakeholder capitalism. *Journal of Business Ethics, 74*(4), 303–314.

Gregory. (2020). *Planning and managing public relations campaigns: A Strategic Approach*. Kogan Page Ltd.

Hambrick, D. C., & Wowak, A. J. (2021). CEO sociopolitical activism: A stakeholder alignment model. *The Academy of Management Review, 46*(1), 33–59.

Heath, R. L. (2018a). How fully functioning is communication engagement if society does not benefit? In K. A. Johnston & M. Taylor (Eds.), *The handbook of communication engagement* (pp. 33–47). Wiley Blackwell.

Heath, R. L. (2018b). Strategic issues management. In O. Ihlen & R. L. Heath (Eds.), *The handbook of organisational rhetoric and communication* (pp. 383–399). Wiley.

Heath, R. L. (2022). The processes-to-end(s) paradox of public relations. *Public Relations Review, 48*, 5.

Ihlen, Ø., Bartlett, J., & May, S. (2011). *The handbook of communication and corporate social responsibility* (1st ed.). Wiley-Blackwell.

Ihlen, Ø., & Raknes, K. (2020). Appeals to 'the public interest': How public relations and lobbying create a social licence to operate. *Public Relations Review, 46*(5).

Ihlen, Ø., & Raknes, K. (2022). *The game of goodwill: An exploratory study of discursive strategies of interest organizations in a consensus democracy*. Interest Groups & Advocacy.

Kjærgaard, A., & Morsing, M. (2010). Strategic auto-communication in identity-image interplay: The dynamics of mediatising organizational identity. In L. Chouliaraki & M. Morsing (Eds.), *Media, organisations and identity* (pp. 93–111). Palgrave Macmillan.

Klopčič, A. L., Hojnik, J., Bojnec, Š., & Papler, D. (2020). Global Transition to the subscription economy: Literature review on business model changes in the media landscape. *Managing Global Transitions, 18*(4), 323–351.

Koya, N., Hurst, B., & Roper, J. (2021). In whose interests? When relational engagement to obtain a social licence leads to paradoxical outcomes. *Public Relations Review, 47*, 1.

Melloni, G., Patacconi, A., & Vikander, N. (2019). *CEO activism as communication to multiple audiences*. SSRN.

Minow, M. (2021). *Saving the news: Why the constitution calls for government action to preserve freedom of speech*. Oxford University Press.

Mintzberg, H. (1973). *The nature of managerial work*. Harper & Row.

O'Connor, A. (Ed.). (2023). *The Routledge handbook of corporate social responsibility communication*. New York.

Olkkonen, L., & Morsing, M. (2022). A processual model of CEO activism: Activities, frames and phases. *Business & Society, 62*(3).

Page. (2019). *The CCO as pacesetter what it means, why it matters, how to get there*. Page research report.

Rendtorff, J. D. (2020). Corporate citizenship, stakeholder management and sustainable development goals (SDGs) in financial institutions and capital markets. *Journal of Capital Markets Studies, 4*(1), 47–59.

Reuters. (2021). Reuters Institute & University of Oxford. https://reutersinstitute.politics.ox.ac.uk/snap-judgements-how-audiences-who-lack-trust-news-navigate-information-digital-platforms, 2021

Rumstadt, F., & Kanbach, D. K. (2022). CEO activism. What do we know? What don't we know? A systematic literature review. *Society and Business Review, 17*(2), 307–330.

Travis, E. S., & Lordan, E. J. (2021). Public relations models. In *Public relations theory* (p. 98). Sage.

Yim, M. C. (2019). CEOs' political tweets and perceived authenticity: Can expectancy violation be a pleasant surprise? *Public Relations Review, 45*, 3.

Communication Must Create Contact   5

The professional communicator must connect at a time when stakeholders want not just information but a relationship with real contact. This is not easy and requires clever orchestration of all the voices of the organisation, from the top manager's statements to the tone of the article on the intranet and the post on social media. This chapter looks more closely at the facilitation of organisational presence and the demands it places on the professional communicator.

In this case, Maersk provides insight into how the strategic producers work to facilitate the organisation's presence both in concrete terms on social media and when a strategic change makes it necessary to engage entirely new stakeholders.

The chapter's international expert is Professor Chiara Valentini, Professor of Communication at the University of Jyväskylä in Finland, who focuses on the opportunities and challenges of technology for communicators.

In the age of stakeholder capitalism, all organisations must understand how to meet stakeholders with respect and at eye level in order to succeed, which constitutes a new 'bottom line' that is not mainly economic. This requires a key change in the content, form and tone of communication, which presents professional communicators with a major task of change in the production of communication itself. Contact with stakeholders has changed. It has become both easier and more difficult. Easier because the many digital possibilities offered by communication technologies make it possible to be in direct contact with stakeholders. Such as the over 3.7 billion active social media users worldwide, which is expected to rise to 4.4 billion by 2025 (Statista, 2022)—or half of the world's population.

Whilst there are more and more platforms and opportunities for engagement, this also means that competition for attention has increased and that it has become more difficult to hold the attention of stakeholders. Neurological studies show that the human ability to focus or our 'attention span' has become shorter (Eanes, 2020). Attention is short-lived, and stakeholders are easily distracted. In practice, this means that it takes more to attract and retain stakeholders. At the same time, studies on both media habits (Reuters, 2022) and trust (Edelman, 2023) show that there is a greater polarisation of stakeholders, with some paying close attention to what is happening in the world and others dropping out altogether, making it even more difficult to make real contact with all stakeholders—and not just those already interested and supportive. Results that a number of internal studies in organisations can also confirm. All of this requires great communicative skills from the communicator. Classic communicative skills that should not give way to strategic communication work. A good communicator must fundamentally master how to communicate in an engaging and convincing way and how to help others to do the same. This chapter identifies some of the tools that the professional communicator can use to connect, from mental shortcuts to storytelling and dialogue-based communication.

5.1 Mental Shortcuts as a Tool

One of the tools that professional communicators can draw inspiration from to attract even potentially polarised stakeholders is the so-called 'mental shortcuts' to contact, derived from a major study by The Reuters Institute for the Study of Journalism (2022). A study that investigated what could make even distrustful and sceptical stakeholders who do not trust news media read something in a digital information environment. It found that stakeholders made quick judgements on six elements, namely brand, headlines, social signals, platform signals, advertising/sponsor signals and visual signals (Table 5.1).

The six signals are perhaps not so surprising, but they are a good reminder that we need to think broadly in terms of mental shortcuts to stakeholders today and are useful to integrate into the professional communicator's toolbox. For example, how can you ensure in the orchestration of communication that you send clear 'social cues' so stakeholders identify with the organisation and want to read or watch? Or how can you ensure in your channel mix that you reach stakeholders on their preferred platforms and in the form they prefer? And how can you ensure up-to-date knowledge about how your brand is perceived and whether this is a headwind or a tailwind in relation to stakeholders? And how can you ensure that your tone of voice is inviting and at eye level? What signals do you send when advertising or

Table 5.1 Six elements that engage stakeholders

Cue	
Brand	Pre-existing ideas about news
Headlines	Tone and word choice
Social signals	Who shared the information?
Platform	Presence of likes, labels and the order in which information appears
Advertising	Cues related to sponsorship
Visuals	Images, video or presence of URL

Source: Reuters Institute for the Study of Journalism (2022)

sponsoring messages? How do you use the headline of the communication to retain stakeholders? And how do you work visually to make the communication inviting and attractive?

All six mental shortcuts are areas of work for the professional communicator and are a clear example of how communication is much more than the choice of words and content. The communicator must be able to put themselves in the stakeholders' shoes and use the mental shortcuts that capture and retain attention and ensure that good contact is established.

5.2 Changing Criteria for Selecting Content

When communicating with stakeholders, the professional communicator must naturally weigh up and prioritise which content will be perceived as relevant, pertinent and interesting. For many years, the classic news criteria have been an often unspoken point of reference for organisational communicators. Communication was centred on what met the five news criteria, namely (Galtung & Ruge, 1965):

- Topicality
- Materiality
- Identification
- Sensation
- Conflict

But even this traditional approach is worth revisiting to update the professional communicator's toolbox. In media research, the news criteria have since been expanded to include the categories of 'celebrity' and 'entertainment' in order to embrace media developments and stakeholder demand. In recent years, the approach has also been challenged by journalists themselves, who have questioned whether it is sufficient. Because ought the media only be a watchdog, passively recording whether representative democracy is being upheld, and in the active form also be a hunting dog that draws attention to challenges, or should the media also be both shepherd and rescue dogs, looking after the flock and perhaps even helping to find the right 'salvation'? (Bro, 2019). As Haagerup (2014) puts it, journalism should have a constructive criterion and look for potentials and not just for problems. Or as Gyldensted (2015) emphasises: Adding positive psychology to news reporting and not just mirroring but moving the world with a kind of proactive neutrality, where journalists must seek to shed light on solutions in the world. A journalistic development that has resonated across media.

If we supplement this with studies of what works journalistically on social media (Jensen, 2019), it turns out that it is important that news are framed with sensation and increased emotional appeal, just as the social signals in the form of likes and shares help to ensure the impact of a news story with stakeholders (Meyer and Maltin 2010). Whilst other researchers emphasise that 'celebrity' (Ekman & Widholm, 2014) and 'sensation' (Highfield, 2017; Kilgo et al., 2016) are more important for whether content is shared on social media, whilst Harcup and O'Neill (2001) add exclusivity, conflict, drama, audiovisual elements and shareability as news criteria.

The points from news and social media are immediately translatable to the professional communicator's work in organising the cross-channel mix of organisations that are increasingly struggling to capture and retain attention and need to provide stakeholders with more transparent insight into organisational life in order to emerge as credible corporate citizens (see also Chap. 4). So the expanded approach to what content may create contact with stakeholders is very important. The communication must continue to be, for example both significant and topical, but it must also be carried by an organisational voice that can capture stakeholders not only by 'celebrity' but also by simple human identification. It may also easily be content that speaks of ambition (so-called 'aspirational talk') in order to activate stakeholders to new solutions, just as constructive journalism tries to create change through proactive and positive content. It can also be content that provides insight into processes and actions that can help bring about the desired change and thereby fulfil the transparency that stakeholders demand today.

Content is thus composed on the basis of a much wider palette than what has traditionally been the case, and professional communication often requires the orchestration of many more organisational voices than the individual communicator can create at the keyboard, which has increased the work load of training other staff in the organisation.

5.3 Cross-Cutting Story Universes

Another important point of inspiration for the professional communicator is storytelling across all media platforms. The professional communicator does not only work with one message in one channel but has an eye for all platforms and channels internally and externally. That is why it is often an advantage to work with story universes that have the same core narrative but can be used in many forms across platforms. This could, for example be the story about the organisation's focus on inclusion in everyday life or psychological safety, which is not only an internal effort in day-to-day management but also a cross-cutting story universe, as it can help position the organisation as an attractive workplace.

In terms of theory, cross-cutting storytelling is called a 'transmedial narrative approach' (Coombs & Holladay, 2018). The idea is that, based on the organisation's strategy and purpose, you define some key cross-cutting stories that are communicated across all platforms. They combine two well-documented, effective approaches to storytelling, 'transmedia' and 'narrative'. Coombs and Holladay exemplify the transmedial with the Star Wars universe. At first it was just a film, but then it evolved into an entire universe, with each film, series, figure and game contributing with its version of the story and reinforcing the universe. In the same way, an organisational

5.3 Cross-Cutting Story Universes

narrative can work transmedially. This is done by organising a universe with the same core story but with varied voices, platforms and elements. This approach has already been implemented by many organisations in their strategic communication work, both because stakeholders navigate across channels and because it creates an opportunity to amplify the impact of a message. In addition, it is also often time-saving for the professional communicator, because communicative elements can be reused or simply versioned for multiple platforms.

The second element of transversal storytelling is narrative, which has been shown to be highly effective. The so-called 'narrative transport theory', for example has documented how effectively stories move from a narrator to a changed agency in story listeners (Van Laer et al., 2014). By using a story universe with a storyteller and a classically composed story, it is thus possible to transport the content very effectively to stakeholders who understand it better and respond more actively to what the story has evoked in them. If it is a strategy story, for example, instead of a bunch of abstract slides, employees are better able to understand what the strategy calls for in concrete terms. They can achieve a better understanding and a direct motivation to act themselves because the story moves in as new agency within them.

A story is defined as a sequence of events created by a storyteller. It contains a plot, protagonists, a climax and an outcome. At the same time, it is a story receiver who interprets the story through his or her own biases, thereby giving the story a new 'receiver agency' (Coombs & Holladay, 2018: 386). The story has more impact the more stakeholders can identify with the characters and the more credible and plausible they perceive the plot to be.

The transmedia and narrative perspectives are then brought together in the theory 'Transmedia Narrative Transportation' (TNT), where the main idea is that a story universe is created that is closely linked to the organisation's purpose and strategy. 'Narrative transportation theory provides a theoretical rationale for the value of stories in strategic communication. It can explain why and how stories can have a persuasive effect on stakeholders. By merging transmedia storytelling with narrative transportation theory, an innovative lens for viewing public relations can be created' (Coombs & Holladay, 2018: 387).

The process can also be refined by inviting stakeholders to tell their own stories within the universe, helping to establish more symmetrical co-creation in line with the stakeholder-capitalism approach.

By working with cross-cutting story universes, the professional communicator can strengthen cohesion and the co-creative connection with stakeholders. In practice, you can organise the potential stories that, for example a new strategy or a new purpose calls for in a universe and define a strong core narrative. This narrative can be creatively developed within the universe so it can work on multiple platforms and with multiple voices in play. For example, if the organisation's strategy includes a new focus area where the organisational position and contact with stakeholders are not yet strong, you can put together a universe across platforms and find the stories that can begin to create the position, possibly in collaboration with your stakeholders.

5.4 Communication in Dialogue with Stakeholders

Much organisational communication has traditionally been information made available to a recipient—whether it was an annual report, a website or a customer email. Communication was more monologue than dialogue, although quality criteria such as recipient orientation have meant that much effort has been made to make the monologue relevant and appetising but without really knowing whether it was successful. Those days are over now, when the possibilities for interaction are entirely different. Monologue has become potential dialogue, information has become potential communication, and recipients have become co-creating stakeholders.

The changes are largely driven by the evolution of technology and the new set up of the platforms, where likes, shares and comments invite new forms of contact: 'The social media have improved the communications between the organisations and their publics. Organisations are using them to engage in two-way communications with their followers on social media (Camilleri, 2018). It also enables them to evaluate the effectiveness of their communication exchanges as they can track the online users' engagement, in terms of their likes, comments, shares, mentions, etc. (Gregory, 1996)' (Capriotti et al., 2021: 34).

But what qualities of communication are essential to create this truly dialogic communication? Capriotti et al. summarise the current research in a simple overview that derives five crucial dimensions for dialogic communication (2021: 38), namely active presence, interactive attitude, interactive resources, responsiveness and conversation, which will be discussed in Table 5.2.

The first three criteria for dialogic communication are the prerequisite for creating communication that facilitates dialogue in the first place. Organisations must have an **active presence** on social media. This means being present with posts and activity at a frequency that creates the perception of a clear presence. Exactly what this is may be a matter of opinion, and of course it varies from platform to platform, e.g. Kemp (2019) recommends one to two Facebook posts per day, but only one to two videos per week on YouTube. The active presence also supports the brand's

Table 5.2 Key dimensions of dialogic communication via social media

Presence	Active	Predisposition	Dialogic
Activity	Presence	To interaction	Communication
Informational	Interactive		
Interactive	Attitude		
Graphic resources	Interactive		
Audiovisual resources	Resources		
Hypertextual resources			
Support	Responsiveness	Effective	
Viralisation		Interaction	
Intensity	Conversation		
Reciprocity			

Source: Capriotti et al. (2021)

5.4 Communication in Dialogue with Stakeholders

recognisability that makes even sceptics trust the brand more (Arguedas et al., 2022). Success depends on content that creates value for stakeholders and that they themselves are ready to engage in dialogue about in order to co-create added value (Picard, 2012: 841). This brings the next criterion into play, the **interactive attitude**. Here the shift from monologue to potential dialogue is most evident because it is a requirement that the organisation directly encourages interaction in both content and form. It is about sharing concrete content that invites response and directly encouraging interaction by, for example directly inviting comments, ideas or suggestions in the comments, designing interactive polls or inviting direct co-creation (Lee et al., 2019; Capriotti et al., 2021).

In addition, the **interactive resources** are crucial. This is about the hooks that are thrown out to get stakeholders on board with the communication itself. The researchers divided them into three types:

1. Graphic elements from images to text and emojis
2. Audiovisual elements such as videos, podcasts or GIFs
3. Hypertextual elements such as # and links

All elements need to be brought into play to make content accessible and appealing, capture attention and invite dialogue. In recent years, audiovisual content media such as Instagram and TikTok have boomed, partly because of the technical feasibility of sharing such 'heavier' content, with better Internet connections in most parts of the world and better mobile phones.

But having the foundations in place in the post itself is far from enough. It is also about actual effective interaction in real time. Here Capriotti et al. point to the last two crucial dimensions of dialogic communication as responsiveness and conversation.

Responsiveness and engagement are the success criteria for dialogic communication. It is by assessing responsiveness, engagement and response from stakeholders that you can judge the quality of your efforts. Social media communication is not good just because it is there and can be counted—but because it generates engagement with the right stakeholders.

Last but not least, the fifth dimension is highlighted as actual **conversation**, and it is about actually showing your presence and your readiness to listen and engage in dialogue by reacting and responding to what happens in contact with stakeholders. The time when you could put up a nice post and then check interactions every now and then is long gone. An active presence requires a readiness to engage in the contact that you as an organisation have invited. An active presence and readiness for dialogue are basic requirements, which is partly about the processes and resources you have ready in connection with your communication. It is a break with classic production workflows, where you were finished and could concentrate on other tasks once you had printed or published. Now, a new set of communicative tasks begins as soon as, for example a post on social media has been published.

These five criteria for dialogic communication on social media can inspire professional communicators to produce contact-creating communication through all channels and platforms. Because in the age of stakeholder capitalism, it is precisely the dialogue-creating and respectful communication that gains a hearing, creates credibility and establishes trust. It is not enough that the signals are sent in the more controllable written or visual outputs for the communicator, they must also be sent when the professional communicator needs to use spokespersons as part of the orchestrated output. That is why the role of the trainer has become increasingly important for the professional communicator to master, something the next section looks at in more detail.

5.5 Training Others for Contact

Media training, press training, message training. In classical communication work, many of the communicator's activities have also been about getting spokespersons ready to communicate. Often they need to be prepared for traditional media or events such as a news broadcast, an interview for the printed press, a presentation at a conference or an internal meeting. Similarly, they also need to be prepared for social media and the rules they each need to follow to communicate authentically and well at the same time, for example on Twitter and LinkedIn.

Communication training remains highly relevant because it is the only way professional communicators can orchestrate the voices of the organisation and thereby 'quality assure' the overall communicative expression. But classical training has often been characterised by the old monological mindset: 'You need to be ready for X situation and try to take as much control as possible by preparing these points, rehearsing them and practicing until you can perform like this'.

An ambition that often made training linear and manageable for the trainer and helped the trainee to feel a sense of control and 'upper hand' that made her/him more confident. This approach is of no use today, where being too monologic risks appearing arrogant, rigid and manipulated. That is why the trainee must learn to be present and also learn to react intelligently and attentively in dialogues.

In other words, the communicative training work must also be updated to the new standards of contact, authenticity and dynamism. A spokesperson must learn not only to inform but to navigate and communicate wisely in interaction with the world around him/her. He/she must get to know him/herself as a 'channel' and know how to present him/herself in the best way. What should the preparation be practically and mentally? What can support being present in the moment? What personal pitfalls should be avoided, e.g. not being misunderstood?

Spokespersons need skill development so that they have the knowledge, tools and self-awareness to be the best versions of themselves in the contact sport of communication. This requires new approaches and new trust between trainer and trainee, because, all things being equal, technical training is simpler than facilitating self-awareness in terms of how one is perceived or preparing dynamic interaction instead of a controlled presentation.

5.6 Communication in Contact

In a mediatised reality, being in touch is not a choice for most organisations—it is a necessity for success. As Falkheimer and Heide summarise the influence of social media: 'What is clear is that social media's emergence has highlighted the fact that communication rarely can be controlled in the way that organisations wish' (2018: 346). Engaging with stakeholders across all platforms is crucial, and it is about more than just looking good. It is about creating robust credibility and a presence which means that you also have something to go on during crises or changes. Today, that credibility is nurtured by an authentic presence with strong organisational voices, both human and mediated, direct and indirect. It is nurtured by genuine dialogue not as a mechanical reaching out, but as a quality of the communication and as an ideal for a relationship with stakeholders (Ihlen & Levenshus, in Austin & Jin, 2022). For the professional communicator, this means important work to ensure a content, a form and a human subtext that is genuinely dialogical. The communicative toolbox is thus very versatile, ranging from working to ensure the mental shortcuts that reach out, to the concrete choice of the right content, prioritising the right storytelling and working to send the right dialogical signals in all formats. It requires an attentive and courageous professional communicator who ensures the right decisions and reminds all organisational senders that they are not senders but reach out for contact with stakeholders.

5.7 Case 4. In Touch with the World

Maersk has long been in the midst of a cultural transformation that includes a focus on greater openness and engagement with the world. Part of this development has been facilitated by the hard work of professional communicators across all platforms and channels to open the windows to the organisation and communicate ambitions and values with lots of examples. The strategic changes in the organisation have also meant that it has been necessary to position themselves in relation to new agendas, including the tech agenda. The communication department has thus had to think of new ways to meet new stakeholders at eye level. The following pages provide insights into social media communication, guerrilla journalism and training managers to actively engage with stakeholders.

For Maersk, the work for stronger contact with stakeholders has been underway for a long time, and one of the areas where the work can best be illustrated is on social media. Here, the communicative work includes organising content so that it is clearly linked to key strategic story universes, expanding the news criteria for what is communicated and finding a form of communication that is genuinely dialogic.

On social media, Samantha Almon Adeluwoye, Head of Social Media & Storytelling at Maersk, is in no doubt: 'The most important thing on social media is to be social and part of society. You can't work in your own corporate bubble. It is crucial that you are not only focused on what is going on in your own organisation, but also in the industry and in society as a whole'.

The foundation of all communication is understanding the situation—and it's often an eye-opener to take stock: 'Our recipients follow many, many organisations and individuals, so when they scroll down their screens, they see personal, professional and organisational content. We need to realise what makes them stop scrolling and spend time with us? And more importantly, what is the take-away we want to give them? What feeling or impression do we want to leave them with?' This understanding is fundamental to Maersk's approach to all social media and is a way of working with 'mental shortcuts' in the form of various signals, see Table 5.1, such as 'social cues', 'brand experience' and 'tone of voice' (Reuters, 2022). For Samantha Almon Adeluwoye, it is crucial to connect wisely and create engagement—and this requires, amongst other things, working deliberately with tone of voice every time so that it matches content, channel and target audience. This may necessitate communicative training of some of the organisation's voices: 'Sometimes we see these long, long posts that are structured so that they slowly move towards a conclusion in the very last line, or someone speaking in Maersk jargon'. If she sees this kind of thing, she is happy to lend a hand, just as she regularly trains spokespersons. 'We sometimes train our organisational spokespersons—just like you do with media training, because that's what this is too. But I can also easily reach out and help if I see someone who is trying but could use a hand to do better. It's actually always well received, because many people are still a little unsure about what it takes to do this well'. In this way, the strategic producers seek to work concretely with communication becoming dialogical, from presence and responsiveness to a more conversational style of communication (Capriotti et al., 2021).

Occasionally, there is also a need to address someone who simply does something that is not appropriate in terms of content. 'It's usually someone who has written a post or two out of emotion and hasn't realised that it could backfire on them personally. So it's important to act quickly so it doesn't do any damage'. It may sound like a difficult situation as a communicator to have to do this kind of outreach, but Samantha Almon Adeluwoye finds that these talks turn out well: 'Often it hasn't occurred to them that their posts could be read in that way, so they actually find it helpful', she emphasises.

5.7.1 Catch the Eye

Like all other organisations, Maersk also works closely with the visual part of social media (Capriotti et al., 2021; Reuters, 2022). That is also very much about catching the eye of the stakeholders as they scroll down the various feeds. This means that the entire social media team works very much as strategic producers, creating visual content, including with colleagues at the Maersk Studio (Fig. 5.1). 'We try to create authentic and relevant content', says Samantha Almon Adeluwoye. 'It shouldn't be too polished, but should have a personal edge. Of course, there is also differences between the media here, because a reel on Instagram is something entirely different from a TikTok, for example'. In this way, the strategic producers work deliberately to expand the news criteria for their content, so the content both matches the platform and has an edge, which can, for example show examples of 'aspirational talk'

5.7 Case 4. In Touch with the World

Fig. 5.1 Examples of Maersk's media presence

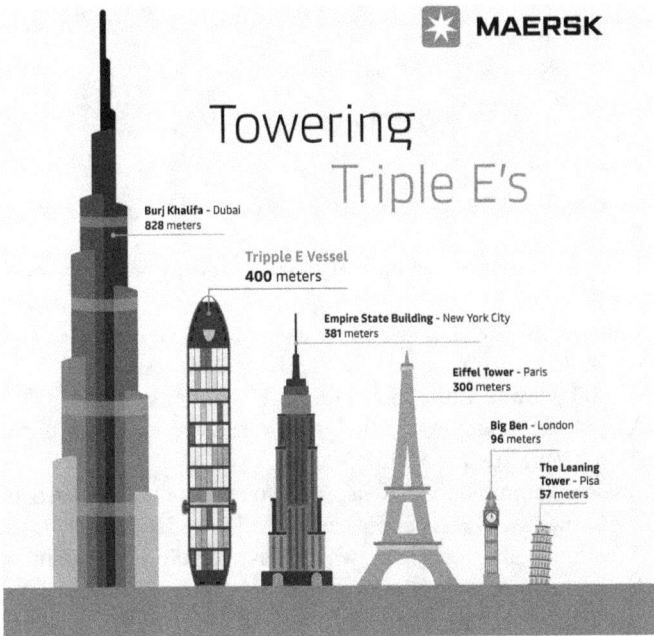

Fig. 5.2 Example of Maersk's use of infographics on social media

about visions or provide insight into work processes, not just results (Gyldensted, 2015; Haagerup, 2014; Harcup & O'Neill, 2001).

5.7.2 Eye-Catching Infographics and Facts

Another important element is the use of infographics: 'We have great experience with using infographics in our social media work. In many ways, it works as a shortcut to convey facts and sometimes surprise a little', Samantha Almon Adeluwoye emphasises. One example could be an attempt to illustrate how big the Maersk ships really are. Using creative graphic thinking, a ship was put on a pedestal and

Fig. 5.3 Example of Maersk's contact-establishing communicative content on social media

compared to the world's tallest, legendary towers, so both the Eiffel Tower and the Empire State Building were beaten by the Tripple E Vessel (Fig. 5.2). The post received 501,000 views, 7605 interactions, 77 comments and 328 reposts on LinkedIn. A concrete example of how graphic resources help to ensure dialogic communication (Capriotti et al., 2021).

The professional communicators also work on posts that approach stakeholders as consumers, but with a Maersk angle, such as a short video on where apples come from—and how to ideally store them, which was shared on Instagram as #Funfacts (Fig. 5.3). Again, an example of the expanded news criteria in the selection of content and the experiments in getting close to stakeholders in a concrete way with simple communicative approaches.

5.7.3 A Step Forward as a 'Thought Leader' in a New Field

As part of Maersk's strategic transformation to become more digital, it was very actively decided to position the company more clearly on the tech agenda. This was a natural consequence of how Maersk's business model would evolve in the next steps of the strategy, so it was important to be noticed externally with a credible voice. This is not something that can be done with a magic wand on the already crowded tech agenda but requires a targeted and patient effort, especially when you are initially associated more with large ships than with software and data. In other words, Maersk must be at the forefront of the digitalisation of global supply chains and thus needs to attract the right IT skills to a much greater extent than before, which is difficult for all organisations—and perhaps even more difficult for an organisation that is not immediately associated with advanced IT. So a crucial task for the strategic producers was to position Maersk in the field and secure an attractive position as one of the voices to be listened to in the field, a so-called 'thought leader'. This required active work on a core narrative of being an attractive IT workplace and a story universe (Coombs & Holladay, 2018) that could challenge prejudices and create new awareness.

Maersk realised that they were starting from a relatively low baseline and that they needed more than traditional campaigns. 'We wanted to make a point of doing something unexpected—surprise, inspire and only then try to convince people that Maersk is a visionary tech company', says Sam Poulter, Head of Corporate Branding and Channel Development. Together with his team, he started looking at the possibilities: How can we surprise? One of the surprises was sponsoring esports (Fig. 5.4). Maersk made an active choice to be visible in the world of young gamers in particular: 'We chose to actively sponsor Blast, who organise gaming events all over the world. We honestly didn't know much about that world, so it was a bit of an experiment', says Sam Poulter, but it was a risk they took in order to reach new stakeholders.

> After one year, we've seen pretty good results. We have sponsored the MVP award for the most valuable player at all events. The MVP is voted by all fans. Maersk has received 2 million impressions across channels for that target group in 2022 alone. We have also been able to see in before and after surveys that the target group's readiness to work for Maersk

Fig. 5.4 Images from the gaming event where Maersk sponsored the Most Valuable Player (MVP) award

has gone from 15% before the event to 54% after the event. This is a huge development and a good step forward in terms of being perceived as a relevant company in a very important target group.

But it was also about orchestrating the voices in Maersk so that they were talking about this agenda and being heard. 'We actually mapped all of our key senior leaders in a matrix with an x-axis going from role with local agendas to taking a seat on the global tech agenda and a y-axis from business-specific statements to visionaries. It was a working tool to set our teams: Who is to be active where? And what should they focus on?' emphasises Sam Poulter, who explains that personal elements such as an individual's passion for the field and communication strengths were also part of this mapping.

At the forefront of the visionary positioning was CEO Vincent Clerc, who was responsible for the largest business area at the time. He personified the great ambitions, especially on behalf of customers, in terms of making it easier and better to be a Maersk customer, partly as a result of increased digitalisation in the supply chain.

Maersk's first appearance on the global tech scene was at the world's biggest tech event, the Web Summit in 2021 (Figs. 5.5 and 5.6). There was a bit of a struggle behind the scenes to get Maersk on the podium, but it worked—and now it was time to surprise. 'We had worked on a very specific presentation that gave everyone an impression of what Maersk is and how big a role IT plays in our delivery', says Sam Poulter. The response was positive. The surprise was delivered.

Fig. 5.5 CEO Vincent Clerc at the 2021 Web Summit

5.7 Case 4. In Touch with the World

Fig. 5.6 Maersk's stand and TV studio at the 2022 Web Summit

Maersk chose to come back in 2022 with a stand at the conference. The top floor was a TV studio, where communicators during the conference interviewed many tech leaders and industry experts in the Maersk Studio for use on multiple channels. 'It was a very positive experience, with thousands of people visiting our stand, attending a lot of talks and judging start-up competitions, for example', says Sam Poulter.

A years-long positioning exercise is underway, but the first steps were about making new choices in an effort to become visible on new stages and help set the agenda. For example, some of the traditional shipping industry meetings were dropped at CEO level in favour of tech summits. The following year, Maersk was invited back as a more central speaker, and reputation surveys show that Maersk has moved significantly ahead of traditional shipping companies on the tech parameter. After the surprise phase comes the work of inspiring and convincing, so that Maersk becomes a natural and credible voice in tech in the future.

5.7.4 Training Managers with Sharp Data from Students

It is one thing to want to position yourself as a key tech organisation, sponsor events and be invited to tech summits. It is another thing to be able to approach various occasions in the right way with presence, contact and conviction. That is why the communicators at Maersk have also worked intensively to train top managers in communication—and have not been afraid to use unconventional means to keep them in good communication shape. Specifically, they have trained managers to be even better able to live up to the dialogic criteria in practice (Capriotti et al., 2021).

'As a manager of up to 100,000 employees, it's hard to get a realistic picture of how your communication is working. Leaders are so familiar with their own messages that it's easy to underestimate the reach of the next level of the organisation and overestimate the organisation's ability to absorb all the communication that is constantly coming at them, and it can be difficult for employees to give their senior leaders 100% honest feedback. That's why we decided to base our training of spokespersons for the tech agenda on an experience analysis of how the top managers were actually perceived by a group of IT students, which is one of the stakeholder groups we want to reach at eye level', says Jesper Løv, Head of Media Relations & Leadership.

In the experience analysis, a number of students from the IT University of Copenhagen were selected for qualitative interviews, where they watched short film clips with Maersk's managers. They commented on their experience. The statements were very honest and specific. They reacted promptly, for example when it seemed too corporate or impersonal. They said things such as: 'This is too politically correct', 'It seems a bit too corporate' or 'I would have taken out my phone and checked something else if I wasn't watching this'.

The many specific statements were edited into a short film that was part of the training. At first to the surprise and then to the amusement of the top managers, who were not used to this kind of evaluation. But it became an important fact-based starting point for a training that demanded entirely different contact requirements than they were used to, but which they were given new tools and individual sparring to master better. At the same time, it became a reference point for communicators to use in their continued individual work with organisational voices.

5.7.5 Guerrilla Journalism at Eye Level with Stakeholders

Another tool in the communicative toolbox of the strategic producers in creating real contact with stakeholders was to bring more voices into play on their social media channels, showing the world that Maersk was part of the dialogue on the future of tech and taking on the role as a source of inspiration on the tech agenda. This effort has been extensive on social media, and one specific occasion was one of the world's trendiest tech events, the South by Southwest conference in Austin, Texas (Figs. 5.7, 5.8 and 5.9). Here, many of the world's creative professionals come together to inspire each other in tech, film, music, education and culture. Maersk considered whether it was a place to be visible to engage in the tech discussion and position themselves to attract a new type of employee. 'Of course, we could have got out the big bucks and paid for an expensive sponsorship, had our logo plastered somewhere or put a speaker in one of their sessions, but in 2022 we decided to think in a different way entirely', says Sam Poulter. 'We decided to experiment a bit and develop something that could be used across all our platforms and had more edge and eye level with our stakeholders'.

Unsure whether South by Southwest was even a relevant forum for Maersk, the strategic producers decided to try a creative solution that was both very flexible and

5.7 Case 4. In Touch with the World   107

Fig. 5.7 Interview with economic futurist Jason Schencker at the South by Southwest conference in Austin, Texas 2022

Fig. 5.8 Example of Maersk's spontaneous interviews with speakers at the South by Southwest conference in Austin, Texas 2022

Fig. 5.9 Examples of Maersk's vox pops at the South by Southwest conference in Austin, Texas 2022

very cheap. They put together a team with their head of business intelligence and chief data officer, along with two of the communications department's own profiles, Sam Poulter and Samantha Almon Adeluwoye. They bought regular conference tickets and hired a local cameraman in Texas with a giant camera. And so they were ready for 'guerrilla journalism', telling the undiscovered and underexposed stories.

'In fact, we kind of hijacked their brand and used the conference as an opportunity to send a lot of good stories', says Sam Poulter. 'It helps a bit to walk around with a huge camera following us everywhere. It attracted attention, and a lot of people immediately wanted to get in front of the camera and take part in our live broadcasts and short films for our social media', he adds. Samantha Almon Adeluwoye continues: 'We planned a lot of good content, but we were also ready to seize whatever was happening in the moment, and whoever we could lure in front of the running camera'.

One example of content planned for the South by Southwest conference was an interview with one of the world's leading economic futurists, Jason Schencker. 'We had asked him to be part of an interview with our Head of Business Intelligence, Graham Slack. He invited us to his home. Of course, that took a bit of preparation with our own spokesperson, who was quickly reassured that this wasn't going to be some perfect news interview, but an authentic conversation where he was there in his own right as our in-house Maersk expert. Once we arrived, Jason Schencker suggested a little walk—so we made a quick decision and seized the opportunity for a walk-and-talk'.

Other examples of Maersk's presence at the conference were the more spontaneous little interviews with speakers just after they had taken the podium. The big camera was ready down in front of the podium, the microphone was held out. The style was not meant to be classically corporate either. No suits, just a jumper, a rucksack and the conference lanyard around the neck. No corporate staging—just ordinary presence, where the strategic producer was the stakeholders' representative at the conference and sent inspiration home at eye level.

The strategic producers also chose to do small vox pops, asking, for example other conference participants and random passers-by in Austin what mattered most to them when working for a company ... Salary or ...? These small posts also sparked interaction with stakeholders who offered their own observations in the comments section.

With this communication endeavour, Maersk chose not to sponsor or buy airtime. Instead, they took responsibility for being a Maersk channel that created their own authentic content. This made it possible to link the content directly to their own agendas. There was ample opportunity to bring your own voices into play, both as experts in dialogue with the world's leading influencers, as journalists curious about the world and as specialists commenting on something factual from the conference. There were butterflies and a high degree of uncertainty when leaving Denmark for Austin, but the experiment exceeded all expectations, both in terms of how many and who we actually managed to talk to, the quality of the content produced and the reception of our own channels. It was an instructive step in the ambition to transcend traditional media silos, illustrating that it is possible to opt out of expensive sponsorship or media partnerships and still make a big impact as an independent channel.

The efforts on the tech agenda are many and across all platforms. 'We're nowhere near our goal, but we're working on it stubbornly. Specifically, we want to recruit up to 100 IT people a month at Maersk in the next few years, so we are able to see from the number of applications or unsuccessful recruitments whether we will succeed in taking a step forward on this agenda', concludes Sam Poulter.

5.8 Interview. Have High Ethical Standards and Take Note!

'Quite frankly, I was shocked'. Chiara Valentini, a professor from Italy and a leading expert on strategic communication and new media and technologies, talks about her experience when reading high-quality texts—written by a robot. 'In fact, I couldn't tell that it was actually a robot at the keyboard'. This and many other technological changes make her focus on the important changes that communicators need to be aware of.

'We can't allow ourselves to feel intimidated but must continue to be ready for major changes', stresses Chiara Valentini, closely following the development for communicators from the University of Jyväskylä in Finland. And the changes are major. Technology gives us huge opportunities to reach out directly to a lot of stakeholders. It requires and enables entirely new forms of contact. And it provides us with and challenges us with a whole new transparency. It may even now begin to relieve us of some of the production that has taken up a lot of communicators' time. So, changes are happening—placing new demands on us.

Chiara Valentini has a lot on her mind, but one thing is particularly close to her heart. 'Let's not forget that machines don't have ethics. That is the thing that really sets us apart—and it's increasingly important to communicators. Machines can now do so much—and I'm genuinely impressed by their writing abilities, to mention one example. But how and when texts can, must and should be used is for the communicator to decide. We must be able to assess the context in relation to the organisation's ambitions, the actual situation, the relationship with each stakeholder. And we must be able to include our knowledge of stakeholders when assessing what, how and when to communicate. Everything that is interhuman separates machines from communicators—and commits us now and even more in the future'.

5.8.1 Create Solid Credibility

In the professor's view, the new media also require new orchestration of the organisation's expression and impression—and bring many more voices and dynamics into play. This means that we need to move away from 'only' thinking in terms of public relations. 'In a new, digitally mediated reality, contact between organisations and the outside world is much closer than anything our old theories can match', Chiara Valentini elaborates. 'Contact between organisations and stakeholders is entirely new and much closer and more transparent, and that is a challenge to communicators'.

> Our main responsibility is to help organisations achieve solid credibility in a transparent time. It must be so resilient and rooted that it keeps the organisation on its feet, even when the going gets tough. This requires communicators to constantly work towards strong credibility and a good reputation. The result is resilience in times of crises. The better the reputation, the easier it is to establish contact with media and other stakeholders when facing challenges.

One of the professor's research areas is corporate reputation. That is one area in which she sees the need for organisations to be more visible, leaving no doubt where they stand—which means having a resilient reputation when struck by the inevitable reputational challenges that are bound to arise in reality with this level of transparency. 'It's about making sure that relationships with stakeholders are as strong as possible at all times and that the organisation clearly stands out' she stresses.

Being clear is not only about classical media exposure but also about the way the organisation presents itself and is in contact with the outside world. 'It's increasingly about generating genuine commitment from all stakeholders—and when it comes to digital media, it's also about humanising contact. We listen more to people than to systems'.

5.8.2 Social Media Are Not a Channel

'It's important to understand that social media are not merely a channel, as was the case back when we had fax machines and suddenly were able to send paper documents to each other in a new way. It's not a machine that can transmit messages—it's something completely different', she explains. 'Social media are more SOCIAL than MEDIA. They are not there to send something out but to engage with your stakeholders, build relationships and make smart connections'.

Chiara Valentini has looked at the details of appropriate contact with stakeholders, right down to the details of tone and style in purely linguistic contact. Amongst other things, her research shows that communication cannot and should not be the same across channels. 'We have a dialogue on social media: it's therefore about interacting. I believe that far too few theorists and practitioners think that way' she stresses. When we interact in dialogues, communication is different and more authentic, present and unfinished, because we co-create. 'That is why we should not produce classical, rhetorical masterpieces on social media. We should rather have the courage to have real contact. This means that we often have to prioritise authenticity over perfection'.

As communicators, we need to be more aware of the impact that technology has on direct, as well as indirect, stakeholder contact. 'By better understanding how technologies are changing the behaviour of all of us, we, communication professionals, are better able to advise organisations and bring all the organisational voices into a dialogue. Social media is not something we should *use* but something we should *act in* to constantly strengthen the organisation's social capital and give it a human face. It's more about being in touch than about promoting'.

It is only by acting with relational wisdom that we, as communicators, can facilitate the establishment and maintenance of the organisation's legitimacy and 'licence to operate' as a voice in the world.

5.8.3 Listen Very Carefully

When it is mostly a matter of contact and relationships, it is no wonder that one of the virtues she encourages communicators to cultivate the most is the ability to listen.

'As communicators, we need to be able to understand our stakeholders in order to interact wisely. This includes being good at collecting, understanding and using big data. There are endless possibilities for gaining knowledge this way', Chiara Valentini stresses, 'but it's far from enough. In continuation of the interpersonal track, we obviously cannot simply measure or count all results. Much of the interpersonal aspect is relational, so in addition to our knowledge of technology, communication and strategy, we also need deep psychological insight—and to listen very carefully', she says.

The professor is convinced that constant change and volatility will not diminish in the future, so active listening and trying to really understand what is going on between the lines will be crucial to the ability to work with the right contact. 'The human side is quite crucial. We must not forget that when we are busy or when preoccupied with strategising. As communicators, we must at all times be able to implement a 360-degree perspective on the organisation and on all people involved'.

5.8.4 The Visual Turn

Another key element is the visual turn. The battle for attention has never been greater, and according to the professor, this has meant a visual turn in communication—not just on social media, but in general. 'We need to capture our stakeholders' attention more than ever—and this is where images of all kinds are pre-eminent for capturing focus and arousing curiosity'.

> There is no doubt that the young generations are leading the way in this area. Obviously, we see it in the boom of users on TikTok and Instagram with mainly visual content, but it also applies to all the other platforms in the professional communicator's toolbox.

Strangely enough, it was the visual aspect that got young Chiara started on the communication path. 'I think I've always talked a lot and been curious about people', she says, laughing. 'But it was the visual aspect in advertising, for example, that made me curious about the impact that communication has on people, and that is also the reason that the beginning of my academic career was focused on marketing and advertising, before I switched to strategic communication from organisations. So, it's a bit funny for me personally that the visual aspect is now key to all types of communication, so I'm somehow back at my own beginning'.

The visual aspect must be included in everything that today's communicators plan and produce, regardless of the distribution channel. From vivid images to great photos and illustrative infographics, 'Communicators must constantly think in terms of the power of images when designing the right solutions'.

The professor also finds it important to remember the power of narratives. There is also a fundamental human curiosity here: 'We get caught up in stories. We linger and listen to or read stories. It seems to create contact and receptiveness', she stresses.

What separates communicators from machines is the emotional, the situational, the ethical and the authentically relational aspects, and for the Italian professor based in Finland, we need to take the best from machines to make it easier to get and process data and eventually produce more content. But we must accept and bear the responsibility of creating strong relationships with all stakeholders, based on our psychological sense of what we are listening to and what we feel. Only then can we make real contact on all types of media and channels.

Chiara Valentini

Chiara Valentini is a Professor of Corporate Communication at the University of Jyväskylä in Finland. She specialises in social and digital media, public relations, stakeholder relations, strategic communication, crisis communication, public affairs and public communication.

She has already contributed to research with more than 130 publications and has received many awards for her work. Her research is featured in leading peer-reviewed international journals and international handbooks such as *Public Relations Review*, *Corporate Communication: An International Journal*, *Journal of Communications Management*, *Journal of Public Affairs*, *International Journal of Strategic Communication*, *International Journal of Press/Politics* and the SAGE *Handbook of Public Relations*.

References

Arguedas, A. R., Badrinathan, S., Mont'Alverne, C., Toff, B., Fletcher, R., & Nielsen, R. K. (2022). Snap judgements: How audiences who lack trust in news navigate information on digital platforms. https://reutersinstitute.politics.ox.ac.uk/sites/default/files/2022-03/Snap_Judgements_Trust_in_News_Report.pdf

Austin, L. L., & Jin, Y. (2022). *Social media and crisis communication*. Routledge.

Bro, P. (2019). Constructive journalism: Proponents, precedents and principles. *Journalism (London, England)*, 20(4), 504–519.

Capriotti, P., Zeler, I., & Camilleri, M. A. (2021). Corporate communication through social networks: The identification of the key dimensions for dialogic communication. In M. A. Camilleri (Ed.), *Strategic corporate communication in the digital age* (pp. 33–51). Emerald.

Camilleri, M. A. (2018). The SMEs' technology acceptance of digital media for stakeholder engagement. *Journal of Small Business and Enterprise Development*.

Coombs, W. T., & Holladay, S. J. (2018). Social issue qua wicked problems: The role of strategic communication in social issues management. *Journal of Communication Management*, 22(1), 79–95.

Eanes, R. (2020). Attention span. In J. Silverman (Ed.), *The Sage international encyclopedia of mass media and society* (pp. 110–113). Sage.

Edelman. (2023). https://www.edelman.co.uk/2023-edelman-uk-trust-barometer

Ekman, M., & Widholm, A. (2014). Twitter and the celebritisation of politics. *Celebrity Studies, 5*(4), 518–520.

Falkheimer, J., & Heide, M. (2018). *Strategic communication: An introduction.* Routledge.

Galtung, J., & Ruge, M. H. (1965). The structure of foreign news: The presentation of the Congo, Cuba and Cyprus crises in four Norwegian newspapers. *Journal of Peace Research, 2*(1), 64–90.

Gregory, A. (1996). *Planning and managing PR campaigns: A step-by-step guide.* Kogan Page.

Gyldensted. (2015). *From mirrors to movers: Five elements of positive psychology in constructive journalism.* Ggroup Publishing.

Haagerup, U. (2014). *Constructive news: How to save the media and democracy with journalism of tomorrow.* InnoVatio.

Harcup, T., & O'Neill, D. (2001). What is news? Galtung and Ruge revisited. *Journalism Studies, 2*(2), 261–280.

Highfield, T. (2017). *Social media and everyday politics.* Polity Press.

Jensen, J. L. (2019). News criteria on social media comparing news media use of Facebook and Twitter. *Journalistica (Aarhus.), 1.*

Kemp, S. (2019). https://wearesocial.com/uk/blog/2019/01/digital-in-2019-global-internet-use-accelerates/

Kilgo, D. K., Harlow, S., García-Perdomo, V., & Salaverría, R. (2016). A new sensation? An international exploration of sensationalism and social media recommendations in online news publications. *Journalism, 19*(11), 1497–1516.

Lee, S. Y., Zhang, W., & Abitbol, A. (2019). What makes CSR communication lead to CSR participation? Testing the mediating effects of CSR associations, CSR credibility, and organization–public relationships. *Journal of Business Ethics, 157*(2), 413–429.

Meyer, J. P., & Maltin, E. R. (2010). *Employee commitment and well-being: A critical review, theoretical framework and research agenda.* The University of Western Ontario.

Picard, R. G. (2012). What social media are doing and where they are taking us. In M. Friedrichsen & W. Mühl-Benninghaus (Eds.), *Handbook of social media management.* Springer.

Reuters. (2022). Reuters Institute & University of Oxford: https://reutersinstitute.politics.ox.ac.uk/snap-judgementshow-audiences-who-lack-trust-news-navigate-information-digital-platforms, 2022

Reuters Institute for the Study of Journalism. (2022). https://reutersinstitute.politics.ox.ac.uk/

Statista. (2022). https://www.statista.com/

van Laer, T., de ruyter, K., Visconti, L., & Wetzels, M. (2014). The extended transportation-imagery model: A meta-analysis of the antecedents and consequences of consumers' narrative transportation. *Journal of Consumer Research.*

The Data-Driven Communicator   6

Listening, measuring and evaluating are key elements in the work of a professional communicator. You can only facilitate contact with stakeholders by actually knowing what they think, believe and feel. You can only know whether an intervention is successful if you keep an eye on its impact. And you can only develop and improve initiatives by constructively evaluating what works and what may be done even better. This chapter focuses on the listening, measuring and evaluating part of the communication work of the professional communicator.

The chapter's case study provides insight into some of the methods that Maersk uses to ensure the impact of their communication efforts, e.g. on social media and in internal communication.

The chapter's international expert is the world's leading researcher on organisational listening, Professor Jim Macnamara from the University of Technology Sydney.

A natural starting point for a professional communicator working with measurement, evaluation and organisational listening is to look at the need for that knowledge. What is it to be used for? And what framework does the application set for choosing an approach? It is indisputable that the modern communicator and communications function must be highly data-driven.

Overall, data can be used to clarify the benefits of having a communications function at all. It can be a challenge to establish a shared and solid understanding of the value that communication contributes with, and here the work of illustrating the value creation can be essential in creating and maintaining the organisational mandate (Michaelson & Stacks, 2014).

Today, data in the communication field has become much more accessible for the professional communicator, and it has become easier to conduct surveys with all stakeholders. All this data on, for example 'clicks', 'likes' and 'reach' has become more accessible. But at the same time, the amount of data is also a pitfall for the professional communicator—because what is all this data for? What does it tell us? And can it even be used to measure the success of a given communicative endeavour?

The wealth of data can be collected, interpreted and utilised even better than what is currently the case. In a review of measurement and evaluation in professional communication, Macnamara summarises: 'The interrelated and integrated processes of measurement and evaluation have long been a challenge for public relations and communication management practitioners, with reviews showing "stasis", the use of invalid methods and even a "deadlock" in the reporting of results of projects and campaigns. In particular, the field has struggled to present credible evidence of outcomes and impact, most often reporting activities and outputs' (Macnamara & Valentini, 2021: 249).

Researchers unanimously point out that communicators can face major challenges in creating the right architecture for building metrics and evaluations that could lead to better 'listening' both internally and externally. As Zerfass and his research colleagues conclude: 'Although robust knowledge of empirical research methods and their application for measuring communication effects is indispensable, many practitioners lack the necessary expertise to conduct reliable evaluation and measurement. Communication departments seldom measure communication effects on stakeholders and organisational goals. Many remain focused on media and channels. Last but not least, organisations do not fully exploit the potential of measurement data for strategically planning future communication activities. The findings highlight the need to reconsider current education and training in communication research methods and their application in corporate practice' (Zerfass, Vercic, et al., 2017: 2).

Evaluation and measurement is a field of work that must be incorporated into the communicative work before, during and after a communication effort. A constructive evaluation along the way can, for example help to ensure that the quality is constantly adjusted, whilst a final evaluation can make the communicator wiser about stakeholders, goals and means that can be useful before the next communication challenge. The evaluation along the way is of course particularly important when the communicator facilitates longer processes such as positioning the organisation in relation to a new agenda, a new strategy or a change process. Here, it is crucial that you are in continual contact with the key stakeholders to keep an eye on whether anything needs to be adjusted. Maybe a questionnaire survey needs to be carried out, addressed to a changing sample of stakeholders, so the professional communicator can gain insight into how a communicative effort is being received. It may also be expedient to organise focus group interviews two or three times along the way, or participant observation may be a solution where the professional communicator visits stakeholders x number of times along the way, to enable listening, reading and learning more about how things are going and whether anything needs to be adjusted.

Evaluations after a given action are valuable, but it is an endeavour that many communicators are unfortunately often too busy to take the time for. New things are waiting on the to-do list. But the professional communicator should set aside time for the task and realise from the start how and when to evaluate whether a given communication has succeeded and what may be done better next time. In the vast majority of communication tasks, you communicate with stakeholders with whom you need to maintain a relationship, and if you do not evaluate on an ongoing basis, you risk both wasting a lot of time and losing an understanding of the importance of the effort in the organisation. That is why this chapter looks at the fundamentals of taking a systematic approach to being data-driven as a professional communicator.

When working with data, systematisation is necessary for both the collection and interpretation to ensure valid data that can be brought into play and provide insight. It is thus not surprising that it is consistently cited by communicators as one of the most complex things to work with in a constructive way. For example, data from the European Communication Monitor shows that more than 80% of professional communicators still evaluate mainly by counting press clippings (Zerfass et al., 2015: 72). Complemented by Page's (2019) US surveys, where more than half of respondents state that they are only at a basic level in terms of using communication technologies (CommTech). So according to Page, communication technologies are mostly used to monitor social media. Eighty-two percent report using a 'social media management tool for listening'. Overall, it is suggested that the main reason for monitoring is to identify what is happening with one's own activities, press coverage and reputation in order to react. Communication technology thus appears to be used more for monitoring than, for example for listening to stakeholders' preoccupations or concerns about other agendas.

It is difficult to master the methods needed to conduct valid measurements, as Zerfass et al. state: 'Overall, the results of this study emphasize that respondents do not possess high experiences and capabilities to conduct robust measurement in practice. Communication professionals particularly lack the ability to utilize valuation methods for reporting how communication contributes to organisational goals at the outcome and outflow level. For that reason it may be hard to defend, explain and legitimise investment into communication to top decision-makers' (Zerfass, Tench, et al., 2017; Zerfass, Vercic, et al., 2017: 8).

Volk and Buhmann (2019) point to many of the pitfalls that can be identified in research in this field. These include the ongoing uncertainty about common standards and a lack of agreement on what we define as, for example measurement and evaluation, which results in a lack of clarity in the use of data. In addition, they point out that too many people get caught up in the instrumental part of the studies themselves and fail to put analyses and measurements in the right context, making them more self-justifying than clarifying. They also point out that the unforeseen effects on stakeholders are often overlooked and warn against communicators working too much in silos, whereby important learning from other people's measurements and methods is lost.

Nevertheless, data-driven work does not have to be an insurmountable barrier for professional communicators. At its core, it is all about being systematic and following the rules of the game of each method, from facilitating focus groups to semi-structured interviews or data from online panels. Each method has its 'recipe' or instructions for the professional approach, which is almost only a literature search away, such as a handbook for qualitative methods (Flick, 2022; Jensen, 2021).

Research also highlights that there is far too little focus on organisational listening: 'Despite theorisation of the disciplinary practices of public relations and corporate, organizational, government and political communication as two-way communication involving dialogue and engagement with stakeholders and publics, a transdisciplinary literature review of these fields reveals that little attention is paid to listening' (Macnamara, 2017: 1).

6.1 Data-Driven Stakeholder Knowledge

Fundamental to the success of any communicative endeavour is stakeholder knowledge, where measurement, evaluation and listening can be very useful in the planning process.

With large amounts of data, a good starting point is often to begin data-driven work with curiosity. What do you know about this stakeholder? Where does the data come from? It does not always have to be surveys conducted in the communication function but could be a survey about an organisation's customers conducted in the sales department, a survey of HR staff or something else entirely. This research phase can make the professional communicator much more knowledgeable about the relevant stakeholder because there is an infinite amount of useful knowledge in the many surveys and data that can be generated based on behaviour. At the same time, it can mean that you can obtain the relevant knowledge without necessarily having to initiate a large collection of data yourself, which is not only a lot of work but also risks disturbing stakeholders unnecessarily.

All knowledge must be weighed in terms of its factual, behavioural and psychological weight. Often, for example, you will only have gained knowledge about what stakeholders read, how long they linger in communicative video material or their opinion in a questionnaire survey. In communication work, however, it is also important to get input on the experience-based and sometimes somewhat complicated psychological element of stakeholders' responses. For example, in a survey, stakeholders may respond dishonestly or incompletely. So it is important to design the surveys to include, for example qualitative experience analyses. The professional communicator must involve intuitive human understanding in designing surveys, interpreting data and assessing whether more organisational listening is required to gain a real insight into stakeholder perspectives. Active listening can be, for example through direct contact with representatives of this stakeholder, where more in-depth knowledge can be gained by asking, listening and interpreting what is at stake. It can also be by designing qualitative studies with, for example focus groups with selected stakeholders, or by looking at all the interactions you have with a given stakeholder and specifically following what is called the 'customer journey' or perhaps conducting a smaller qualitative interview study, where you as a professional communicator talk confidentially with stakeholders one at a time. Or perhaps this situation calls for a quick sounding out, where the professional communicator simply calls a few people, or if it is internal stakeholders, sits down with them in the cafeteria or gets coffee on another floor of the building. The qualitative data can often complement the quantitative when there is a need for more knowledge about why, a better sense of psychological barriers to contact or perhaps there is a desire to involve stakeholders in developing quality solutions.

6.2 A Measurable Basis for Communication Work

In order to work in a data-driven way, the professional communicator must be very aware of working systematically in a goal-orientated way, so all efforts have a goal against which they can be assessed. So a natural starting point is to ensure that all communication efforts are measurable. A widely used method in this context is to work with the so-called SMART objectives. These are goals that live up to being:

- **S**pecific
- **M**easurable
- **A**ttainable
- **R**ealistic
- **T**ime-bound

By setting goals for the work, the professional communicator can both ensure the strategic anchoring of the work and make it easier to evaluate whether the endeavour has succeeded.

The field of measurement and evaluation has been challenged by a lack of common standards, but both in Europe and the USA, associations such as the Association for the Measurement and Evaluation of Communication (AMEC) have attempted to work towards standardising analytical approaches, parameters and scales to make them more useful and comparable. Part of their work rests on the so-called Barcelona Principles, most recently updated with a 3.0 version in 2020 (Fig. 6.1).

The summarised principles emphasise that measurement is not just about collecting data and tracking, but about creating insights and learning from the collected material so it can be applied to the production of future communication. AMEC also warns that bias can skew results in terms of choice of methods, tools and interpretation.

> **Barcelona Principles 3.0: an overview**
>
> 1. Setting goals is an absolute prerequisite to communications planning, measurement and evaluation.
> 2. Measurement and evaluation should identify outputs, outcomes and potential impact.
> 3. Outcomes and impact should be identified for stakeholders, society and the organisation.
> 4. Communication measurement and evaluation should include both qualitative and quantitative analysis.
> 5. AVEs [Advertising value equivalency: media coverage converted to $/€/£ are not the value of communication.
> 6. Holistic communication measurement and evaluation includes all relevant online and offline channels.
> 7. Communication measurement and evaluation are rooted in integrity and transparency to drive learning and insights.

Fig. 6.1 An overview of AMEC's Barcelona Principles. Source: AMEC

6.3 The Theoretical Basis for Evaluation

There is a wealth of theoretical evaluation models that may be applied when designing an evaluation. The theoretical root of most of them, according to Macnamara (2021a), is the psychological theory of change, which has provided insights into the stages in which processes occur: 'How a program is intended to work, identifying the basic stages that lead from planning to demonstration of effectiveness in achieving its objectives, with particular emphasis on outcomes and impact' (Macnamara, 2021b: 251).

The psychological theory of change is complemented by programme theory, which can describe the chain of activities that need to be monitored in order to evaluate a process. One of the more nuanced representatives of this is the Henert and Taylor-Power model (2008), which we will spend a little time expanding on below.

In measurements and evaluations of public relations, you ought to take an interest in inputs, outputs and effects, the latter termed 'outcomes-impact' by Henert and Taylor-Power. They emphasise that outputs can be both organised activities and participation in existing activities, just as it may be relevant to look at the effect both in the short, medium and long term.

In the design or architecture of an evaluation, it is crucial to balance it carefully, so you do not just count the countable but look at the mix of methods that are actually needed to say something accurate about stakeholders' responses to communication initiatives.

Table 6.1 Parameters in measurement work

	Social and cultural change
Impact	Number who repeat behaviour
	Number who behave as desired
	Number who change attitudes
	Number who change opinions
	Number who learn message content
	Number who attend to messages and activities
Implementation	Number who receive messages and activities
	Number of messages placed and activities implemented
	Number of messages sent to media and activities designed
	Quality of messages and activity *presentation*
Preparation	Appropriateness of messages and activity *content*
	Adequacy of background *information* base for designing program

Source: Broom (2012)

Another model that has been widely used in the field of communication comes from Cutlip and Broom (2012), who provide an overview of the parameters that might be taken into account in the preparation, implementation and in terms of impact (Table 6.1).

The idea of the model is for you as a communicator to meticulously map out each step. In preparation, for example how you are doing with the quality of background information, content and messages. Whilst in implementation, you need to measure the number of messages sent and received. In assessing the real impact, on the other hand, measurements of stakeholders who, for example change their position and change their behaviour should be the focus of the data-driven communicator.

6.4 An Agile Evaluation Model

However, the world is rarely as linear as models suggest, and it can be too simplistic to design your measurements and evaluations without taking into account the dynamic processes that often characterise reality. In addition, many of the models are old fashioned in their preoccupation with essentially one-way communication: An organisation wants to achieve something and tries to convince a recipient. In this respect, evaluation theory has not moved forward, as communication with stakeholders has long since become two-way and symmetrical. This is one of the reasons why Macnamara has developed a new model to guide organisations when professional communicators need to plan measurement and evaluation in a more dynamic or agile way (Fig. 6.2). The model attempts to integrate existing theory and also to allow for the fact that unintended effects of interventions often arise, or that organisational listening can lead to learning and continuous adjustment, making the model more flexible and agile.

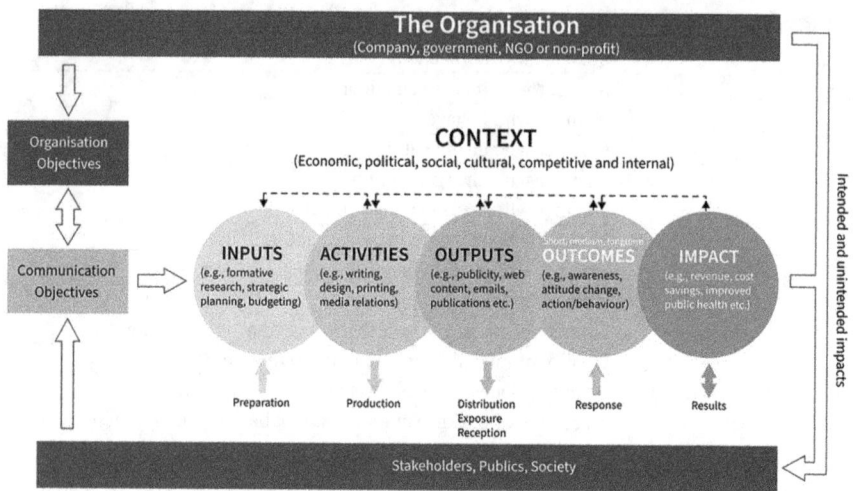

Fig. 6.2 Integrated evaluation model for PR and communication. Source: Macnamara (2018a, 2018b)

The model highlights that the SMART communication objectives are directly linked to the organisation's objectives, and the bottom left arrow illustrates that stakeholders have influence and impact here too.

The arrows on the far right highlight unforeseen effects that are also worth paying attention to in evaluation processes.

The model illustrates with overlapping circles that the phases are in motion and that they all need to be contextualised both organisationally and in contact with stakeholders at all times.

- **'Input'** is the planning and research phase.
- **'Activities'** are everything that is created and made ready to be communicated.
- **'Output'**, on the other hand, is the externally visible activities such as events, social media posts and press coverage.
- **'Outcomes'** is the effect. Here, Macnamara brings together both what AMEC calls 'outtakes' (reactions) and 'outcomes' (effects), i.e. for example both awareness and changes in attitude and behaviour in the short, medium and long term.
- **'Impact'** is the influence of the communication effort, i.e. changes in reputation, relationships or whatever you have worked to evaluate.

6.5 AMEC Recommendations for Measurement in Practice

When the international industry association AMEC summarises the theoretical input and recommends how they believe professional communicators should measure, they set it out in this wheel (Fig. 6.3). The model is designed to follow a communication effort from conceptualisation to evaluation.

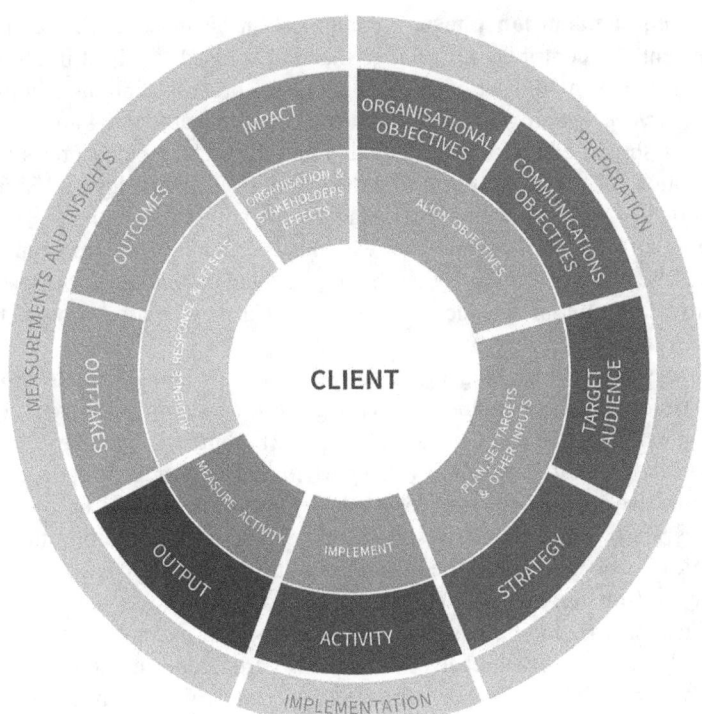

Fig. 6.3 AMEC's recommended approach to measuring communication in practice. Source: www.amecorg.com

As a starting point, AMEC recommends that measurement is not something that is only invented after you have communicated something, but that it is incorporated into the work process from the very beginning, so evaluation is a natural part of the professional communicator's working method, just as it is also recommended. In the following, the various phases of the evaluation process are described.

In the **preparation phase**, the first step is to focus on the business and communication objectives of the organisation. Only by being aware of these from the outset can the professional communicator ensure both the right communicative solution and the ability to evaluate it properly.

Next, it is important to design the communication solution and measurement by focusing on what you already know about strategy and target audiences to make sure you get the right content in the first place. This could include specific knowledge about the target audience's preferences, drivers, media habits and influences. It is also in this phase that budget, time frame, technique and timing need to be organised. It may well be that the first measurements are already integrated here. For example, pilot studies of key messages on a sample of the target audience or qualitative interviews to learn more about it.

In the **implementation phase,** communication is underway. Here, real-time measurement can contribute knowledge that can be used to adjust in all channels where possible. Can you, for example in a change process continuously use questionnaire surveys that provide the professional communicator with knowledge along the way, or should ethnographic methods be used, such as being present at large meetings along the way and observing the response from employees? Should you use experience analyses with representatives of individual employees to get in-depth input on what needs to be better explained? In short, there are a multitude of methods. The important thing is that the professional communicator assesses what could provide useful knowledge along the way that may be used constructively in the work.

Then, the final overarching phase focuses on measurement for **learning and insight.** Here, AMEC recommends dividing the process into four steps, one step more than in Macnamara's model above (Fig. 5.2): 'outputs', 'outtakes', 'outcome' and 'impact'. The first three steps evaluate whether the effort has met the communication objectives, whilst the last step evaluates the actual impact on the organisation's overall business objectives and thus points back to both the specific communicative objectives and the objectives of the organisation as a whole.

In the **'output'/results phase**, roughly speaking, countable data must be collected. That is, what can be seen in concrete terms? For example, how much press coverage did a given action receive? How many participants turned up to an event? How many views did a video get? How much website traffic can be recorded?

You look at how many stakeholders were exposed to the communication and whether it actually succeeded in exposing the message to all relevant stakeholders. It is also important to look at whether it was the entire message of the communication effort that was shown, or whether there was, for example a journalistic adaptation that meant that it was an adjusted message that was communicated.

This measurement phase provides knowledge about what content was communicated to whom, but only the next phase assesses the reactions to it. Each measurement phase requires a positive outcome before moving on to the next stage of the work process. In practice, this means that you do not look for reactions until you have confirmed that the target audience was actually exposed to the message ('output').

In the **'outtakes'/reaction phase**, the professional communicator must look at what stakeholders do with the communication and take away from it. What do they understand and how do they react to it? After all, a 'positive reaction' can be very different depending on the communication objective pursued and how the activities themselves were organised. So in the outtakes/reaction phase, you may, for example, seek to measure recipients' reactions in terms of:

- Attention
- Awareness
- Understanding
- Interest/liking

- Commitment
- Participation
- Consideration (Andersen, 2019)

Reactions can be measured in many ways, depending on what is being analysed. For example, if it is communication on social media, it could be likes, positive comments or shares. Is it click-throughs to more info on a website? Or is it whether the stakeholder 'does' something in relation to the specific communication? It can be both quantitative measurements or the use of qualitative methods that can help the communicator gain useful knowledge. Qualitative methods such as interviews, focus groups or experience analyses may, for example be used to find out how the communication has been experienced by stakeholders.

The **'outcome'/impact measurement phase** is about documenting the impact of a communication endeavour. That is why it can often be a time-delayed measurement activity because it takes time before an actual effect can be traced amongst stakeholders. For example, what impact has specific communicative content had on the trust and credibility of an organisation? What impact can you see in the behaviour you want to change? In short: What effect did you aim for, and how did it go?

This phase presents important knowledge for the professional communicator, because a communication effort is ultimately not successful until an effect is traceable, no matter how much quality communication has taken place along the way. The key question to start with is thus: Why do not stakeholders already do what you want them to do? The answer allows the professional communicator to zero in on what stakeholders are missing in the communicative expression, and then you know what outcome or effect you can aim for.

On the basis of all this data, it is possible to take stock of the process in relation to both the communicative objectives and the organisational objectives of the **impact/influence phase**. What has the communication influenced? It is not always the communication alone that has had an impact, but in this phase you nevertheless look at the bigger picture: What has it meant for, e.g. reputation, relationships or whether a stakeholder fulfils a specific agenda? Unlike many of the earlier phases of M&E, measurement in the 'impact' phase will often require data from other parts of the organisation, such as sales figures, records of actions and major population surveys.

In the case of COVID-19 communication, the 'inputs' were the knowledge of citizens' knowledge about hand washing, face masks and behaviour, the 'activities' were the communicative campaigns to teach us all to wash our hands, keep our distance and use face masks. 'Output' was how much all the films, articles and campaigns were seen. 'Outtakes' were how much attention the material received: Did people seek more knowledge, were posts shared etc. 'Outcomes' were stakeholders' new knowledge, attitudes and intentions, whilst 'impact' was the overall trust in the health authorities, our behaviour in the public sphere and ultimately the spread of infection and vaccination rates in society.

6.6 When an Audit Is the Ambition

One particular measurement and evaluation that many organisations undertake on a regular basis is something called a 'communication audit' (Yamaguchi, 2017). The name is inspired by financial reviews of the strengths and weaknesses of an organisation—and the method has similarly been used in communication to diagnose and clarify the quality of communication.

'The main purpose of a communication audit is to evaluate an entire organisation's communication system and to acquire information on its strengths and weaknesses' (Goldhaber, 1993; Hargie & Tourish, 2000). According to Dickson et al. (2003: 37) an audit is 'fundamentally an evaluation of some designated process' (Tkalac Verčič, 2021).

A communication audit is typically a quality review, where, for example based on a mapping of channels, qualitative analyses of text qualities and perhaps the perception of stakeholders are carried out.

An audit can easily follow a model like Macnamara's above and can include a variety of methods from qualitative interviews, quantitative surveys, reach mapping and focus groups to diary studies where, for example employees write down what they experience every day (Zwijze-Koning and de Jong, 2007 in Tkalac Verčič, 2021).

They often have the same basic structure as a financial audit, with data collection in a diagnostic phase to identify basic trends, then prescribing recommendations on *where* and *how* to take action to control, maintain or improve communication quality and finally comparing data with, for example an industry benchmark, standard or similar (Tkalac Verčič, 2021).

As it is the 'health status' that is to be analysed, an audit is often an analytical pit stop and not an ongoing and continuous measurement and evaluation. They are often carried out, for example as a prelude to new communication strategies in order to have a data-driven starting point for new goals and initiatives.

6.7 Data as Driver, Feedback and Mandate

Several researchers speak of communication having become 'datafied' (Tench et al., 2017: 87). More than 40 years ago, Grunig already stated that it ought to be paramount for any communicator to be able to document impact and ensure the right data-driven starting point for the communication profession. Measurement has only become easier and cheaper with the development of technology since then and can increasingly be done in-house rather than through external agencies. It is crucial not to measure blindly or incorrectly, as is unfortunately often the case. So the methodological knowledge of smart measurement and evaluation architecture is important. In addition, it is also crucial to be careful about what you are able to interpret from your data, so you do not end up in one of the many fallacies that often occur.

The data-driven communicator today has better and simpler options when it comes to:

- Ensuring the right mandate by being able to demonstrate impact.
- Ensuring the right starting point for their interventions.
- Keeping quality and impact high by continuously adjusting based on data.
- To learn from experience.

Macnamara (2014a, 2014b) identified four factors that were part of the reason for the many challenges with fallacies in measurement and evaluation of communication efforts:

1. Communicators forget to work systematically on measurement and evaluation, e.g. using recognised models.
2. The field has not evolved enough, so the interaction between, for example sociological measurement experts and communicators has not produced properly grounded solutions.
3. We are still looking for the magic formula that fixes everything.
4. Commercial pressure from external providers of, for example media clip counting, keeps organisations stuck in outdated measurement regimes.

The professional communicator must make measurement and evaluation a natural part of their work and not be reluctant to dig into data from other units or to find or create the necessary data themselves to constantly quality-assure their efforts. There are many methods—from the intuitive presence with curious questions, big ears and empathic antennae that provide real knowledge and understanding of stakeholders' perspectives to the more systematic measurement and evaluation methods. Each task calls for the data-driven communicator to take an interest in how data may contribute this time around.

6.8   Case 5. Being Data-Driven Must Be Useful

At Maersk, data is a natural part of the communications unit's work, and the basic attitude is clear: It must be useful, otherwise, it should not be collected. The organisation should not be burdened with data collection unnecessarily. Data is used in three areas: to drive the unit in a goal-oriented way and to document impact and value creation; as organisational listening in relation to stakeholders; and in practical terms to ensure the highest possible quality and impact of communication efforts at all times.

One of the areas where data is collected and plays an important role in the work of the communications unit at Maersk is in the work on the organisation's reputation. 'We probably do the same here as many other large organisations', says Communications Director Mette Refshauge. 'For example, we keep an eye on our reputation in the so-called 'Global RepTrack' survey, which measures and compares reputation using a number of common, well-established parameters. It is also possible to combine the standard analysis with special questions that reflect our specific ambition and identify a specific target respondent group, which the research organisation then reaches out to on our behalf. Data can be carved across geographies and topics. As well as giving us an indication of whether we are succeeding in our ambitions, we also get interesting insights into how market dynamics or geopolitical situations affect our reputation'.

The data Maersk gets from reports like these are used as a basis for prioritising efforts. 'Of course, measuring our stakeholders is not something we do alone', emphasises Mette Refshauge. 'For example, we work closely with colleagues in sales and marketing, investor relations and HR, who have other types of data and insights from investors, customers and colleagues. They have different end goals in mind than the company's reputation—it could be confidence in the stock, sales or customer and employee satisfaction, but it's all connected when you work in an integrated way with communication'. However, it is important not to just blindly use external metrics, as the organisation's experience is that they vary greatly in quality: 'There are countless metrics, analyses, "hit lists" and awards that score companies on this and that—it's a whole industry in itself. Some are interesting and scientifically based, others are more superficial, whilst others are somewhere between hocus-pocus and science. In my experience, it is a good idea to make some very deliberate choices about which measurements and data you value and follow. This should preferably be justified and agreed on with the executive board, because there will always be someone who has read that Maersk has moved up or down on some list, and as a non-communication professional it can be difficult to distinguish what to go for and what is valuable to us', she emphasises. That is why she has regularly aligned her recommendations for goals and metrics with the executive board to ensure a shared understanding of which metrics are the most valid and relevant to use as benchmarks for Maersk's communication ambitions.

6.8.1 KPIs as Direction and Motivation

The communications function works internally to define targets for both the positioning of Maersk, the transformation of the communications department and the individual professional communication areas—these are the so-called 'Key Performance Indicators' or 'KPIs' for short.

'It's a good chance for taking stock every year and realising how far we've come since last time, while adjusting and renewing our ambitions for the future. We look at which goals are linked to the business strategy, which external trends dominate the world of communication, and how we as a department deliver', emphasises Mette Refshauge.

The focus is on impact targets rather than effort targets. So it is not enough to deliver a lot of effort within the agreed time frame to meet your targets. It is the effect of the effort that will determine whether the objectives have been achieved. At the same time, there is an ambition not to burden the organisation with special measurements and, as far as possible, to avoid basing targets on personal estimates from stakeholders, such as how satisfied management is with the work of the communications department. As far as possible, targets should be built on the insights and research that the organisation already has. For example, progress on the ambition to create understanding and ownership of the strategy is better reflected in some of the responses from the employee satisfaction survey than in the number of articles and town halls produced on the subject. 'We have a set rhythm for how and how often we communicate on the larger themes, and we follow up on it regularly. But the success must be measured in terms of the effect we are able to see, for example in attitudes or behaviour', says Jesper Løv, Head of Media Relations & Leadership.

'We also use it actively when we want to develop the perception of what Maersk is', he says. For example, the press team has been measured on whether they have succeeded in increasing the proportion of stories that were about integrated logistics rather than traditional shipping stories, and most recently the development of stories related to the tech agenda is being monitored. 'Here we have used data actively. We create a so-called 'coin score' that tells us something about how the press coverage is. And here we first put logistics and then tech as separate parameters in both the Danish and foreign media. It gave us a place to look—even when we thought it was a bit difficult to get publicity. Fortunately, it was quite visible that progress was being made. In this way, data can also become a motivating factor internally', he elaborates. Jesper Løv also emphasises that the coin score tells us nothing more than that the messages have been visible and that the publicity has been positive, neutral or negative. The real influence is, for example, to look at whether Maersk is perceived as a natural and credible voice in the forums where tech profiles meet, and whether the company is able to attract and retain talent for tech positions.

6.8.2 'Social Listening' on Social Media

Maersk's strategic producers are not only data-driven in their work with KPIs, they are also data-driven in their organisational listening on social media to ensure that we are not living in our own world but are aware of what others think and

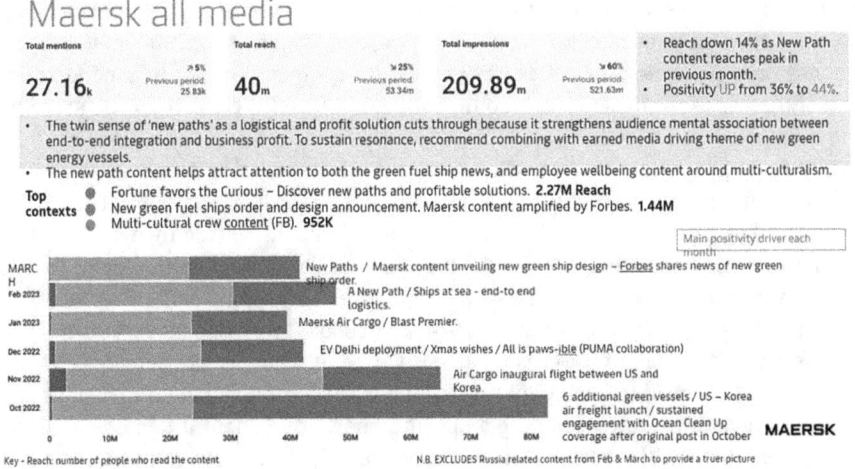

Fig. 6.4 An extract from Maersk's monthly report on social media activity

Fig. 6.5 An extract from the monthly social media activity report

experience (Figs. 6.4 and 6.5). They are thus provided with a detailed report from an external company every month that gives them a comprehensive overview and allows for detailed dives into what is happening on social media. An example of some of the data can be seen here:

Amongst other things, the report provides insight into the publicity Maersk has received over the past month. The data shows, for example that many people were interested in the fact that Maersk changed CEO in December 2022, but also that a small story about the use of a small, quirky electric vehicle in India generated a high level of interaction. The insights can provide communicators with input on what content generates interest and which narrative forms penetrate, so they can constantly develop content and formats to match.

At a very basic level, the report provides insight into what was the most read content on Maersk's channels in a given period. The data can also be broken down to allow the communicator to track the response of specific stakeholders to a given agenda or to generate a so-called 'word cloud', i.e. an automatically generated figure of the words most used when commenting on Maersk's content on social media (Fig. 6.6).

'There are really almost overwhelming possibilities of going deep with data. And it's not something we should drown in or spend an inordinate amount of time on', says Head of Social Media & Storytelling, Samantha Almon Adeluwoye, who uses data to drive social media. That is why the team has decided to use the report to take stock every month and look at the overall direction of the team, and also to use data specifically when they are working on a given agenda. 'We use data very actively to assess where we need to prioritise—just as we use it when we are actually producing content and need to ensure that we hit the mark communicatively. Then we can open the data treasure chest and get specific knowledge about the interests of the key stakeholder on the current topics, or, conversely, what does not interest them. This is a very important tool also in the concrete communication work'.

6.8 Case 5. Being Data-Driven Must Be Useful

Fig. 6.6 Example of data-driven 'word clouds' based on social media comment traces

6.8.3 Data-Driven Processes

Another data-driven field of work at Maersk is large-scale change processes. 'In change processes, we will often set up some indicators that we keep an eye on along the way to ensure that we do not lose focus on the stakeholder perspective. This is important because in extensive processes there is a risk of losing sight of the stakeholder perspective', says Jesper Løv.

That is why the professional communicators, together with the managers of the change project, typically set up parameters that are monitored on an ongoing basis, where the response is measured at a fixed frequency, typically in a sample of employees to gauge the temperature (Fig. 6.7). The next measurement is carried out on a new respondent group, so as not to burden your organisation with too many measurements. These pulse measurements act as a kind of reality check in the engine room, so you know whether adjustments need to be made in relation to planned changes.

6.8.4 Data Related to Events

When Maersk's communicators facilitate large events, they work with data to a wide extent along the way. For example, when organising a big kickoff, it is a natural part of the planning to discuss what data can be used as input along the way to ensure they are on track with the overall goal.

It may, for example be simple data about participants in an online event or data about people who might drop out along the way (Figs. 6.8 and 6.9). It may also be the registration of questions and comments that are categorised so you can follow up on something that may be unclear or that needs to be actively addressed in later webinars.

'Retaining the interest of online participants has become increasingly important as more of our events have become fully or partially virtual. In addition to creating

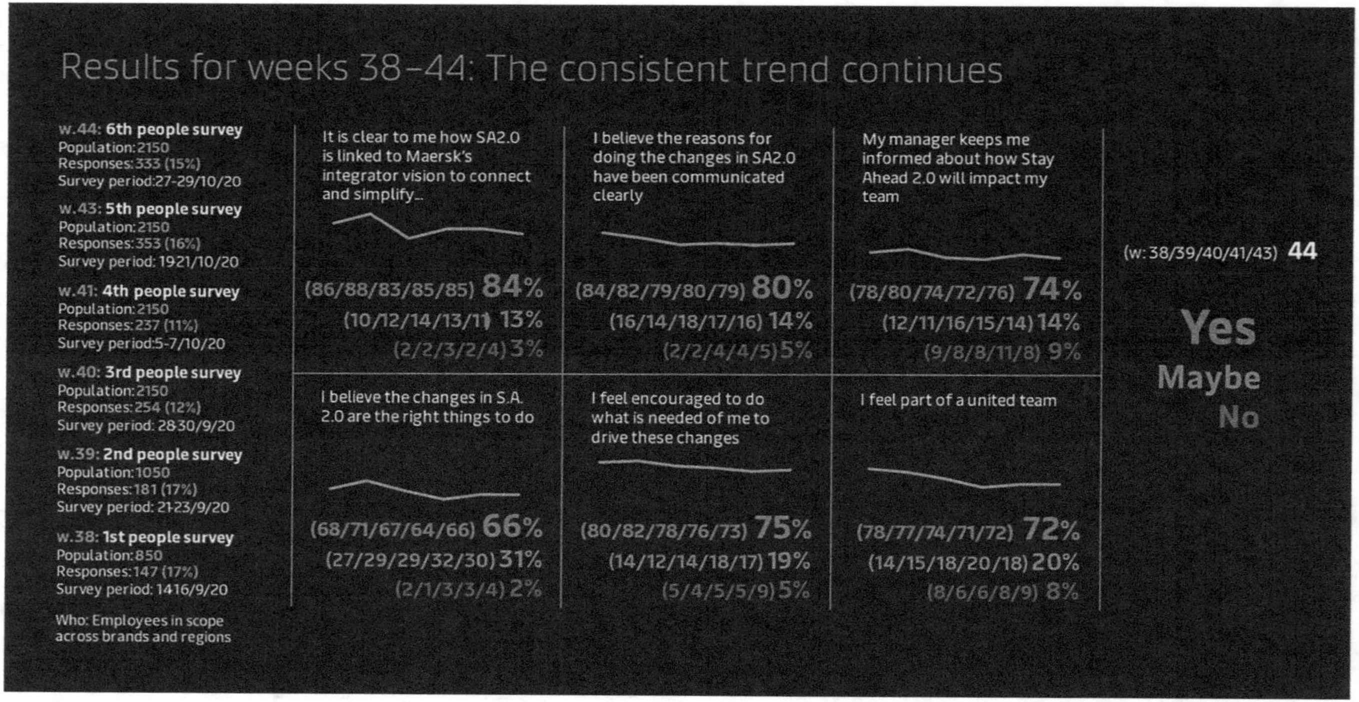

Results for weeks 38–44: The consistent trend continues

			(w: 38/39/40/41/43) **44**
			Yes
			Maybe
			No

	It is clear to me how SA2.0 is linked to Maersk's integrator vision to connect and simplify...	I believe the reasons for doing the changes in SA2.0 have been communicated clearly	My manager keeps me informed about how Stay Ahead 2.0 will impact my team
w.44: 6th people survey Population: 2150 Responses: 333 (15%) Survey period: 27-29/10/20	(86/88/83/85/85) **84%** (10/12/14/13/11) 13% (2/2/3/2/4) 3%	(84/82/79/80/79) **80%** (16/14/18/17/16) 14% (2/2/4/4/5) 5%	(78/80/74/72/76) **74%** (12/11/16/15/14) 14% (9/8/8/11/8) 9%
w.43: 5th people survey Population: 2150 Responses: 353 (16%) Survey period: 19-21/10/20			
w.41: 4th people survey Population: 2150 Responses: 237 (11%) Survey period: 5-7/10/20			
w.40: 3rd people survey Population: 2150 Responses: 254 (12%) Survey period: 28-30/9/20	I believe the changes in S.A. 2.0 are the right things to do	I feel encouraged to do what is needed of me to drive these changes	I feel part of a united team
w.39: 2nd people survey Population: 1050 Responses: 181 (17%) Survey period: 21-23/9/20	(68/71/67/64/66) **66%** (27/29/29/32/30) 31% (2/1/3/3/4) 2%	(80/82/78/76/75) **75%** (14/12/14/18/17) 19% (5/4/5/5/9) 5%	(78/77/74/71/72) **72%** (14/15/18/20/18) 20% (8/6/6/8/9) 8%
w.38: 1st people survey Population: 850 Responses: 147 (17%) Survey period: 14-16/9/20			
Who: Employees in scope across brands and regions			

Fig. 6.7 An example of a weekly temperature check during a change, enabling Maersk's strategic producers to monitor the response at all times

6.8 Case 5. Being Data-Driven Must Be Useful

Fig. 6.8 An example of the communication of at an online event

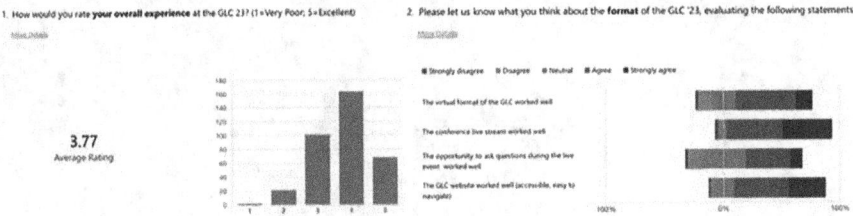

Fig. 6.9 Examples of post-event evaluative data that can be used for future planning

greater engagement with participants, our tools also aim to facilitate an active dialogue through the screen and to collect feedback that can be used to improve the experience and content of the next event', says Thomas Søndergaard, Head of Digital Enablement.

Data is also typically summarised after the specific event in a simple overview that can be actively used the next time you plan a similar event.

6.8.5 Data in Channel Work

Equally straightforward use of data can also be found amongst many of the communicators who are primarily responsible for various specific communication channels. 'I use data actively in my text work on all our internal media', says Anne-Katrine Bostrøm, who works with internal communication at Maersk (Fig. 6.10). 'It is simply an integral part of my work processes that I follow data closely. How many people read an article? How many comments does a post get on Yammer? What are people writing, or is there a deafening silence? I keep an eye on it and use it actively to adjust as needed', she emphasises.

For example, this internal post, first shared as a more localised post, with the headline 'How the humble Papad is creating waves—a story of hope'. It was felt that the headline did not give enough information about what the story was about, so it was initially shared on LinkedIn globally with the title 'Empowering women in Murbad Taluka, Maharashtra 🇮🇳' (see LinkedIn post). 'On LinkedIn, the headline

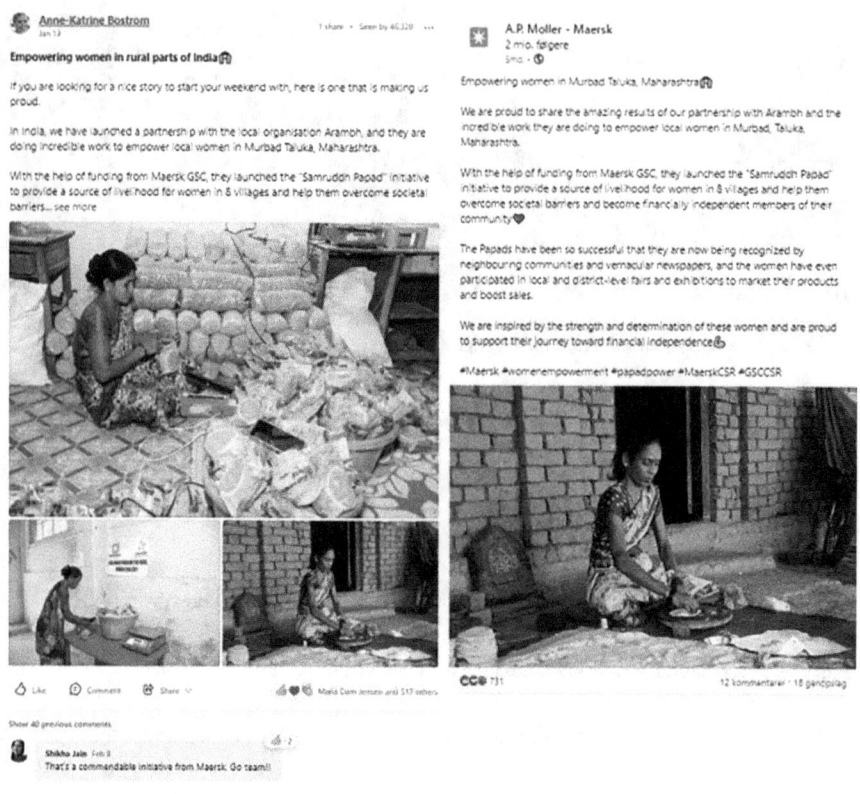

Fig. 6.10 Examples of data-driven internal communication

worked well as it reached a huge Indian audience. However, I could see from the data that it was completely stagnant internally, so I adjusted it again to 'rural parts of India'—and then it really took off and became a post that performed better than I would in any way have expected', says Anne-Katrine Bostrøm.

Data use in internal communication does not rely on sophisticated 'SharePoint reports', which are never really used constructively. 'We could probably have struck gold there too, but our days are very busy, so it often slipped into the background. So instead of being annoyed, we've started to work more simply and constructively with data'. This is both in the concrete, practical production, where data is actively used for adjustments and in the weekly newsletters that are sent out. 'Every week we send out a newsletter with the most important news from the past week, so we are sure that even colleagues who have not had much time for internal media can get an overview and insight by us pushing it out to them'. Here, Maersk has a basic principle that the newsletter should not be used to 'fix' stories that have not been seen by many. If a story does not deliver, it should be edited into a new and better version before it is shared again: 'The newsletter should be used to ensure that the most important things get out. But of course we also look at the data to find our own blind spots, if there is something that we haven't been aware of but that is important for the organisation, we can use the newsletter to share it'.

In addition, the statistics on the most viewed content are, for example also used for inspiration at editorial meetings across channels. What do people read? And where do they prefer to read it? The communicators work with a 'newsroom approach' where, instead of gathering in channel silos, editorial meetings are held to discuss and coordinate across communication channels. 'We very much work towards using the same channels externally and internally, for example, if we publish a video, we use the same source link to YouTube. We believe that many colleagues use e.g. LinkedIn as much as they use SharePoint (or more)—and this way we get a single place to pull data from. It also fits really well with our newsroom approach, where we think story first. I am sure that in the future we will also integrate external posts into the internal content flow much more than we already do', concludes Anne-Katrine Boström.

6.8.6 A Data-Driven Future

At Maersk, they are also in no doubt that data is an area where professional communicators can become even better. The headache for many communication functions is how to identify and use exactly the data that can be translated into action and improvements in everyday routines. It is a balance between using data, without being overwhelmed by it, and taking data seriously, without getting lost in the infinite number of data sources available. Data can improve both quality and impact, but data cannot replace, only supplement and anchor the professional judgement of the individual communicator.

6.9   Interview. Choose Communication!

It is a choice. We can keep informing, or we can step up and communicate. If we do, we need to listen, measure and evaluate. This is one way to sum up the advice of Australian communication professor Jim Macnamara to all future communicators. He is one of the world's leading researchers and advisors and is currently helping the WHO learn from the global pandemic. But it requires something new from communicators.

'I saw 'the light' myself some years ago. That it's about a choice. A choice between continuing to inform and produce a lot of information materials or to genuinely step into communicating. Communication means exchanging and sharing, and that requires genuine engagement and receptiveness'. There's no doubt that the professor from the University of Technology Sydney is keen for all communicators to see this difference and develop the skills to turn it into action—and there's a long way to go.

Jim Macnamara is a researcher in the evaluation of public communication and organisational listening, and from his perspective, we are not good enough. 'Way too many people get the very definition of listening wrong. It's *not* about collecting data or even just listening, it's about the process of interpreting data into real knowledge and insights that the communicator can use to make a difference', he stresses.

6.9.1 Drop the Recipients – and Rethink 'Audiences'

Dropping the term recipients may sound provocative, but the professor's important point is that as long as we see others as audiences or recipients, we fail to understand communication: 'I simply don't like the concept of *audience*.[1] We need to see others as stakeholders with whom we need to engage and not simply bombard them with information', he stresses, saying with a smile that he himself has also informed lots in the past. The professor himself started his career as a journalist and later worked in corporate communications, and a lot of one-way communication found its way into the columns and fancy brochures and campaigns for many years.

But it is a fact that communicators love to make creative publications and other outputs and forget that communication is a two-way interaction with stakeholders. That does not mean that Jim Macnamara underestimates the importance of producing good information: 'It's important that we have talented writers everywhere— I'm the biggest advocate of smart, independent journalists. And we need information to be distributed on issues such as health. But today it takes more than putting out information. We need to look beyond outputs to succeed. Even journalists today must keep an eye on views, time spent on articles, etc., to be efficient'.

Receivers do not sit around passively and wait for information in today's media landscape: They are active stakeholders, and some researchers even talk about the communication of active citizens as 'citizen journalism' and 'the fifth estate': 'More than 200 countries in the world now have democracies where citizens have a voice and use it. They are the ones we need to engage with, based on respect and understanding, if communication is to succeed', he stresses. 'It's probably the biggest change at the end of the 20th century that citizens want to be consulted: they want to have a say, they want to exercise their rights. That is why it is not expedient for neither public nor private organisations to spend 90–95% of their budget on sending out information. They need to listen more and engage in two-way communication'.

A 50–50 target might be a little naive, Jim Macnamara believes, 'But we should at least reach a level of 30% of our time and budgets spent on listening properly as organisations, and that should be achieved by researching properly'.

6.9.2 Learning Is Essential

Listening, measuring and evaluating are all about learning. Jim Macnamara has just helped the World Health Organisation (WHO) learn from the pandemic. The focus should not be on whether information was provided, but on whether it had an impact: 'Counting how many fancy brochures about face masks, campaigns about social distancing or vaccine advertisements had been made is not enough. We have to look at whether face masks are being used, whether people are keeping their distance and accepting vaccines'.

---

[1] Audience.

The WHO has adopted the process of MEL—Measurement, Evaluation and Learning—to emphasise that measurement and evaluation are not an end in themselves but that rather they lead to learning. Learning is one of the key results of evaluation and organisational listening.

Jim Macnamara personally learned that in a rude awakening. After his time as a journalist, he started a successful PR consulting business. One of his major clients was Microsoft, and 1 day the CEO asked him to provide a report summarising what value Macnamara's consultancy had provided to Microsoft.

Jim Macnamara quickly set about writing a report, which he happily handed over at a meeting. The CEO flicked and browsed through the first pages, then lifted his head and said 'This is what you've done for us. But we don't care about how much work you have done. We want to know what is the impact and the value'.

It is clear that the memory is still vivid, perhaps also because that excellent question became a turning point in his career. This got Jim Macnamara on the track towards evaluation, with a focus on identifying outcomes and impact and applying the learning gained through evaluation and organisational listening.

Inspired, he switched his own career path, got a master's degree in research, then a PhD and sold the PR consultancy to establish a research company focusing on evaluation using computer-aided research. That company was successful to the point that after a decade he sold it to a larger international company. With his appetite for research whetted, he then took a position as a professor at UTS and has worked there since 2007.

6.9.3 Lift the Heavy Weights

Communication is much more than distributing information. It is one thing to write press releases, plan campaigns and produce creative videos and publications, but communicators need to do more than produce information material and send it out. The hard task in communication is to achieve results and impact.

'In the WHO project, I work closely with researchers and scientific health professionals, and frankly, their work is not always fun or visible, but it is infinitely important. That's what we need to do as communicators, move from being creative producers of information material to being effective communicators', he says.

6.9.4 Interpret Data Wisely: Even on the Move

Some of the heavy lifting required in strategic public communication involves becoming skilled in measurement, evaluation and organisational listening which must—in Jim Macnamara's perspective—be a part of each of the communicator's processes. Technology has made it easier. He highlights, for example how much easier it is to monitor the response to communication outputs in real time on social media or websites: 'We can tell how people are responding by the minute. Based on learning gained from measurement and evaluation, we can identify if information is being used and understood, and whether it is producing an outcome such as increased awareness or behavioural change. If not, we can adjust our approach or try something different', he says.

Evaluation should not just be about looking backwards to report what was done in the past. 'When you change your understanding of evaluation from passive retrospective reporting to progressive learning, it starts to make a crucial difference'.

Digital technologies give us access to so much data. 'Data can tell us who is looking at a website, for example. How long do they stay there? What do they click? What do they download? If, for example, we produce a video and can see that only few people are watching it, then we can take it down and do something. Attention can be difficult to capture, and we need data to ensure that we work wisely. Simply putting something online and then waiting a year to see if it had an effect is a waste of time and money'.

We need to master a range of methods to conduct the necessary analyses, and Jim Macnamara finds it important to remind us that it is not only the quantitative data that we get from questionnaires, for example, that is important; in communication, the qualitative aspect is also very important. He gives an example of a large organisation that conducted a public consultation. 'They received 127,400 submissions that were up to seven pages long. It's impossible for anyone to manually process that much data, so machine learning software for textual analysis was necessary to process the data and produce usable findings. The trick is not just to get a lot of data, which can be overwhelming, but to interpret and analyse that data, for example to identify themes and issues that need to be addressed. We don't just listen with our ears and through collecting piles of data; we have to use our brains to interpret what the data means and develop appropriate strategies'.

6.9.5 Skills of the Future

> Don't worry, I'm not suggesting that communicators of the future should be data experts. Not at all. But communicators of the future must use technology even more and then add human interpretation and ethics. We need to put together teams in communication functions to create quality content, collect data and, above all, analyse the data so it can be turned into something constructive.

Analysis and interpretation require many skills. The professor smiles and says that you almost have to be 'part psychologist, part sociologist and part data analyst' to master translating all the quantitative and qualitative input into useful learning that can be translated into real stakeholder insights and communication.

'Many other professions have evolved', he stresses. 'Companies are trying to become customer-centric, hospitals try to become patient-centric—and of course we, the communicators, need to be stakeholder-centric. The moment we choose to communicate and not just send out information, the need for real listening becomes essential and the evaluation of measurements is a form of organisational listening. We must have a clear sense of the concerns, needs, interests and expectations of our stakeholders, and this calls for new skills, either in the individual communicator or at least represented in the communication team'.

Jim Macnamara

Jim Macnamara is a professor in the School of Communication at the University of Technology Sydney (UTS). He is also a Visiting Professor at The London School of Economics and Political Science (LSE) Media and Communications Department and a Visiting Professor at the London College of Communication (LCC) in the University of the Arts London (UAL). He is internationally recognised for his research on evaluation and organisational listening. Before choosing an academic career, he was an active entrepreneur, analyst and communicator for more than 30 years as a writing journalist, consultant, advertising expert and, not least, analyst.

He is the author of more than 80 academic articles, book chapters and numerous books, including: 'Beyond Post-Communication: Challenging Disinformation, Deception, and Manipulation' (Peter Lang, New York, 2020); 'Evaluating Public Communication: New Models, Standards, and Best Practice' (Routledge, UK, 2018); 'Organizational Listening: The Missing Link in Public Communication' (Peter Lang, New York, 2016); and 'The 21st Century Media (R)evolution: Emergent Communication Practices' (Peter Lang, New York, 2014).

References

Andersen, J. (2019). https://quantumprmeasurement.com/
Broom, G. M. (2012). *Cutlip & Center's effective public relations* (11th ed.). Pearson/Prentice Hall.
Dickson, D., Rainey, S., & Hargie, O. (2003). Communicating sensitive business issues: Part 2. *Corporate Communications: An International Journal., 8*, 121–127.
Flick, U. (2022). *The Sage handbook of qualitative research design* (Vol. 2). Sage.
Goldhaber, G. M. (1993). *Organizational communication*. Brown & Benchmark.
Hargie, O., & Tourish, D. (2000). *Handbook of communication audits for organisations*. Psychology Press.
Henert, E., & Taylor-Power, E. (2008). *Developing a logic model: Teaching and training guide*. University of Wisconsin-Extension Programme. Retrieved from https://fyi.uwex.edu/program-development/files/2016/03/lmguidecomplete.pdf

Jensen, K. B. (2021). *A handbook of media and communication research: Qualitative and quantitative methodologies* (3rd ed.). Routledge.

Macnamara, J. (2014a). Organisational listening: A vital missing element in public communication and the public sphere. *Asia Pacific Public Relations Journal, 15*(1), 89–108.

Macnamara, J. (2014b). Journalism-PR relations revisited: The good news, the bad news and insights into tomorrow's news. *Public Relations Review, 40*(5), 739–750.

Macnamara, J. (2017). Toward a theory and practice of organizational listening. *International Journal of Listening., 32*, 1–23.

Macnamara, J. (2018a). *Evaluating public communication: Exploring new models, standards and best practice* (1st ed.). Routledge.

Macnamara, J. (2018b). A review of new evaluation models for strategic communication: Progress and gaps. *International Journal of Strategic Communication, 12*(2), 180–195.

Macnamara, J. (2021a). A 'macro' view of strategic communication management: Beyond 'siloes', dominant paradigms and pandemics. *ESSACHESS, 14*(1), 65–91.

Macnamara, J. (2021b). New insights into crisis communication from an 'inside' emic perspective during COVID-19. *Public Relations Inquiry, 10*(2), 237–262.

Michaelson, D., & Stacks, D. W. (2014). *A professional and practitioner's guide to public relations research, measurement and evaluation* (2nd ed.). Business Expert Press.

Macnamara, & Valentini. (2021). *Public relations measurement and evaluation*. Public Relations, 249-273. De Gruyter Mouton.

Page. (2019). *The CCO as pacesetter what it means, why it matters, how to get there*. Page research report.

Tench, R., Vercic, D., Zerfass, A., Moreno, A., & Verhoeven, P. (2017). *Communication excellence: How to develop, manage and lead exceptional communications*. Palgrave Macmillan.

Tkalac Verčič, A. (2021). The impact of employee engagement, organisational support and employer branding on internal communication satisfaction. *Public Relations Review, 47*(1).

Volk, S. C., & Buhmann, A. (2019). New avenues in communication evaluation and measurement (E&M): Towards a research agenda for the 2020s. *Journal of Communication Management (London, England), 23*(3), 162–178.

Yamaguchi, I. (2017). Instruments for organisational communication assessment for Japanese care facilities. *Corporate Communications: An International Journal, 22*(4), 471–485.

Zerfass, A., Tench, R., Vercic, D., Verhoeven, P., & Moreno, A. (2017). *European Communication Monitor 2017. Excellence in strategic communication: How strategic communication deals with the challenges of visualisation, social bots and hypermodernity. Results of a survey in 50 countries*. EACD/EUPRERA, Quadriga Media Berlin.

Zerfass, A., Vercic, D., Verhoeven, P., Moreno, A., & Tench, R. (2015). *European Communication Monitor 2015. Creating communication value through listening, messaging and measurement. Results of a survey in 41 countries*. EACD/EUPRERA, Helios Media.

Zerfass, A., Vercic, D., & Volk, S. C. (2017). Communication evaluation and measurement: Skills, practices and utilization in European organisations. *Corporate Communications—An International Journal, 22*(1), 2–18.

Zwijze-Koning, K. H., & de Jong, M. D. T. (2007). Measurement of communication satisfaction. Evaluating the Communication Satisfaction Questionnaire as a communication audit tool. *Management Communication Quarterly, 20*(3), 261–282.

7 Internal Stakeholders in Focus

Results, engagement and well-being. As a professional communicator, there are countless reasons to pay particular attention to internal stakeholders. This chapter looks at some of the key factors in creating direction, meaning and engagement through strategic communication.

The case study in this chapter provides insight into one of internal communication's key areas of work: turning the strategic ambitions of top management into meaningful signposts for internal stakeholders. After all, what can you do to get an organisation's long-term ambitions across to over 100,000 employees?

The chapter's international expert is Croatian Professor Ana Tkalac Verčič, who has, with a background in psychology, put internal communication on the agenda as a field of research and action and has even found links between internal communication and individual quality of life.

For many years, research and practice have focused mostly on the external and powerful stakeholders of organisations, but this perspective should not obscure the fact that internal stakeholders are crucial to the success of an organisation. The reasons abound: Fundamentally, internal stakeholders are the ones who make up the organisation, who have to deliver the results, and at the same time they are also very much the ambassadors and the face of the organisation—they are the ones who have to build trust with all stakeholders. They are in contact with all customers and partners, and in the new media landscape they are also very important internal ambassadors as voices on social media, also called 'employee advocacy' (Thelen, 2020). The competition to get and retain the right labour force has also meant a much greater awareness of creating an internal commitment that can retain and attract talent. In addition, internal stakeholders have also come into focus following challenges during the coronavirus pandemic, the balancing act of new hybrid workplaces and so-called 'quiet quitting' (Scheyett, 2022). According to researchers such as Tkalac Verčič (2021), it is high time for the professional communicator to prioritise internal stakeholders even more. That is why this chapter identifies key areas of work in relation to internal stakeholders in terms of communication culture, channel mix and strategic anchoring.

7.1 Communication with Internal Stakeholders

The transmission paradigm has long characterised the practice in relation to internal stakeholders. This means that the perception in many organisations has roughly speaking been that the internal stakeholders needed to be informed—that information had to be transmitted—when something new happened and that there was no need to make a special effort to communicate in an interesting way. Because they *had to* read along. Fortunately, this is changing with the realisation of the importance of symmetrical two-way communication with employees as internal stakeholders. There is a move away from the more functionalist view of communication, where a management approach has seen information as something to be controlled and channelled out. Instead, this view is replaced by a more constitutionalist view of communication as interaction, where communication is seen as an exchange process. Always in motion, influenced by many factors and actualised by what is happening at any given time, planned or unplanned, i.e. emergent (Aggerholm et al., 2020: 26).

Another significant shift is one from seeing organisations as 'containers' in which communication takes place, for example between managers and employees, to looking at the creative power of communication. Namely, the organisation is to a large extent created by the communicative exchanges in what Heide and Simonsson characterise as a processual approach:

> The process view focuses on organisations as a continuous process of becoming, while the entity view centers on how an organisation comes to be through an organizing process (Cooren et al., 2011; Putnam et al., 2009; Putnam & Nicotera, 2010) (Heide & Simonsson, 2018: 209).

It is a symbiotic relationship where the communication creates the organisation, whilst the organisation mediates the communication, which results in four communication flows (see also Table 2.1 in Chap. 2):

1. Membership negotiation
2. Self-structuring
3. Activity coordination
4. Institutional positioning

In other words, the communicator has to work in all four flows. How to negotiate with 'members' (1)? How to structure oneself in the organisation? (2) Which activities need to be coordinated (3)? And how to position the organisation externally (4)? These are points of attention that must kept in mind when planning any initiatives.

The definition of internal communication is thus often quite broad, for example: 'Internal communication is defined as integrated internal communication, i.e. all formal and informal communication taking place internally at all levels of an organisation' (Kalla, 2005: 304). And this is precisely how broadly the professional communicator must think when organising communicative solutions that can realise ambitions for good communication with internal stakeholders. For example, if a new initiative is to be announced, it may be appropriate to use a mix of channels, where the manager presents a news item in a short film externally and internally at the same time ('institutional positioning'). At the same time, all managers may have been equipped with background knowledge and good arguments on a webinar, so are able to call meetings with all their employees immediately after an announcement. Here, the immediate manager can create a good framework for actual dialogue ('membership negotiation'), where everyone can have their say— and where the communicators may simply have created a few slides and some good questions for opening the conversations. The otherwise classic informative article on the intranet can be replaced by an event report from one of these departmental meetings, which employees can then reflect on. At the same time, the official descriptions and procedures can be updated on the intranet, perhaps with a new quick guide to make it easy to turn words into action ('self-structuring'). Such an orchestrated mix ('activity coordination') aims not only to inform but also to facilitate communication, meaning-making, identification and engagement.

The concrete value of internal communication has been documented by a number of researchers, as Tkalac Verčič summarises in this way in her comprehensive summary of international research in the field:

> It is clear from research that there is a significant link between internal communication and organisational climate and productivity (Joshi & Sharma, 1997), as well as employees' ability, motivation and commitment (Nakra, 2006). Internal communication can help improve corporate reputation and credibility since employees represent a highly credible source for all external publics (Dawkins, 2005; Hannegan, 2004; White et al., 2010) and can add significant insight into leadership communication (Men, 2015; Jiang & Men, 2015; Men & Stacks, 2014) (Tkalac Verčič, 2021: 243).

The field of work for the professional communicator is increasingly becoming communication with internal stakeholders. It is no longer just about informing but about communicating *with* and ensuring that strategies make sense, that commitment is motivated and that psychological safety (Edmondson, 1999) and well-being are supported. This means that the field of work includes supporting strategic change, major projects and changes, managing crises and creating an engaging culture because communication helps to glue together the organisation.

7.2 The Culture of Communication as a Field of Work

Communication culture can be defined as the way the organisation interacts communicatively (Lund, 1999). It is very much part of the self-structuring flow mentioned above, but although it is called self-structuring precisely because it is driven by many of the voices of the organisation itself, this does not mean that it is so self-structuring that it should be left to itself. This is also a field of work for the professional communicator. It is very much here that communication functions can take co-responsibility, in sound interaction with HR functions, for facilitating a healthy culture of quality knowledge sharing and effective communication channels, underpinned by internal trust.

So, the professional communicator cannot only ensure his or her own anchoring of any planned communicative effort with an analytical, organisational view but use the same analytical skills to ensure insight into whether there is a need for a professional communicator's facilitation of an even better communication culture.

The level of trust in the communication culture is crucial for the professional communicator to succeed in communicating with internal stakeholders. Compared to employees in so-called 'low-trust' organisations, employees in 'high-trust' organisations have:

- 74% less stress
- 106% more energy at work
- 50% higher productivity
- 13% fewer sick days
- 76% more engagement
- 29% higher satisfaction with their life
- 40% less burnout (Zak, 2017)

As a communicator, this kind of data can inspire what is important to show and promote with communication in order to build trust.

Often, a serious indicator of a lack of trust and a need to examine the communication culture is the noisy silence from internal stakeholders when dialogue is invited. Morrison and Milliken (2000) identify a number of parameters that create organisational silence—and they can serve as key points for further investigation of the professional communicator:

- Is the view of employees from management accurate, or does it need to be influenced and changed so the signals are more open and invite engagement and dialogue?
- Is there a real openness to input?
- Is there a link between what you ask and what you listen to?

Not everything is within the scope and mandate of the communicator, but these are issues that are worth taking an interest in and seeking to influence. Because silence cannot be fixed with quality communication from the communication department—it is the organisation and communication culture that needs to be changed in the long haul.

In an analytical view of communication culture, a focus on trust, effective channels and appropriate behaviour is essential. Communication knowledge can be brought into play in many parts of organisations, if professional communicators are given or assume a mandate in the communication culture. An example could be using managers as a communication channel. Many communication functions provide media training, but few have taken real co-responsibility, such as facilitating managers' communication awareness and skills. When this happens, it can often be essential for employees' sense of belonging to an organisation with a clear direction and a meaningful everyday life. Psychological safety also often increases if managers' awareness is raised regarding how inappropriate communication habits and a lack of feedback can create negative experiences and mistrust (Lund, 2008). Similar potentials could be found by looking at other elements of the communication culture, from time-consuming meeting cultures to inboxes that indicate a challenging email culture.

These tasks require a professional communicator with an analytical eye and a facilitating and instructing role, where professional skills are brought into play to influence the habits and patterns of the organisation. This is a field that is not always prioritised, but it is an area that is increasingly being put on the agenda, partly driven by challenges such as stress and dissatisfaction.

7.3 The Organisation's Communication Infrastructure

The communication function has often been responsible for organising the communication infrastructure, i.e. all the channels that need to be available for communication with internal stakeholders.

As a result of the shift from the transmission paradigm to a more constitutionalist communication approach focusing on symmetrical communication, this channel picture is changing. Communication is not just about top-down communication from top management to employees at town hall meetings or news articles on the intranet. It is also about creating an infrastructure that supports exchange and dialogue.

Tkalac Verčič et al. (2022) have developed an overview of traditional and newer communication channels focusing on this interaction.

Figure 7.1 clearly shows that an updated infrastructure must focus on more than just channels for mass communication. The professional communicator must thus broaden the channel perspective to far more channels in order to be able to engage in symmetrical dialogue with the internal stakeholders. This also means that in many channels, the communicator is not necessarily the producer of the communication but takes on entirely different roles. This may be as moderator in a video conference, facilitator of an internal meeting or sparring partner for a manager before a major meeting.

	Traditional	New
Not interactive	Newsletters	Digital newsletters
	Magazines	Information on LCD or other screens
	Information boards	Podcasts
	Posters	Blogs
	Memos	Video posts
	Mail sent to home	Group emails
Somewhat interactive	Meetings in larger groups	Intranet
	Live events	One-on-one emails
		Live web-casting
		Video conferencing in larger groups
		Social networks
		Internal communication applications (apps)
Interactive	Meetings in smaller groups	Video conferencing in smaller groups
	Team building	One-on-one video conferencing
	One-on-one interactions	
	Rumour mills	

Fig. 7.1 Overview of traditional and new internal communication channels. Source: Tkalac Verčič et al. (2022)

At the same time, channel development is part of the extended work function of the professional communicator, whose task it is to orchestrate the communicative expression with an analytical view of the existing channels, which must be constantly developed and supplemented with new ones. Not to chase every trend, but to focus on 'commtech' possibilities that can often help increase internal stakeholder engagement. Commtech is a new approach to communication that uses the possibilities of digital technology such as machine learning, artificial intelligence and big data analysis to organise communication efforts. However, the starting point for updating an organisation's channel infrastructure should never be technology enthusiasm alone but rather the needs of stakeholders and any challenges in getting their attention. This requires continuous analytical channel development, preferably based on data from both quantitative statements of reach, reading time, etc. supplemented by qualitative input from surveys of stakeholders, e.g. experience analyses, focus groups and the like.

One way to work with quality assurance of internal channels is to make internal social media *multivocal*, i.e. multi-*voiced*, so internal stakeholders interact and not just inform. In his research, Madsen (2022) summarises three reasons why it is not always possible to make internal social media (ISM) multivocal:

- The purpose of ISM is unclear (Denyer et al, 2011; Laitinen & Sivunen, 2020; Madsen, 2017; Amelia, 2016; Trimi & Galanxhi, 2014);
- ISM lacks support from (top) managers (Chin et al., 2015; Trimi & Galanxhi, 2014); or
- employees interpret and understand the social technology in a different way than anticipated (Högberg & Olsson, 2019; Madsen, 2017; Rice et al., 2017) (Madsen in Tkalac Verčič, 2021: 62).

7.3 The Organisation's Communication Infrastructure

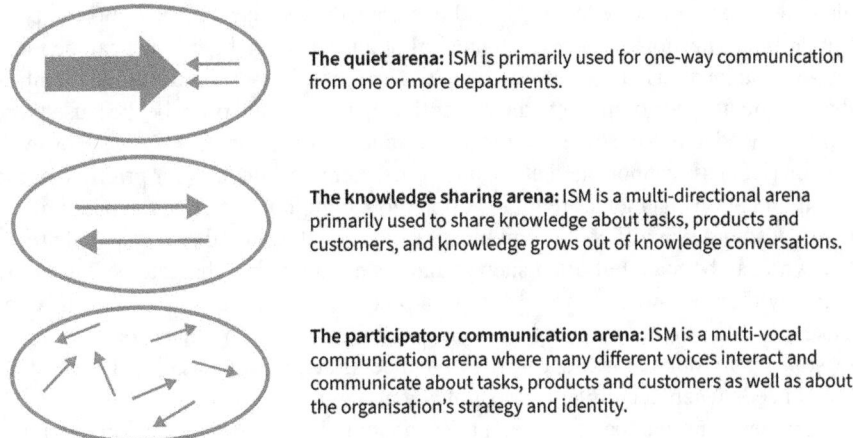

Fig. 7.2 Three types of communicative arenas on internal social media. Source: Madsen (2018) in Tkalac Verčič (2021)

These are challenges that indicate that the framing of a communication channel should not be underestimated for the professional communicator. Specifically, Madsen (2022) suggests a clearer framing of different areas of internal social media to make it easier to navigate. This is visualised in Fig. 7.2 with 'the quiet arena', 'the knowledge sharing arena' and 'the participatory communication area'.

The three areas in Fig. 7.2 show just how multifaceted the work of the professional communicator is in relation to communication channels: They need to be developed, quality assured, framed and mobilised in very different ways. In the 'quiet area', the communicator's role is often to help communicate clearly and engagingly, whilst the other two can be about helping to orchestrate the internal voice in the best possible way or perhaps moderating some of the interaction that takes place.

Analysing the trust and credibility of the individual channels is an important part of the communicator's quality assurance of communication. For example, have the town hall meetings become too long and boring? Are the only questions the ones prepared in advance? And does data show that people only stay on the live broadcast for 7 min? Or is there no interaction on the Yammer post—or maybe it is only the same 12 employees who are always active? The professional communicator ensures that the organisation has the best possible channels available and develops or deploys them as needed.

In the practical work of putting the channels into use, the aim is broad use across platforms to ensure the optimum effect in relation to stakeholders. An important consideration here is also the so-called 'media richness', which is an expression of 'the capacity of a channel to deliver potential information' (Daft & Lengel, 1986). How quickly does the content arrive? How many possibilities are there for reading signals? How much personal presence is possible etc. A face-to-face conversation, for example provides the possibility of reading many levels of communication, e.g.

also the subtext of body language and eye contact, and there is the opportunity to ask probing questions, whereas a flat email or an article on the intranet can be more one-dimensional. Tkalac Verčič et al. (2022) emphasises that the rule of thumb is that the greater the complexity, the richer the channel should often be, because there will be a need to be able to read more signals and ask questions (2022: 59). However, 'media richness' cannot stand alone as a professional benchmark for prioritising the communication channel, as reality is often more complex. A virtual town hall meeting may sound like a 'rich' communication situation because there are people there live who can be read, but often such situations end up being characterised more by one-way than two-way communication in practice and thus a poor opportunity for stakeholders to create meaning by asking and interacting. In other words, the professional communicator must always balance strategic, organisational and situational needs when deciding on the right channel mix.

Another important perspective in the channel mix is the external communication about the organisation itself—what is also known as auto-communication (Christensen, 2003). As mentioned, research (Kjærgaard & Morsing, 2010) shows that reading about the organisation in external media and channels can reinforce internal opinion formation. So the external narratives are also an important channel for the internal stakeholders.

7.4 The Strategy as an Anchor in Internal Communication

The strategy is the anchoring point for communication, also when working with internal stakeholders. Purpose, vision and mission are the meaning of the organisation, and this meaning must be transformed from abstract ambitions into direction and meaning in everyday life. Here, the professional communicator must use all communicative means to not only communicate the strategy but to maintain and realise the ambitions.

The skilled communicator not only communicates the strategy on special occasions but orchestrates the communication so it constantly links efforts to the strategic level. It may sound banal, but it is the strategic stubbornness that can make a big difference to the experience of being in an organisation where there is coherence in efforts and direction for everything. The strong organisation is both *univocal*, with a strong voice on direction, and at the same time *multivocal*, so that all employees translate the overall direction into their own meaningful version—it is this translation that is an important part of the communicator's co-responsibility (Dahlman & Heide, 2021).

This view can be complemented by Gulbrandsen and Just's (2020) focus on the need to move away from talking about strategic communication as a top-down, linear process and instead look at it as 'strategising': 'Strategic communication should not be seen as the result of actions taken by organisations, but rather as that which a network of actors does when it strategizes. Borrowing Nietzsche's maxim, one could say that 'there is no doer behind the deed': there is no organisation behind the strategy; 'it' does not 'have' a strategy; strategizing does organizing' (Gulbrandsen & Just, 2020: 12).

An approach that, in the organisational context, shifts the focus from the linear to the processual, the emergent and the co-creative. In most organisations, strategies are traditionally created by top managers but are realised in a joint strategising process, which only becomes stronger if the communication task is not just about informing or translating, but about all actors having their own power and 'agency' to translate the strategy into reality in their area of work. Here, the orchestration of the process is important—and requires a communicator with an eye for stakeholders' wishes as well as those of top management.

With the internal stakeholder in focus, the role of the professional communicator is complex. It requires not only professional communication skills to create good communication but strategic skills to ensure that it anchors the organisation's ambitions. In addition, relational skills are also important to ensure that internal communication is properly involved and integrated into all the key projects and ambitions of the organisation. Furthermore, ethical skills are crucial, as summarised by Tkalac Verčič et al., (2022):

Fifteen years of research on the communication profession in Europe led Tench et al. (2017) to propose that excellent communication professionals in Europe must be 'sagacious (knowledgeable, with reflective wisdom and good judgement), linked (with people, media and networks) and solid (strong, sensitive and savvy)'. They should also understand 'that conflicts of interest are a fundamental part of living together as humans and therefore also of organisational life' (Tench et al. (2017): 187). This highlights the importance of ethics in internal communication and raises the question, 'How are internal communication experts equipped to deal with it?' (Tkalac Verčič et al., 2022: 156).

How can professional communicators work with ethics? This is a question that is of course also worth keeping in mind as a professional communicator with a focus on the internal stakeholder, as they are co-responsible for internal trust and thus have an obligation to ensure coherence with both strategy and the organisation's values. Communication takes place at the intersection between what is said and what is done, and there must be consistency. This requires an ethical, analytical view of communication work and sometimes some 'do-overs' even in senior management, who may, for example, have been too busy to realise that some announcement could undermine trust. The communicator must help to draw attention to this, which requires sound professional judgement and personal courage.

7.5 Case 6. A Shoe Ready to Make Its Mark

An often difficult and always important part of communicating with internal stakeholders is communicating the organisation's strategy. This was the challenge facing the strategic producers at Maersk at the beginning of 2023. With a newly appointed CEO and a newly expanded executive board at the helm, the

next steps of Maersk's strategic transformation towards 2030 had to be announced in a big way. In collaboration with the executive board and the strategy function, the communicators have thus worked to design a simple and effective starting point for communicating the strategy, which both creates immediate attention and recognisability, and at the same time builds on elements that may live for many years to come.

A large part of the work behind implementing a strategy for the internal stakeholder is to ensure the right communicative starting point. This requires close interaction between communicators and management to ensure that ambitions are communicable and that there is agreement on how best to create meaning with internal stakeholders. At Maersk, the communications team followed the Executive Board closely when a strategy update was underway: 'We had a very good preparation process with the Executive Board. The strategy document itself, which was presented to—and approved by—the board, was close to 200 pages. A large part of the work has thus been focused on processing and condensing the document into something that was simpler to communicate and easier to relate to for our 100,000 colleagues', says Jesper Løv, Head of Media Relations & Leadership Communication.

It was not just a matter of communicative simplification but of ensuring that the strategy was crystallised into a coherent narrative that all managers could pass on to their employees and describe in more or less the same way. 'In the past, we have had some experience of, with the best of intentions, inventing too many different metaphors for the strategy, and this compromised recognisability and resulted in too many interpretations and perceptions of what the strategy was or was not about', Jesper Løv elaborates. This experience meant that it was important for the strategic producers to establish a shared story universe with a number of simple elements that can be recognised by everyone and help create an understanding of what the strategy is about and what it means for the individual parts of the organisation (Fig. 7.3).

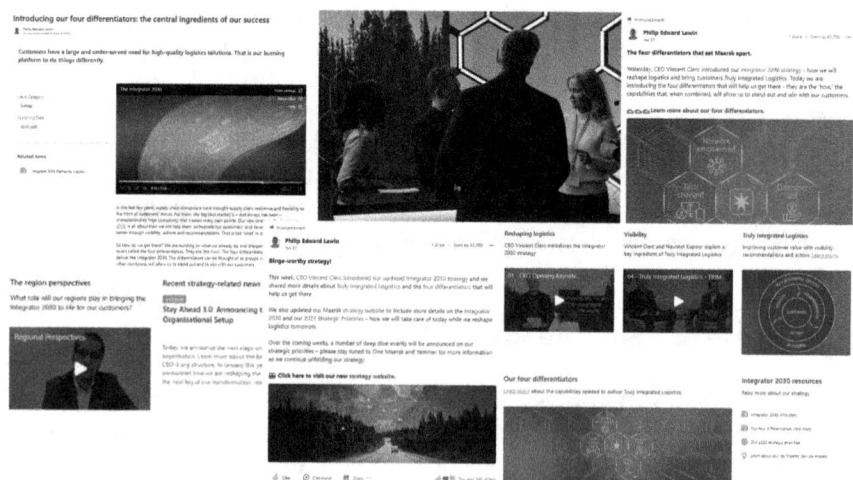

Fig. 7.3 Examples of internal communication in connection with the updating of a new strategy in Maersk, 2023

7.5 Case 6. A Shoe Ready to Make Its Mark

The concrete translation in the line communication from top manager to middle manager to employees had to be made as simple as possible, whilst at the same time leaving room for and encouraging individual managers to take co-responsibility for the communication and, for example add their own local examples to the narrative.

In other words, the channel mix of the strategic products emphasised a joint launch with a unified narrative with clear and easy-to-use elements. The communication effort was launched from the top management level, bringing together 1200 top managers for a virtual meeting over several days with time to listen, ask questions and discuss. At the same time, all internal channels were followed up with everything from partial live broadcasts of elements from the virtual leaders' meeting to films on Yammer and in-depth articles on the One Maersk intranet. A mix of channels ensured that no one felt left out and that line communication had depth and was supported by mass communication. So the strategic producers were busy with all types of communication tasks from studio design to training managers, creating articles, films and posts on the internal social media, Yammer.

7.5.1 A Visual Framework for the Strategic Narrative

The first phase of work for Maersk's communicators was to transform the 200 pages of strategy into a single, simple narrative with a clear *why* and *what*. Here, the strategic producers worked closely with colleagues in the strategy department to find the best ingredients for the simple, grand narrative. The ambition was to create some communicative building blocks that could be used for strategy communication on all channels and platforms in the coming years (Fig. 7.4). 'The visuals should never be underestimated, neither the concrete physical images nor the mental images you create with your framing of the strategy. That's why we like to spend a lot of energy to begin with, talking about which images should be the mainstay', says Jesper Løv.

It was an update of the existing strategy and not an entirely new strategy, so the strategic producers deliberately chose to reuse one of the elements that were already well known in the organisation: the Maersk shoe. As mentioned in Chap. 2, all 100,000 employees received their own pair of Maersk shoes produced by Puma in 2022 to signal quite specifically that employees would walk in the customer's shoes.

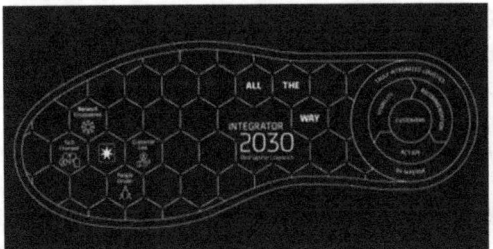 

Fig. 7.4 The sole of the Maersk shoe with the new strategy's key concepts together with Maersk's brand platform 'All the Way'

This had kindled great enthusiasm, so it was decided to keep the shoe as a visual anchor for the launch of the updated strategy: 'The updated strategy has a very clear starting point in the customer-centric, so we decided to use the shoe as a starting point for the new narrative. On the one hand, it was a good image of customer focus and the fact that we will walk the next many miles of the journey together. Secondly, the shoes have provided a collective identity, and they were already tied to positive associations'.

The solution was to create a visual identity that integrated the core elements of the strategy into the shoe. Specifically, all the key elements were built into a visualisation of the sole of the shoe.

As can be seen in the image, the so-called 'growth wheel' with the customer at the centre is seen in the sole of the foot, whilst the toe of the shoe has a visualisation of the four key areas that will act as 'differentiators' to drive the strategy. Being: 'Customer-led', 'People-driven', 'Network-empowered' and 'Tech-charged'.

'In this way, we visualise it all in a very simple way—and we make it loud and clear that this is the way to go as Maersk employees', says Jesper Løv. However, the strategic producers are also in no doubt that the shoe cannot walk all the way on its own, but ventured that it could function as an important artefact in the work of making the strategy tangible.

The visual anchoring of the shoe became the mainstay of the entire strategy universe that the strategic producers built up to the launch.

7.5.2 Virtual Leaders' Meeting as a Kickoff

It was important to make the framework for the actual launch of the updated strategy as visually clear as possible so that the framework could support the visual framing of the strategy from the start. The strategic producers thus designed a Maersk studio which in itself contributed to unfolding the strategy narrative (Fig. 7.5). The core elements of the strategy were, for example present as physical models in the studio and functioned both as large eye-catchers and as smaller physical blocks that the managers could take in their hands and use to physically support points. In this way, a degree of depth and 3D experience is created despite the virtual space, which reinforces the dialogic element in the communication.

The images show that the studio was set up like a TV studio, with two scenes that could be customised in different ways by varying the furniture etc. On the main stage, a large LED screen was used as a backdrop to bring the visual identity into play. The second stage was more intimate and designed for 'fireside chats' to create a more informal setting for conversations about the strategy with the executive board.

The whole event was managed by two internal hosts: the heads of Branding & Channel Management and Social Media & Storytelling, Samuel Poulter and Samantha Almon Adeluwoye, who often team up for internal events of this kind and are known as Sam & Sam. They have both been key communication staff in the preparatory work and thus know the strategy in depth. At the same time, they have good advisor relationships with the executive board (Schein, 2016), so they know

7.5 Case 6. A Shoe Ready to Make Its Mark

Fig. 7.5 Photos from Maersk Studio, where the updated strategy was launched

how to help unfold the points in the best possible way and how to get as close as possible in order to create good contact as proxies for all the internal participants at the screens.

The virtual management meeting was designed with a focus on variety and a strong desire for good contact with the internal stakeholders. This was one of the reasons why the studio included a conversation section, which afforded the possibility of varying the form of communication and talk in many ways about the next chapters of the strategy (as described in the theoretical section of this chapter in connection with dialogical elements and 'media richness').

The key communicator in the launch of the updated strategy was the then-new CEO Vincent Clerc, but as he expanded the Executive Board when he took office, it was also important to give as many Executive Board members as possible a role in the launch and to build confidence that the Executive Board as a team can come together to lead the organisation through the next crucial steps of the organisation's transformation.

Only Vincent Clerc had actual one-way presentations to the camera. All other sessions were designed as conversations between moderators and members of the Executive Board, something that served several purposes: Firstly, it was more informal and allowed the dynamics of the new management team to be shown, and secondly, the moderators could incorporate questions from the virtual participants along the way, allowing for direct dialogue.

In addition, to ensure further opportunities for engagement in the virtual format, breakout rooms were scheduled several times along the way, where participants could discuss in small groups what they had heard. After each workshop, feedback was provided so the communicators could help the Executive Board to make adjustments, answer questions or prioritise an underexposed topic. In this way, data was actively used in real time for quality assurance. All breakout rooms were conducted in MS Teams, and the feedback was collected via MS Forms.

Throughout the live event, there was also an open Q&A track where communicators could elicit questions for the conversations during the event.

'We did what we could to make the experience dynamic and animated. We wanted to create conversation and get all voices heard and all areas seen, but of course there were many limitations in the virtual space. We made it simpler by making a number of decisions from the start, e.g. that we would not use PowerPoint, that a session could only last 20 minutes, that we would only use formats that were structured as interviews rather than presentations, etc.', Jesper Løv elaborates.

In the subsequent evaluation of the event, participants expressed great satisfaction with both the format and the content, which greatly contributed to the understanding of the strategy. However, it was also clear that even with an ambitious virtual format, it is not as good as physical conferences where everyone from around the world meets.

7.5.3 Continuous Strategic Communication

The presentation of the next phases of the strategy was only the starting point for the communicative work of supporting the strategy in creating meaning and action. The strategic producers were acutely aware that there is a big difference between communicating something and hearing it, let alone implementing it. So a comprehensive implementation plan was developed to help ensure that the strategy came into play and that there was also 'strategising' in the sense of Gulbrandsen and Just (2020). In the sense that it is not just an announcement of strategy but the start of an involving, engaging and meaning-making cascade of dialogues. Employees need to hear their managers talk about the strategy, and they need to engage in dialogue with managers and each other about what it means for them. It is the task of communicators to ensure that managers are given the knowledge and tools to make that cascade work as well as possible.

The top 300 managers were already privy to the updated strategy as soon as it was approved by the board. 'That way, we made sure they knew what was coming and could start thinking about what it would mean for them', emphasises Jesper Løv.

Following the broad announcement at the virtual leaders' meeting for the top 1200 leaders, they were given access to a site with key documents, slides, films and practical recommendations on how to approach the communication and dialogue on the strategic update (Fig. 7.6).

'We tried to make it as easy as possible for managers to do it well and take up their role in the line communication', Jesper Løv emphasises. 'And we made sure that they are not doing it alone. The new management team will all be reaching out

7.5 Case 6. A Shoe Ready to Make Its Mark

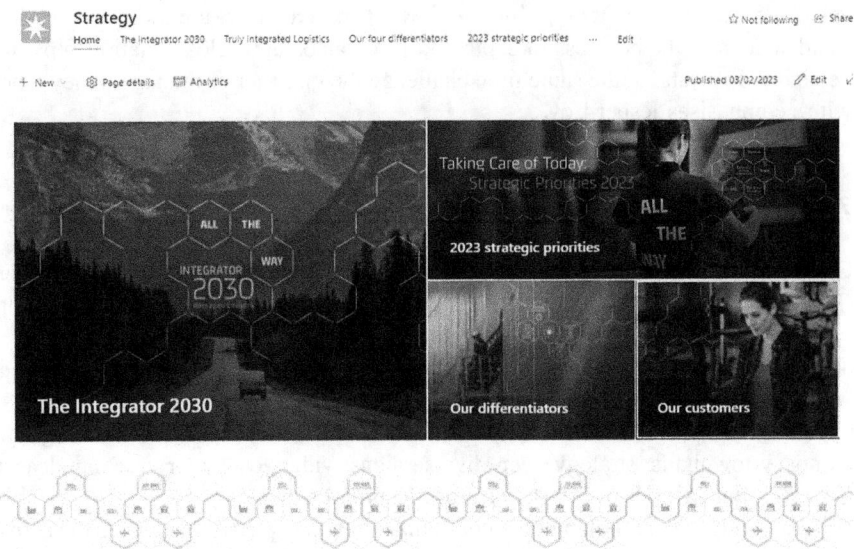

Fig. 7.6 At the launch of the updated strategy for Maersk, a site for managers was available to help communicate the messages

actively in the coming period, going out to local meetings and discussing the new ambitions'.

The entire Asian management team, for example subsequently held a management meeting in Bangkok, at which Vincent Clerc also participated. This opportunity is seized to put the strategy on the agenda so internal stakeholders there can hear him articulate the strategy and link it to their local reality. By creating opportunities and activities over an extended period of time to talk about the strategy, the strategic producers seek to keep the focus on concretising the strategy. These activities are supported by internal mass communication to ensure that the overall priorities remain on the agenda.

All the advising communicators across the group also share the responsibility for helping with local translation and training managers in effective relevant communication. 'Here, we have good experience with being almost like catalysts for the individual strategy narratives for each manager', says Jesper Løv. In sparring sessions, the strategic producers help individual managers to find the core of their part of the strategy story. It is a lot of very specific localised translation and communication of relevance. It is basically about answering two questions: What does the strategy mean to us? And how do we contribute to the overall ambition in our daily routines? This is accomplished through a combination of sparring, advising and training, which requires both skilled strategic producers and managers who are willing to let the advisors into their confidential space. This is something that the strategic producers work on through ongoing relationship building. The ambition is that the managers have seen and experienced that the strategic producers contribute value and can be of great help. 'In my view, the best advisers are those who understand an area of the business in depth and who can create a close relationship with key individuals and at the same time challenge the manager or managers they work with', emphasises Jesper Løv.

7.5.4 Keeping Your Nose to the Grindstone

Of course, internal mass media are also an important part of the implementation (Fig. 7.7). The internal media ensure a continuous flow of articles, posts and short videos. 'We want to keep an eye on what people are seeing, commenting on and asking for, so that we are always in sync with the needs. It's organisational listening, where we use data actively in our work', says Jesper Løv.

Other examples of elements planned to be utilised include top 300 meetings, all company townhalls, strategy deep dive sessions, video, customer cases, podcasts, Q&A sessions, stories of efforts for cross-inspiration etc.

An entirely different element in communicating the updated strategy is the active use of auto-communication. 'We know that by communicating externally about internal things, we also create a lot of internal meaning. So it's also a natural part of our plans, both on our own channels and in contact with the media when relevant', concludes Jesper Løv.

Strategy implementation is not easy, but it is important—and is one of those organisational occasions where communicators can really show how, with thorough and patient effort, they add value to the organisation and forge even stronger links with key stakeholders. On the whole, technological developments will hopefully also improve this more symmetrical interaction. Because whilst external social media platforms have become increasingly simple, the internal versions are not nearly as well developed yet. The lockdown gave everyone a quantum leap in the use of virtual collaboration technology, and now development should continue so

Fig. 7.7 Examples of the follow-up strategy communication internally after the launch of the updated strategy in Maersk

that it becomes increasingly easier to facilitate an internal communication infrastructure focused on co-creation and an internal, interactive community where the communication channel and the collaboration tool can merge.

7.6 Interview. With the Individual as Key

'Managers have not realised how much they need to invest in internal communication'. As one of the world's leading researchers on the impact of internal communication, Ana Verčič has no shadow of doubt in her voice. Internal communication is crucial to employees' productivity, commitment and quality of life. For organisations to succeed, retain and attract the right people, this is where to invest.

The new generations' demands for meaning and direction in the workplace, the challenges of capturing attention internally, the ever-growing scepticism and mistrust. According to the Croatian professor, there are numerous reasons for keeping a firm eye on how internal communication is prioritised. Ana Verčič has researched the impact and challenges of internal communication for many years and is internationally recognised for her well-documented projects, most recently the book 'Internal Communication and Employer Brands' from late 2022, which she co-authored with her husband, who is also a researcher, and another colleague. With a background as a psychologist, Ana Verčič's focus is clear: The individual is key, and the understanding of the individual must drive internal communication.

7.6.1 Forget About the Suggestion Box in the Corner

'We have too narrow a view of internal communication', the professor stresses. 'People very nearly used to think that it was simply a matter of letting people know when something was happening and then putting up a box for good ideas in the corner of the cafeteria', she says with a smile, but there is no doubt that she is quite serious. This field is important, and Ana Verčič was also quick to identify her research focus when she spotted employees as stakeholders. After her studies in psychology, she first got involved in marketing by chance, but after a study visit to the USA with Professor James Grunig and an even deeper understanding of symmetrical communication and PR, employees as stakeholders were on her mind. Here, psychological insight meets communication tools—and both are essential.

In classic terms, the challenges of focusing properly on internal communication are largely rooted in a lack of insight. 'Managers simply have not grasped how crucial employees are as stakeholders and how important a role internal communication plays in this context', explains Ana Verčič.

'It becomes obvious when looking at the priority of internal communication. In far too many places, it is somewhat haphazardly placed organisationally and only sporadically staffed. But fortunately, this is changing and is becoming part of the agenda of the management and is included early enough in internal processes', she says.

Some places include it in the management secretariat, in HR or in communications. From the professor's point of view, the latter is preferable unless it is established as an independent function—focus and organisational positioning are crucial.

7.6.2 Strategic Acumen and Communication Skills Are Not Enough

Some of Ana Verčič's recent research projects have looked at nothing less than the link between internal communication and quality of life. The conclusions seem clear—and are being explored in a major new research project. 'We were able to conclude that when internal communication is good, it has a major impact on job satisfaction. Job satisfaction is directly linked to our quality of life, so this is a very important area', she stresses.

In Ana Verčič's own classes of students, the focus for many years has been on strategy, as it became clear that internal communication was lagging behind because the necessary coherence and direction were not provided for employees. 'It's important that communicators have the strategic understanding necessary to drive our communication work. We must never compromise on that'. But we must not neglect the psychological aspect: Here, she cannot help but laugh a little, because it collides with an internal banter with her husband, who is also one of the world's leading researchers in strategic communication. He also runs a consultancy business alongside his research and teases her about being so preoccupied with psychology and well-being because she lives exclusively in the academic world: Is not it mostly about productivity in the 'real world'?

But productivity is only one of the factors, and if it is to be nurtured effectively by internal communication, it requires a deep understanding of the individual as a receiver. What does it take for us to listen? What does it take to motivate? And what does it take to reassure when crises are beginning to bite or change is rolling? 'As a communications student today, you need to make sure you have a solid understanding of both culture and psychology', stresses Ana Verčič. 'Only with that knowledge can we help organisations succeed strategically and effectively, because people are our receivers: They are embedded in their culture and respond through both their emotional and cognitive functions all at once'.

7.6.3 Listen, Interpret and Understand

Ever since Ana Verčič was introduced to the basic understanding of symmetry with James Grunig's basic academic education, she has argued that symmetry only comes about if we truly understand one another, and that starts with listening and interpreting other people wisely. 'Communicators must base their choices on a real understanding of the receivers. That's why you need to listen actively to understand what's going on out there among your stakeholders. It's important—but not sufficient—to ask about and measure these things' says the professor.

'The problem is that people don't always know exactly what they lack or what they need, so asking is not enough. Internal communicators must develop good psychological antennae and analytical skills to understand what's really at stake', she stresses, because we also need to be able to figure out when they say one thing but really need something else. And we must also have the courage to fight for this understanding upwards in the organisations as well. 'Managers are often a little too blind to needs. That's where they need internal communicators to make sure they gain the insight into what is needed'.

Ana Verčič's research includes work to develop and test possible measurement tools for guiding organisational listening: 'We have no doubt that important parameters to monitor include the experience of feedback, communication with immediate superiors, horisontal communication, informal communication, information about the organisation itself, the quality of internal communication channels and also communication in meetings'.

7.6.4 The Internal Communication Elements

Looking at the factual flows of information when running internal communication effectively is not enough. We also need to take an interest in the more informal and communicative climate; elements that often fall outside the classic internal communicator's field of work. 'It's good, but not enough, for the internal communicator to be in charge of effective communication of new strategies, changes or internal crisis management. We also need to take an interest in, for example, management communication, feedback and meeting culture, just to name a few of the large important fields' stresses Ana Verčič.

In their new book on internal communication, Ana Verčič and colleagues summarise the fields of work of internal communication into four key areas:

- A strategic leadership role responsible for guiding and managing organisational processes, carried out by professional communicators with psychological understanding.
- A leadership role for all managers in organisations to drive local internal communication and communication culture. Here, communicators can only assist.
- The functional expertise necessary to drive communication policies, channels, messages, media and relationships, and the professional expertise of the communicator is central here as well.
- Last, but not least, the employees' own communicative skills, which can only be indirectly influenced by the internal communicator, for example through practice or facilitated processes to activate them.

7.6.5 Not Cosmetic, but Necessary

The complexity is great and the importance enormous, obliging us to act as professional internal communicators. 'We have to create internal communication that is not just considered and working as a cosmetic addition to the real thing. We need to take our seats at the right tables and create the understanding that internal communication is crucial to the future of organisations', Ana Verčič stresses. It makes demands on professional internal communicators.

> Not to sound patronising about all the good things that are already being done, but it is important that we think outside the box. If we only think in terms of classical communication in our solutions, we will not succeed. Our toolbox must hold a great deal of knowledge and tools about strategy, psychology and communication, and we must bring it all into play every time in order to succeed.

The professor has no doubt either that it takes courage to get it right. 'We have to understand that it's rarely ill will but more often a lack of understanding that makes internal communication a low priority, and we have to help create that understanding'.

Ana Tkalac Verčič

Ana Tkalac Verčič is a professor of Marketing and Public Relations at the University of Zagreb, Croatia. She is a former Fulbright scholar and recipient of the Chartered Institute of Public Relations diploma. She is an internationally recognised researcher within internal communication and the author of several books, most recently 'Joy: Using strategic communication to improve well-being and organizational success'; 'Current Trends and Issues in Internal Communication: Theory and Practice'; 'Internal Communication and Employer Brands' and the first Croatian textbook in public relations.

She has published more than 100 articles in academic journals and serves on several editorial boards, including *International Journal of Strategic Communication*, *Journal of Public Relations Research* and *Public Relations Review*.

References

Aggerholm, H. K., & Thomsen, C. (2020). *Change management and communication in public sector organisations. The handbook of public sector communication* (pp. 197–213). John Wiley & Sons, Inc.

Amelia, M. (2016). Communicating the "Social" organization: Social media and organizational communication. https://doi.org/10.1057/9781137585356.0007

Chin, C. P. Y., Evans, N., Choo, R. K. K., & Tan, F. B. (2015). What influences employees to use enterprise social networks? A socio-technical perspective. In *Proceedings on PACIS, Singapore, July 6-9* (p. 54).

Christensen, L. T. (2003). Corporate identity as seduction and self-seduction. In J. Helder & B. Kragh (Eds.), *When the company opens its window—A corporate perspective* (pp. 87–100).

Cooren, F., Kuhn, T., Cornelissen, J. P., & Clark, T. (2011). Communication, organizing and organization. *Organization Studies, 32*(9), 1149–1170.

Daft, R. L., & Lengel, R. H. (1986). Organisizational information requirements, media richness and structural design. *Management Science, 32*(5), 554–571.

Dahlman, S., & Heide, M. (2021). *Strategic internal communication: A practitioner's guide to implementing cutting-edge methods for improved workplace culture*. Routledge.

Dawkins, J. (2005). Corporate responsibility: The communication challenge. *Journal of Communication Management, 9*, 108–119.

Edmondson, A. (1999). Psychological safety and learning behaviour in work teams. *Administrative Science Quarterly, 44*(2), 350–383.

Gulbrandsen, I. T., & Just, S. N. (2020). *Strategising communication: Theory and practice* (2nd ed.). Samfundslitteratur.

Hannegan, C. (2004). Employees as reputation makers. *Strategic Communication Management, 8*(6), 5.

Heide, M., & Simonsson, C. (2018). *Internal crisis communication: Crisis awareness, leadership and coworkership* (1st ed.). Routledge.

Högberg, K., & Olsson, A. K. (2019). Framing organizational social media: A longitudinal study of a hotel chain. *Information Technology & Tourism, 21*. https://doi.org/10.1007/s40558-019-00141-6

Jiang, H., & Men, L. (2015). Creating an engaged workforce: The impact of authentic leadership, transparent organizational communication, and work-life enrichment. *Communication Research*. https://doi.org/10.1177/0093650215613137

Joshi, R. J., & Sharma, B. R. (1997). Determinants of managerial job satisfaction in a private organisation. *Indian Journal of Industrial Relations, 33*(1), 48–67.

Kalla, H. K. (2005). Integrated internal communications: A multidisciplinary perspective. *Corporate Communications, 10*(4), 302–314.

Kjærgaard, A., & Morsing, M. (2010). Strategic auto-communication in identity-image interplay: The dynamics of mediatising organizational identity. In L. Chouliaraki & M. Morsing (Eds.), *Media, organisations and identity* (pp. 93–111). Palgrave Macmillan.

Lund. (1999). *Det sku´ vær´ så godt – organisationskommunikation: cases og konsekvenser*. Samfundslitteratur.

Lund. (2008). *Lad gå videre*. Bedre strategisk lederkommunikation.

Madsen, V. T. (2017). The challenges of introducing internal social media—The coordinators' roles and perceptions. *Journal of Communication Management (London, England), 21*(1), 2–16.

Madsen, V. T. (2018). Participatory communication on internal social media—a dream or reality? Findings from two exploratory studies of coworkers as communicators. *Corporate Communications: An International Journal, 23*(4), 614–628.

Madsen, V. T. (2022). Making sense of internal social media and participatory communication: Exploring the employee perspective in a change process in a public sector organisation. *Journal of Communication Management (London, England), 26*(4), 420–435.

Men, L. (2015). The internal communication role of the chief executive officer: Communication channels, style, and effectiveness. *Public Relations Review., 41.* https://doi.org/10.1016/j.pubrev.2015.06.021

Men, L. R., & Stacks, D. (2014). The effects of authentic leadership on strategic internal communication and employee-organization relationships. *Journal of Public Relations Research, 26*(4), 301–324. https://doi.org/10.1080/1062726X.2014.908720

Morrison, E. W., & Milliken, F. J. (2000). Organisational silence: A barrier to change and development in a pluralistic world. *The Academy of Management Review, 25*(4), 706–725.

Nakra, R. (2006). Relationship between communication satisfaction and organizational identification: An empirical study. *Vision: The Journal of Business Perspective, 10,* 41–51.

Putnam, L. L., & Nicotera, A. M. (2009). *Building theories of organization : The constitutive role of communication* (1.ed. ed.). Taylor and Francis.

Putnam, L. L., & Nicotera, A. M. (2010). Communicative constitution of organisation is a question: Critical issues for addressing it. *Management Communication Quarterly, 24*(1), 158–165.

Rice, R. E., Evans, S. K., Pearce, K. E., Sivunen, A., Vitak, J., & Treem, J. W. (2017). Organizational media affordances: Operationalization and associations with media use. *Journal of Communication, 67*(1), 106–130. https://doi.org/10.1111/jcom.12273

Schein, E. H. (2016). *Humble consulting: How to provide real help faster.* Berrett-Koehler.

Scheyett, A. (2022). Quiet quitting. *Social Work (New York), 68*(1), 5–7.

Tench, R., Verčič, D., Zerfass, A., Moreno, Á., & Verhoeven, P. (2017a). *Communication excellence: How to develop, manage and lead exceptional communications.* Palgrave Macmillan.

Thelen, P. D. (2020). Internal communicators' understanding of the definition and importance of employee advocacy. *Public Relations Review, 46*(4).

Tkalac Verčič, A. (2021). The impact of employee engagement, organisational support and employer branding on internal communication satisfaction. *Public Relations Review, 47*(1).

Tkalac Verčič, A., Verčič, D., & Špoljarić, A. (2022). *Internal communication and employer brands.* Routledge.

Trimi, S., & Galanxhi, H. (2014). The impact of Enterprise 2.0 in organizations. *Service Business., 8.* https://doi.org/10.1007/s11628-014-0246-x

White, C., Vanc, A., & Stafford, G. (2010). Internal communication, information satisfaction, and sense of community: The effect of personal influence. *Journal of Public Relations Research, 22,* 65–84.

Zak, P. J. (2017, January-February). The neuroscience of trust. Management behaviours that foster employee engagement. *HBR Magazine.*

Facilitating Change   8

Never before have organisations wanted or needed to change more frequently than today. That is why it is crucial that the professional communicator is skilled at driving change—from clever design to effective communication in large meetings, films or slideshows. This chapter thus zooms in on the basic knowledge of change and strategic communication that can help turn ambitions into reality.

In the chapter's case, the strategic producers in Maersk describe the challenge with the acquisition of LF Logistics, where 10,000 new employees had to be integrated into the organisation within a few months.

The chapter's internationally recognised expert is Professor Mats Heide from Lund University, who specialises in strategic communication, also with a focus on change.

Never before has the need for change in organisations been more urgent. Change can come from outside, as when the coronavirus pandemic transformed organisational reality, and technological developments, in particular, accelerated the pace of change. But change can also come from alterations in the market, in the organisation's strategy or in expectations for organisations to engage in societal issues, such as the green transition. Change is necessary to keep up with the demands and challenges of the times.

> Change is necessary to advance innovation, address injustices, remedy failing or poor practices, revitalise the energy of participants, maintain competitiveness, create variety, experiment and adapt to environments. Without change, organisations would eventually fail to adapt to their changing environments, stakeholders and participants and would at some point become so mismatched with the demands made on them that they would likely become obsolete. Organisations are embedded in multiple streams of processes and thus are surrounded by change. Organisations must change to adapt and survive. They spend significant time, energy and money on selecting and launching change initiatives every year (Lewis & Sahay, 2018: 1).

The many changes increase the risk of the organisation becoming exhausted and that internal stakeholders even develop a so-called 'BOHICA mentality', which stands for 'Bend Over—Here It Comes Again' (Alvesson, 2013). A mentality that can arise due to too many or inexpediently driven changes that simply tire out the organisation's employees (Dahlman & Heide, 2021) or changes that are not realised after all, resulting in indifference amongst internal stakeholders. As in Aesop's fable, where a little boy shouts 'mummy, mummy, the wolf is coming' so many times that she does not come to save him when the wolf actually appears. The cry has lost its impact and trust in its relevance has broken down.

'Meaning fogs' may also occur because too much is going on at once, creating confusion, doubt or even conflicting messages, also known as 'sense-dimming' (Järventie-Thesleff et al., 2014). That is why the professional communicator is crucial because change needs to be supported by wise, clear and trust-building communication.

Research divides change into types—Dahlman and Heide (2021), for example, categorise change into six types:

1. Policy changes (e.g. new regulation)
2. Technical changes (e.g. new IT system)
3. Demographic changes (e.g. changing customer profile)
4. Economic changes (e.g. crisis or boom)
5. Significant organisational changes (e.g. new CEO, acquisitions or cultural changes)
6. Management trends (e.g. a sudden focus on efficient workflows with the LEAN business philosophy)

In addition, changes are often grouped according to size (Argyris et al., 1978). First-order changes are the incremental and predictable ones, whilst second-order changes are major transformations that require many behavioural changes in the organisation. Some even talk about third-order changes as processes that fundamentally change organisations, which thus have to reinvent themselves, such as the disruption that the music industry went through when streaming became a possibility.

All changes are planned, by any means. There are plenty of small and large changes that occur suddenly in busy organisation routines, where a need to act differently arises. This type of change is often called 'emergent' (Burnes, 2004) and is defined by Weick (2000) as follows: 'Emergent change consists of ongoing accommodations, adaptations and alterations that produce fundamental change without a priori intentions to do so. Emergent change occurs when people reaccomplish routines and when they deal with contingencies, breakdowns and opportunities in everyday work. Much of this change goes unnoticed, because small alterations are lumped together as noise in otherwise uneventful inertia' (Weick, 2000: 237).

Emergent change is often driven by bottom-up action, with top management supporting and facilitating the change (Bamford & Forrester, 2003). The change process is rapid, continuous and open-ended, employees constantly learning and adapting (Edwards et al., 2020).

The emergent approach to change involves recognising that the need for change can arise suddenly and may call for action. The quote from Weick points to the small changes in everyday routines, but larger organisational changes may also arise as sudden realisations that need to be acted upon quickly (Burnes & Randall, 2016). It will typically be in connection with major change processes that the professional communicator will be involved to help orchestrate the process.

Case studies of successful change suggest that it is not an either-or between planned and emergent change, but a question of both-and: 'Successful change requires the reconciliation and integration of top-down and bottom-up approaches. Top management must set the direction and should then step back and allow the diagnosis and solution-development processes to take place in a bottom-up manner. This allows employees to identify and solve the problems that matter to them and that reflect their organisational reality. The implementation of the changes toward the end of the change process should take place in a top-down manner' (Edwards et al., 2020: 342). Thus, integrating top-down and bottom-up approaches to change can ensure that top-down initiatives can work and can engage employees, create transparency and trust.

Research in this field emphasises that communication is crucial for any change to become more than an ambition. For it is communication that translates ambition into meaning and into concrete action. It is often claimed that over 70% of all changes fail (e.g. Kotter, 1990), but Hughes (2016) has checked the figures and this cannot be substantiated by research. However, there is no doubt that most organisations find it difficult to drive change and that the change process is perceived to be too slow. Once the decision has been made or the need for change has arisen—patience is not always so great. The impatience and need for control of, typically, top managers of organisations also means that a large part of the narrative and popular models that prevail in the field of change is linear, so they describe change as a logical, progressive process. At the same time, a focus on a more dynamic, changeable or 'agile' approach to change processes has emerged since two professors from Harvard and Tokyo in 1986 challenged the approach to product development with new agile methods (Takeuchi & Nonaka, 1986). This way of working has inspired change work around the world and has been further developed with a method from tech change called the 'SCRUM method'. The two approaches are briefly reviewed in the following before the chapter takes a closer look at the role of the professional communicator in change regardless of the approach.

8.1   Linear Perspectives of Change

One of the most popular linear approaches to change has been put forward by former Harvard Business School management professor John P. Kotter. His books have sold millions of copies worldwide, and the steps he recommends to create change are quite simple (1996) (Table 8.1).

Table 8.1 Kotter's eight steps of change

	Action	Purpose
Step 1	Create urgency	
Step 2	Form a powerful coalition	Creating the climate for change
Step 3	Create a vision for change	
Step 4	Communicate the vision	
Step 5	Empower action	Engaging and enabling the organisation
Step 6	Create quick wins	
Step 7	Build on the change	
Step 8	Make it stick	Implementing and sustaining change

Source: Kotter (2012)

The idea is fundamentally to motivate your organisation by establishing the 'burning platform' for change (1), ensuring you have the right team to drive the change (2) and creating the vision for the change itself (3). Then you are, roughly speaking, ready. Next, communication acts as a catalyst: The vision must be communicated (4). Then you need to get people to act (5), and you need to be able to show quick results (6) to keep the change engine running. The last two steps are about building on the change (7) and making sure it becomes part of routines moving forward (8).

In his later research and dissemination, Kotter (2014) has sought to clarify that the linear aspect of steps one to eight should not be taken quite so literally. Instead of being based solely on the 'burning platform' (i.e. a 'sense of urgency') for the change, Kotter's focus and the core of the updated version of his research is 'the big opportunity'. This marks a major shift from a more mechanistic view of change to a greater focus on positive motivation as a driver of change. 'The big opportunity' plays a part in every step of the process, not only as a catalyst for a beginning, as the 'burning platform' indicated. However, the model is still linear at its core, with eight steps that follow upon one another, once it has been set in motion. However, Kotter now acknowledges that these processes must be viewed in a more circular way, with Step 1 of each new change taking over, so to speak, Step 8 of the preceding change. Kotter thus recognises that the speed of change means that changes go on in a continuous flow.

8.2 The Agile Change

Agility is not just a buzzword, but an ideology with its own manifesto (https://agile-manifesto.org/). It is a dynamic approach to, first of all, product development (Takeuchi & Nonaka, 1986) and then to all development in organisations, particularly IT-related development. The basic idea is to do away with long, linear processes and instead work more dynamically and constantly develop in co-creation. The ideas have gained widespread acceptance (Clayton, 2021) and have, in IT development, resulted in a whole format for co-creation and change called 'SCRUM'. The word originates from the sport of rugby, where it describes situations where the rugby team comes together to collaborate on moving the ball

8.3 The Human Factor

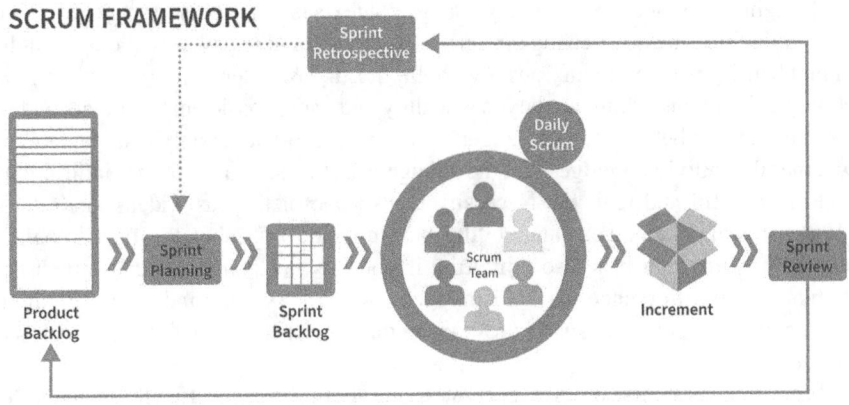

Fig. 8.1 An overview of the SCRUM framework. Source: www.scrum.org

forward. This way of working inspires many organisations to embrace change, as it offers a more agile approach than the classic linear approach. Changes are initiated immediately instead of postponing implementation until after a long series of preparation steps.

The fact that the change is implemented on an ongoing basis means, amongst other things, that the realisation of benefits is constantly in progress and that any resistance can also be dealt with on an ongoing basis, because the change proceeds in serial waves rather than a single one. In the SCRUM approach, we talk about making room for sudden events as a rejection of the imagined control of traditional approaches.

In the SCRUM methodology, specific methods are used to ensure the agile workflow—and that the entire change team is constantly meeting in practice to drive progress.

Figure 8.1 generally illustrates that SCRUM collaboration is an empirical process in which people work together and constantly base their decisions on what they see and experience. Work is done in so-called 'sprints', i.e. delimited sub-tasks where the team prepares and meets for daily meetings where they develop together, take stock and continue towards the next sprint. The process is based on a trusting collaboration with transparency, mutual inspection of ideas and results, and continuous adaptation that constantly moves the change process forward. It is an experimental way of working that emphasises continuous learning along the way.

8.3 The Human Factor

Organisational change is often about getting people to act differently. That is why it is no use having a mechanistic view of change. A professional communicator must thus understand the psychological nuances of getting people to change their behaviour.

A slightly misused word in many change contexts is 'readiness for change'. If we look at this readiness for change in purely psychological terms, it is about the individual being 'sufficiently anxious' (Visholm in Lund & Petersen, 2018). In the psychological understanding, anxiety is a healthy and useful basic emotion that can tell the individual whether there is danger ahead. So, adequate anxiety is a question of whether the individual judges that the change is both necessary (i.e. not indifferent) and meaningful and realistic. Necessity is also one of the basic ideas in Kotter's (1996) model of change, namely 'the burning platform', but the psychological approach warns that it is also inhibiting if you are *too anxious*, because then the human system of defence mechanisms kicks in and makes the individual anything but ready for change, because in response you either become defensive, paralysed or flee.

From studies of the brain, we know more about what specifically triggers the alarm response when a person encounters the world. The brain is provoked to go on chemical alert when a person feels threatened in relation to what Rock and Ringleb (2013) call the 'SCARF model':

- **S**tatus—do I feel threatened on my status?
- **C**ertainty—do I feel my safety/security is threatened?
- **A**utonomy—do I feel that my freedom and self-determination are restricted?
- **R**elatedness—do I feel excluded or restricted from belonging?
- **F**airness—do I feel it is unfair/unjust from my perspective?

A large part of the communication work during changes (Schmitz, 2019) must thus also be based on this psychological knowledge of how to ensure that stakeholders do not become defensive during change but are 'sufficiently anxious' and 'ready for change'. One of the lessons learnt from communication research has long been that this is also about genuine involvement of stakeholders, so that changes are not dictated or take you by surprise, but that key stakeholders feel involved (Armenakis et al., 1993)—as early as possible, otherwise it develops into actual resistance that can prevent or delay much change.

From psychology, we can also draw knowledge about resistance, which in the work of change is often fixed as something negative. But if, as a communicator, instead of seeing it as an obstacle, you see it as part of the change work to ensure responsiveness and reach the constructive scepticism that can often lie behind resistance. Working with resistance and scepticism can be a goldmine of knowledge and even help to facilitate change. It requires very active stakeholder work in the planning and a great deal of agility along the way to ensure a constructive dispute.

It is crucial to the process that you see resistance as something that not only needs to be managed—but also as something that can largely be prevented through well-considered change processes. However, it still makes a lot of sense to be prepared to deal with the resistance that suddenly emerges during a change process—typically related to either the cognitive, emotional or behavioural response of stakeholders. In the midst of a fast-moving change process, resistance can even be provocative to senior and middle managers, something that communicators need to help manage. Very often, resistance is amplified by time lags in change, where managers are further along in the process, because they have initiated and planned the change themselves, but forget that employees only hear about it much later. The managers are thus moving forward too quickly, whilst the employees need to understand and process the new initiatives before they are ready to start acting in a different way. As a professional communicator, it is important to be aware of this time lag as a cause of resistance, but there may of course also be other factors in play. Maurer (2010), for example defines three causes of sudden resistance:

1. Information: 'I don't understand it. It doesn't make sense to me. I need more information, data and more ideas'.
2. Feelings: 'I don't like it. I need to feel more secure.'
3. Trust: 'I don't trust you. I have to see it before I believe it'.

Cognitively, stakeholders may disengage because the change does not make sense, emotions may take over, e.g. because the alarm system is activated, or a lack of trust in, e.g. the manager presenting the change may hinder readiness for change.

There is no doubt that readiness for change can only arise as a positive motivation to change behaviour based not only on trust in the communicator but also on a psychologically safe culture (Edmondson, 2019). This is precisely why a professional communicator facilitating a change must be aware of the cultural facilitators and inhibitors of change.

8.4 Facilitator of Change

Two pitfalls are particularly easy to fall into as a professional communicator facilitating change: the linear pitfall and the producer pitfall. The linear pitfall is when a professional communicator only works to inform about the change and help launch it. This often happens in organisations that work with change in a too-linear way, for example inspired by Kotter. Here, the communicator may only be involved in a fancy communication kick-off with good explanations of where to change and why, but there is no focus on how it is to be realised, and so the change risks never getting from plan to reality because it is not supported communicatively.

The producer pitfall is akin to the linear pitfall but is about the professional communicator only being invited in as a concrete producer and not as a facilitator of change. This reduces the communicator to, putting it bluntly, simply putting down which specific products are to be produced and not contributing to initiating change. It is a reactive role where the communicator is a supplier and thus only succeeds if the 'client' or change manager asks for the right thing, which may be difficult, partly because the change manager is very rarely a communication professional, partly because he/she is often challenged by knowing so much about why and with what goal the change is to be made and thus often has to be reminded to meet the recipients where they are.

The best way to avoid both pitfalls is to make sure that you, as a professional communicator, have and take on the necessary roles in a change—and these may be many different ones. From strategic advisor who helps management to make communicable decisions to the production of vision films, organiser of events, moderator for management talks in front of employees with Q&As, or the person who constantly takes it upon themselves to represent the recipients of the messages.

In addition to the roles, the challenge is also to remember to activate the analytical, planning, implementing and evaluating mindset.

In change contexts, the analytical mindset naturally depends on when the communicator is invited into the process. This could be, for example by conducting a stakeholder analysis, analyses of cultures and subcultures and what can inhibit or promote change, or perhaps strategic sparring with managers about the raison d'etre and framing of the change. The framing of the change itself should not be underestimated because it helps to condense and communicate what the core of the change is and whether it is, for example frightening or motivating.

In other words, the communicator must base his or her help with a change on real knowledge of the rationale behind the strategic decisions and on up-to-date knowledge of the stakeholder landscape. This knowledge can help both when advising management on the overall narrative of the change, with the appropriate planning of the channel mix and contributing to the very practical decisions in prioritising framing, content and form of the communication. The nature of the change is of course of great importance for the communication effort. Is it a positive renewal of workflows, a new strategy or a major round of redundancies that comes as a bolt from the blue? The communicator's design of the best possible change plan also has to do with understanding the size, depth and challenges of the change.

Planning and orchestrating are natural parts of facilitating change—whether the organisation works with SCRUM methods or in a more linear way, the process must be supported by communication. Regardless of the methodology, a change plan must be dynamic, so the professional communicator must be aware of stakeholder preferences and plan across channels and platforms so that the channel mix works. For example, is it wise to start with a town hall meeting? And how can the training of the leaders who are going to present the change be integrated into the plan? Or is it better to have a short film with the top manager and then have managers at top or middle management level in the organisation hold local town hall meetings with dialogue? There is no one model that works for everything. The professional communicator must design a mix of channels each time, based on knowledge of stakeholders, culture and the change at hand.

The channels are many, for example:

- Senior managers on all platforms, e.g. town hall meetings, webinars, films and articles.
- Middle managers in direct contact, e.g. equipped with meeting kits to help along good local meetings.
- Articles on the intranet.
- Q&A sessions with managers on internal social media.

- Auto-communication by communicating the changes externally.
- Direct communication by, e.g. emails or one-to-one meetings.

The communicator has many options and important channel choices to make.

Research clearly shows that early involvement is important for stakeholders' genuine commitment and for the impact of the change. This is the subject of the following sections (Table 8.2).

The above list systematises some of the thoughts the professional communicator may have in relation to selecting and involving stakeholders. Who should be involved and to what extent is this something symbolic or as real resource in the change?

For each of these categories or steps, you can look at how specific or diverse the stakeholders are in a given situation. You must then assess whether the stakeholders should be involved as a resource or only symbolically. If they are only to be involved symbolically, they will, for example be informed about the content of the changes in a pseudo-involvement, whilst some of the groups further down the list may become a direct co-creating resource by, for example, also being given real decision-making competence. Decision-making competence may sound like an unrealistic involvement, and it is also extremely rare that it is a decision-making competence in relation to whether the entire change should be implemented. It is rather involvement in decisions on, for example how best to realise the change, where it is often not the initiating management that knows best, but rather other stakeholders.

The implementation stage naturally depends on the elements of the plan and thus often calls for multiple roles from advisor to film producer and the development of many communicative products, often under massive time pressure.

The evaluative mindset must be constantly switched on by the professional communicator in change processes because of the many reactions that the changes can lead to amongst stakeholders. This means that the professional communicator must incorporate evaluation and adjustment into the communication approach and not

Table 8.2 Reflection on stakeholder involvement

Degrees and purposes of involvement
Stakeholders are told they are considered important participants in change
Stakeholders are provided input channels in order to make them feel more involved
Stakeholders are provided input channels so their complaints, concerns and ideas can be vented
Stakeholders are asked to provide perspectives on change so that implementers can correct misinterpretations of disseminated information and stop or correct rumours
Stakeholders are encouraged to put forward ideas and suggest improvements in the process of implementing change that are then used to alter the implementation
Stakeholders are asked to provide initial guidance and render opinions about change adoption and implementation that are heavily influential in decision-making
Stakeholders are given decision-making power and resource control over whether to adopt change and how to implement it

Source: Lewis and Sahay (2018)

only listen actively but also plan systematic qualitative or quantitative studies along the way to ensure a data-driven basis for the many communication decisions. This could, for example take the form of pulse surveys that ask about employees' experiences at regular intervals.

All this knowledge needs to be integrated into the change plan continuously, so that it is adjusted and nuanced as necessary. Perhaps a top manager needs to moderate or nuance his or her statement, or there is a need to produce more articles with employees talking about their responses and actions. Hearing colleagues tell their stories is important in terms of stress reduction, reassurance and motivation (Lewis, 2018). If you stop communicating about the change as soon as it is announced, it is likely to end up in the poor statistics of failed changes. The professional communicator thus needs both his or her analytical skills, courage and communicative skills to constantly drive the change forward.

Facilitating change with good communication is not only important for the literal success of the change, but also because the way change is managed is often important for the fundamental trust throughout the organisation. During an organisational change, all internal stakeholders are extra vigilant, and if management behaves in a way that is perceived as unfair, it can undermine trust in the long term as well. Research clearly shows that change can both generate and undermine trust: 'Organisational change occasions both trust building and trust destroying. Change scholars have documented that levels of uncertainty coupled with feelings of vulnerability experienced by stakeholders during change often lead to active processing of trust-relevant information. Lack of trust or a decline in trust during change can lead to a chronic response of cynicism by stakeholders' (Lewis & Sahay, 2018: 12). Change is thus an important opportunity for the professional communicator to support the organisation in concrete terms and at the same time work on developing and maintaining trust in the entire stakeholder landscape in the longer term.

8.5   Case 7. Orchestrating Effective Changes

Change is part of everyday life at Maersk, just like in any other organisation—including big changes such as acquisitions. Since 2019 alone, Maersk has made 11 major acquisitions, because part of the group's strategy is to grow through acquisitions. Communicators are part of the core team from the start and help drive the entire change with analysis, effective communication, facilitation, training and responsiveness. One example is the acquisition of LF Logistics, which was finally approved by the competition authorities on 1 September 2022, a major change challenge including over 10,000 new colleagues in Asia with eight different languages. This case explores how Maersk's strategic producers have worked to support the change in practice.

The business rationale for Maersk's acquisition of LF Logistics is simple. It is part of a strategy to become an even stronger transport and logistics partner that can move customers' goods from one end of the supply chain to the other. LF Logistics

8.5 Case for This Chapter. Orchestrating Effective Change

is a Hong Kong-based logistics company with a long tradition and a strong foothold in Asia. The acquisition almost doubled Maersk's warehouses with 223 new warehouses and 10,000 new employees, in addition to a large on-call corps of workers. In addition, the new joint venture is seen as having growth potential in the Pacific region and many large global customers. But two companies will not become a strong growth company simply on the basis of a business decision. It has to be realised through a change process supported by quality communication. The approach to change at Maersk is agile but also incorporates linear elements, with work carefully distributed according to who knows what, when and how.

8.5.1 The Right Mandate for the Communicator

An acquisition involves an unimaginable amount of legal elements, secrecy, regulatory approvals etc., which requires great care and diligence on the communication side of the change. It is thus essential that the person(s) from the communications department who are to support the change becomes part of the confidential space with management, and a strong advisor relationship is a clear advantage. 'In order to be able to contribute in the best possible way, it is important to be in that confidential space from the start', emphasises Anders Nørgaard, Head of Communication, Asia Pacific, who has been in charge of the communication work in the integration of LF Logistics. Specifically, this change meant that he was posted from the head office in Copenhagen to Singapore to be close by and help drive this huge change more or less in the same time zone as the 10,000 new employees. With many years of seniority in Maersk and good relations with the part of the management team most involved in the change, the prerequisites for being able to contribute were in place. One of the first steps was to thoroughly familiarise himself with the current knowledge about the change and all stakeholders, and then to develop an overall plan (Fig. 8.2). 'A key tool for me has been a good, phased communication plan that

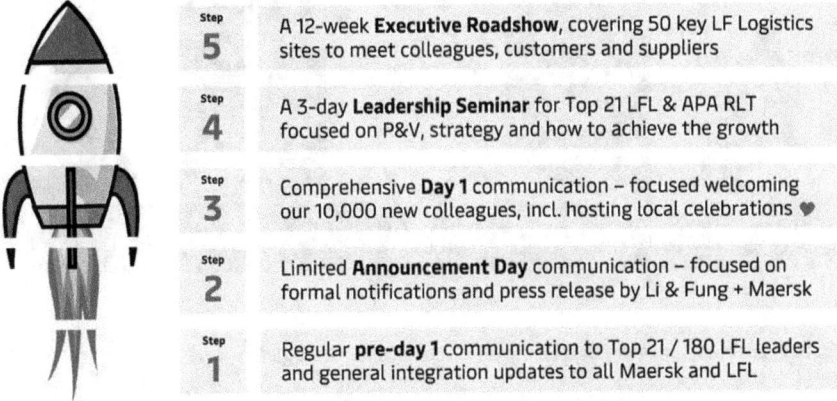

Fig. 8.2 Phased communication plan for Maersk's acquisition of LF Logistics in 2022

is easy to explain to all relevant stakeholders. It's crucial both to navigate it yourself but also to spend a lot of time communicating it so that everyone knows exactly what's happening, when, why and how', he says.

8.5.2 An Analytical Starting Point

In order to create a plan that is sufficiently responsive to the local context, it was important to get out of the head office in Denmark and really understand both local cultures and the corporate culture of the company being acquired: 'It's a long way from the Esplanade in Copenhagen to a distribution centre in Manila, and it was crucial to get a good understanding of Asian cultures to make sure we could meet the new organisation at eye level', says Anders Nørgaard. An analytical basis was thus the first point in the change plan. This was to ensure that communication staff had an understanding of the stakeholders, for example the 'tone of voice' in which communication should take place. The strategic producer's insider knowledge of Maersk was not enough, because 10,000 of the stakeholders came from a completely different organisational culture in LF Logistics. Here, the analytical challenge was to find differences and similarities in order to plan the best possible change. For example, Anders Nørgaard tried to gain insight into the preconceptions that needed to be communicated. The tool was a thorough cultural analysis prepared in collaboration with HR (Fig. 8.3). 'The cultural analysis gave us a very concrete understanding of who the stakeholders were—and what we needed to be aware of when welcoming them. For example, there was a big difference in decision-making and delegation in the two company cultures, while they were very similar in their customer orientation and ambition to go the extra mile. We got a lot of important input that helped us both to create the overall narrative for the change and to make practical decisions along the way', he says.

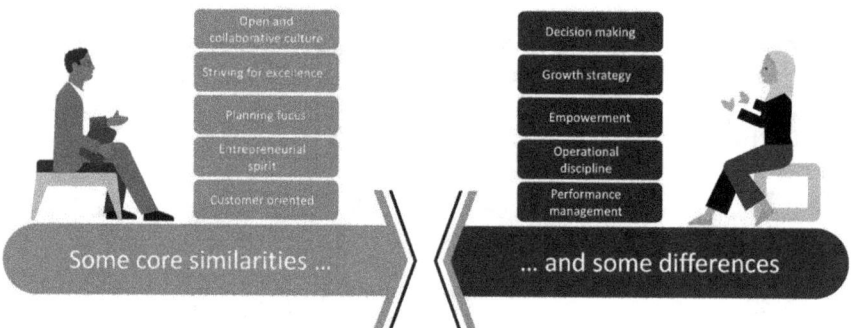

Fig. 8.3 A comparative cultural analysis of Maersk and LF Logistics

8.5.3 A Unifying Growth Narrative

Driving change effectively is about creating a shared motivation, 'the big opportunity' in Kotter's (2014) terminology, which can act as a positive motivation for change and not only work from a 'sense of urgency' and 'burning platform', i.e. the necessity of change. Maersk's strategic producers were very aware of the level of anxiety associated with the change plan, as acquisitions can make stakeholders fearful. 'Here we were really helped by the fact that the ambition was to increase growth, so this was not a change with a lot of redundancies. The two companies complement each other well in terms of business and already share a number of large customers. At the same time, we could see from the cultural analyses that customers and growth were important to employees in both organisations, so these elements quickly became the driving force in our development of the change narrative', says Anders Nørgaard.

A unifying narrative always takes longer to develop than the few words signal, because they have to be chosen carefully and framed wisely, just as the visual part has to be worked on: 'In this change, it took a really long time to get everyone involved, but we insisted that it was something that had to be created together. The solution was two words and a tree (Fig. 8.4): 'Growing Together'', says Anders Nørgaard, who adds that it was of course also complicated by the fact that they had to collaborate very formally because the change had not yet been approved by the authorities, so everything had to go through legal entities to keep within all the rules of the game.

'It was important for us to also visually signal respect for the two strong companies, so we didn't want everything to be Maersk blue overnight. We quickly decided on a tree to symbolise growing together, but which tree? It wasn't going to be a Scandinavian beech tree, nor was it going to be an Asian bonsai tree that grows infinitely slowly: That wasn't the plan'. So they landed on a more generic tree with a trunk of LF Logistics' steel grey colour and Maersk blue leaves. Nothing was left to chance—and Anders Nørgaard has lost count of how many versions of trees they have been through.

Fig. 8.4 The narrative of change became 'Growing Together'

8.5.4 An Advanced Channel Mix

The entire change has required a mix of virtually every conceivable channel during the implementation phase: 'I think we've had the whole toolbox out. It was important for us that everyone could feel that they were welcomed, so we have prioritised as many authentic channels as possible', Anders Nørgaard emphasises. For example, the entire top management from LF Logistics was invited to Denmark, where they met with the entire top Maersk management. Presence was key and, for example Chairman of the Board Robert Maersk Uggla spent half a day with them, where he was also able to talk about the family relations between the two companies back when Mr. Møller was at the helm. 'That presence was important for everyone, and we prioritised talking in depth about the cultures, values and purposes of the two companies so that everyone could be realistic about what it would take for the integration to succeed'. In addition, many events and a management roadshow were organised so that as many employees as possible could physically meet the new management (Fig. 8.5).

From the very beginning, it was important to communicate not only correctly, but also properly. There was, for example a detailed publication roadmap, where announcements to stock exchanges and media had their own section, whilst less formal and more engaging communication to employees were also prepared. 'We had tried to take everything into account, but there were a lot of x's. For example, no one really knew how long it takes to transfer four billion dollars from Copenhagen to New York and Hong Kong, and until the money was in the account, we couldn't make the announcement', says Anders Nørgaard, who was ready with his team of four strategic producers to handle anything. 'Luckily, it was amazingly fast, so we were able to send out announcements, and then we had almost 16 hours to get all the technical stuff in place before the 10,000 new employees started their workday in Asia. We wanted to be ready without any technical hassle, so they could just log in and access all the communication we had prepared'.

Fig. 8.5 Photo from a roadshow with Maersk and LF Logistics management in Vietnam

8.5 Case for This Chapter. Orchestrating Effective Change

For example, a special site was set up where people could find information about the change in their own language and watch short films with employees and managers expressing their ambitions and welcoming them (Fig. 8.6). All managers had been given a change toolkit with everything from videos for screens in the warehouses to PowerPoint presentations and an FAQ with over 250 questions and answers. The managers had been trained beforehand so that they could both describe the changes and answer the most important questions.

The analysis also showed that it was important to mark the change physically: 'We had the budget to make 10,000 white polo shirts for everyone, lanyards and also water bottles with the logo they could use in the hot warehouses (Fig. 8.7). It turned out to be very important for everyone', describes Anders Nørgaard, who has been surprised by how important it is to meet and bring merchandise. 'We've been on roadshows in all the parts of the region where corona rules have allowed it, where we've all arrived in the white polos, and we must have almost looked like a sect', he laughs, 'but locally, colleagues have taken it to new heights. What I haven't seen of

Growing Together | Integration Hub

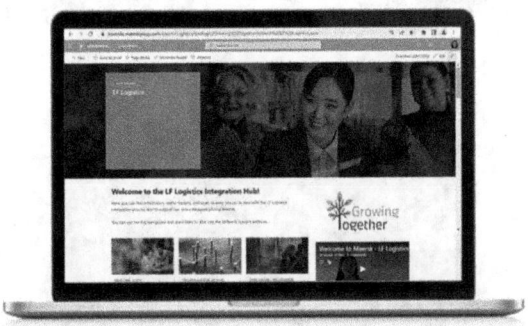

Fig. 8.6 Photo of the welcome site for all new employees after Maersk's takeover of LF Logistics

Fig. 8.7 Examples of artefacts developed to symbolise Maersk's acquisition of LF Logistics

banners with the tree, posters, cakes, even mocktails were developed. I really don't think you should underestimate the value of the visual and tangible physicality of change'.

Not only merchandise, but also food and drink contributed to a successful launch. And that means a lot to keep track of. 11,500 people attended either the physical or virtual events on the launch day on 1 September 2022, which meant serving 3500 hot food dishes in China and the Philippines alone and 1300 mocktails in Thailand. And that is not even counting the sweet treats, with thousands of cakes, cookies and cupcakes featuring the 'Growing Together' tree.

8.5.5 Data-Driven Change

Collecting and interpreting data has been important both before the launch, in order to make the right plan and create the right narrative, but also along the way to ensure that the communication could continuously be adjusted to ensure good contact (Fig. 8.8). It was not supposed to be a one-sided campaign but was meant to meet

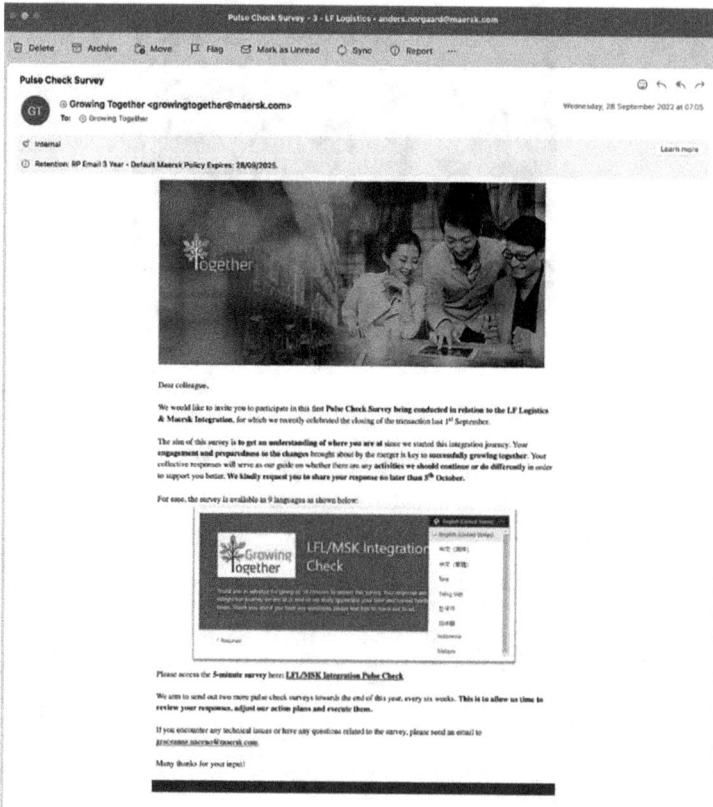

Fig. 8.8 Quantitative pulse measurements of employee response to Maersk's acquisition of LF Logistics

8.5 Case for This Chapter. Orchestrating Effective Change

the needs of stakeholders. For example, the communications team conducted pulse surveys along the way, with 3000 employees answering ten questions every 2 months to indicate whether anything needed to be adjusted.

> 1. I understand the purpose of the acquisition.
> 2. I know what the changes will be in the integration.
> 3. I trust that the changes as part of the integration are the right ones.
> 4. I receive or have access to sufficient information about the integration.
> 5. I am ready for the new ways of working.
> 6. I am confident that the changes are planned with the customer in mind.
> 7. I know how to get help and support.
> 8. I experience leaders are committed to drive the change.
> 9. I am equipped to drive the change.
> 10. I take the lead in driving the change activities to help my team through the integration.

Qualitative methods of analysis have also been employed. For example, legal approval was obtained for 25 staff members to view and comment on the communication on the welcome site before publication. 'We gained really important insights into how our ideas were received and where we might have been misunderstood or needed to adjust our tone of voice. It could also be down to individual words, for example, if something had been called something else in LF Logistics, and where they would feel more welcome if we adjusted'.

Overall, the response to the acquisition has been ongoing, both in the form of input for specific products or the collection of knowledge about stakeholders from some of the other 14 so-called 'workstreams' that drove the change. 'We have held meetings on an ongoing basis and helped one another, and we have continued to do so long after the launch. We have received a lot of questions along the way, including at the many roadshows where we have travelled locally, and in fact only one person has asked whether there would be lay-offs. We are quite proud of that, because that is often a major concern. But we have succeeded in creating a positive growth story that people are happy to be a part of, and that they feel is not being forced on them, but are helping to create themselves'.

With such a big change, the demand for communication is inexhaustible, so it is also been important for the team to say yes and no at the right times: 'There's always something to address when you're driving such a big change, so we've also had to prioritise distinctly to make sure we're spending the time right, and data has helped us with that too'.

8.5.6 Integration Continues

The integration of an acquisition does not happen through a successful launch—no matter how good it is. It requires persistent and steady work. Maersk's communications team has worked to recognise this by, for example keeping the item on the agenda at management meetings, continuing to communicate a lot about the change and sharing input from the pulse surveys. 'We have passed day 100', says Anders Nørgaard. 'The first six months we have called the "discovery phase", where we get to know each other better. Later in the process, when the final regulatory approval of the acquisition is available, and we formally become one company, we will be ready with a new round of communication according to all the rules of the art'.

In addition, a local strategy is to be presented. So large local management meetings have to be planned and, once again, a large repertoire of communication channels and creative solutions is being prepared. The integration must be followed through to the end. Even if it got off to a good start, it is crucial that the communicators are ready for the work that follows. Not with perfect, ready-made solutions, but with the best possible communication efforts, constantly adjusted to the pace of change and the needs of the stakeholders.

8.6 Interview. Involvement Is Key

'We need to listen and engage more'. Professor Mats Heide from Lund University has no doubt that this is the key to good change communications. His research focuses on strategic communication in both everyday routines, during crises and during change, and he publishes an impressive flow of international books because he believes that communicators can become much better.

According to the Swedish researcher, the core of quality change communications is to create coworkership. Employees need to feel that they are part of the change: 'For too long, communicators have followed the old management paradigm of simply passing clear messages from the top. We focus too much on creating 'followership' instead of 'coworkership', and that makes change ineffective', he explains.

Change is a challenge to organisations and must be taken seriously, and the professor has no doubt that communicators must be careful not to think in a way that is too one-sided, old-fashioned or 'efficient': 'If you look up communication in various reference works, you will still all-too-often find a description that says we must send communication from a sender to a receiver', Mats Heide says, shaking his head. 'The old transmission view of communications doesn't seem nuanced enough at all today—and certainly not during change. It becomes too one-sided if we think we can simply send messages from the top and out into the organisation. Communication doesn't go one way—it goes both ways. We must meet in the communication'.

Professor Mats Heide has personally become more interested in the dialogical understanding of communication over time and is currently applying the finishing touches to a new book on strategic listening which, he says with a smile, he is writing with his partner researcher in service management. 'Well, we kept talking about how we all don't listen enough to our stakeholders, and we set out to provide inspiration on how to do something about it', he elaborates. In general, many of the books that leap from the keyboard in Helsingborg seem like attempts to inspire in a very specific way based on insights from Mats Heide's research.

Communications research became his career path somewhat by accident. He studied business economics and planned a career in marketing, management or organisational processes. But he stuck around a bit longer at the university because of his girlfriend at the time and took a few more communications courses—and that was it, he was off to graduate research school. Ever since, he has largely dedicated his working life to research into strategic communications and is now an internationally recognised researcher and facilitator.

8.6.1 Step into the Change

Early involvement is essential for effective change, quite literally at first by communicators: 'There are far too many change processes where communicators get involved way too late', Mats Heide stresses, 'It simply becomes too difficult to drive change if communication is not properly incorporated from the beginning'.

Unfortunately, that is an obstacle in many places because the field of communication is not recognised enough as a strategic discipline, so top management only involves communicators when they need something practical to get done: An event to be planned, a press release to be written or a nice slide show to be produced for internal meetings. 'It's also about the sometimes rather one-sided communication view of top managers—it doesn't make sense to talk about change without communication, and so they need to involve professionals'.

If you ask the professor what to do about it, the recommendation is clear. 'Of course, we need to look inwards and not just take on the role of victim or martyr. Too many communicators I meet whine a bit and say, 'There's nothing we can do, they're involving us too late'. But you can start by asking yourself: Is my value creation as a communicator clear? Does the top management know how I can contribute to make the change succeed? And do I have relations with enough trust for them to involve me—even in the difficult and confidential decision-making processes that often lie behind change? If you don't have a clear answer, you have a specific task in building trust and showing your value so that you get involved properly'.

Mats Heide has no doubt that there are also *too* many communicators who do not prioritise continuously updating their strategic knowledge. 'Simply having communication skills is no good: They are important, but not enough. Business acumen and strategic knowledge are essential to understanding and driving change, and we need to be proactive in our approach to the entire organisation'.

8.6.2 Away from the Campaign Trail

Mats Heide is determined to get us off the campaign trail as change communicators. 'Of course, campaign elements can be part of change processes, but there is a very high risk of falling into too much top-down information if we think in terms of campaigns. For example, research clearly shows that it is important to involve much more than most people do. Employees need more than to simply hear about *why* change is needed and *what* is specifically going to happen; they need to be genuinely involved and heard'.

According to the professor, this requires not only that we, professional change communicators, are good listeners but also that we understand human reaction patterns: 'In change communications, knowledge of interpersonal communication and relational skills is very important. We do not prioritise that enough in the training of communicators. In reality, psychology is very closely linked to communication, and we should be much more interested in that', he stresses.

Mats Heide hopes that the new research focus on strategic listening will also mean a greater understanding of meeting employees, so that they are not just receivers of the change but that change processes can be designed with true coworkership.

8.6.3 We Must Not Fear Authenticity

A current research project at some of the major public authorities in Sweden has also made it even clearer to Mats Heide how crucial authenticity is in effective change. 'One of the top leaders we followed in the project had the courage to be more honest than top leaders often are. She was not afraid to say what was difficult, what had made her doubt and what she herself thought and felt about it all. It was quite clear how crucial that authenticity became to the employees. It made everything much more personal and something you would also get personally involved in'.

It may seem trite to stress that personal impact is rooted in a fundamental presence and authenticity, but unfortunately, it is not. 'This is another area where communicators often help reinforce skewed change communications, where top leaders appear absolutely perfect and confident, rather than allowing or insisting that imperfect and authentic is better' stresses Mats Heide, who sees perfectionism as an enemy to many change communicators and change leaders. 'It has to be too perfect. Too fine. Too finished. And in reality, we lose the possibility of initiating real communication, and the employees are reduced to passive "followers" who simply have to follow the lead of the confident management'.

8.6.4 Psychological Safety as a Foundation

Effective change without trust is not possible in an organisation. This is why Mats Heide is also interested in the concept of 'psychological safety' proposed by American professor Amy Edmondson. 'Being communicators, we need to take an interest in psychological safety when designing successful change. Basically: How are things? And what does that mean to our design of the change process?'

For example, it may be important to facilitate many local meetings with the immediate manager to make sure that staff can talk in a psychologically safe space about their concerns when it comes to change, what they think it will mean and what it requires for them to succeed.

'At its core, much change communication is about facilitating the translation of general change into meaning for each individual. The need to know is a basic human reaction: What does it mean for me?' he stresses. 'And we shouldn't be afraid to give employees the space to vent their emotions, even if it might scare managers a bit. Employees must be allowed to vent—whether they are angry, scared or sad. Otherwise, we'll never get anywhere with a change'.

In other words, effective change is not only about communicative leadership and authenticity but also about facilitating communicative coworkership, which will often be rooted in dialogue about nuances and doubts and with an understanding of the emotional elements. This requires professional communicators who actively accept co-responsibility throughout the process, from decision to execution.

With a final crack of the constructive whip to communicators, Mats Heide also has no doubt that we need to be better at collaboration. 'It's not something we can do alone as communicators, and a lot goes wrong if we don't train our ability to collaborate with other units in the organisation, such as HR, IT and Quality. In addition to management, they are often important actors, as well. We need to get better at understanding our own unique selling point and working on strong relationships within the organisation. Our job is to make organisations understand how we can contribute and how creating meaning in an organisation is a very important and value-creating function'.

Mats Heide

Mats Heide, Professor and Excellent Teaching Practitioner (ETP), PhD at the Department of Strategic Communication, Lund University.

Mats Heide is an internationally renowned researcher focusing on strategic communication, internal communication, crisis, change and strategic listening. He is the author of numerous books in Swedish and English, articles and reports. His work with Jesper Falkheimer is considered to have helped found and define strategic communication as a research field. This work was crowned in 2022 with the publication of both an international textbook: 'Strategic Communication: An Introduction to Theory and Global Practice' (Routledge) and 'The Research Handbook of Strategic Communication' (Edward Elgar Publishing), which they edited to bring together the necessary research methods in the field. Another key area of research, together with Charlotte Simonsson and others, has been the attempt to create much-needed focus on internal communication; for example with publications on coworkership, the communicating organisation and communicative collaboration.

References

Alvesson, M. (2013). *Organisation and management. A somewhat sceptical perspective.* Studentlitteratur.
Argyris, C., Schon, D. A., & Schön, D. A. (1978). *Organisizational learning: A theory of action perspective.* Addison-Wesley.
Armenakis, A. A., Harris, S. G., & Mossholder, K. W. (1993). Creating readiness for organisational change. *Human Relations, 46*(6), 681–703.
Bamford, D., & Forrester, P. (2003). Managing planned and emergent change within an operations management environment. *International Journal of Operations & Production Management, 23,* 546–564. https://doi.org/10.1108/01443570310471857
Burnes, B. (2004). Emergent change and planned change—Competitors or allies?: The case of XYZ Construction. *International Journal of Operations & Production Management, 24*(9), 886–902.
Burnes, B., & Randall, J. (2016). *Perspectives on change: What academics, consultants and managers really think about change.* Routledge.
Clayton, S. J. (2021). An agile approach to change management. *Harvard Business Review.*
Dahlman, S., & Heide, M. (2021). *Strategic internal communication: A practitioner's guide to implementing cutting-edge methods for improved workplace culture.* Routledge.
Edmondson, A. C. (2019). *The fearless organisation: Creating psychological safety in the workplace for learning, innovation and growth.* Wiley.
Edwards, K., Prætorius, T., & Nielsen, A. P. (2020). A model of cascading change: Orchestrating planned and emergent change to ensure employee participation. *Journal of Change Management, 20*(4), 342–368.
Hughes, M. (2016). *The leadership of organizational change* (1st ed.). Routledge.
Järventie-Thesleff, R., Moisander, J., & Villi, M. (2014). The strategic challenge of continuous change in multi-platform media organisations—A strategy-as-practice perspective. *International Journal on Media Management (Saint Gall, Switzerland), 16*(3–4), 123–138.
Kotter, J. P. (1990). *A force for Change: How leadership differs from management.* Free Press.
Kotter, J. P. (1996). *Leading change.* Harvard Business School Press.
Kotter, J. P. (2012). *Leading change.* Harvard Business Review Press.
Kotter, J. P. (2014). *Accelerate: Building strategic agility for a faster-moving world.* Harvard Business Review Press.

References

Lewis, L. (2018). *Organizational change – Creating change through strategic communication*. Wiley-Blackwell.

Lewis, L. K., & Sahay, S. (2018). Change communication. In R. L. Heath & W. Johansen (Eds.), *The international encyclopedia of strategic communication* (pp. 1–15). Wiley.

Lund, A. K., & Petersen, H. (2018). *Strike!: The DNA of the effective counsellor* (1st ed.). Gyldendal Business.

Maurer, R. (2010). *Beyond the wall of resistance, revised 2nd edition: Why 70% of all changes still fail—And what you can do about it*. Bard Press.

Rock, D., & Ringleb, A. H. (2013). *Handbook of neuroleadership*. Createspace Independent Publishing Platform.

Schmitz, D. (2019). Better organisational change through neuroscience. *EHS Today*.

Takeuchi & Nonaka. (1986). *The new new product development game*. Harvard Business Review.

Weick, K. E. (2000). Emergent change as a universal in organisations. In M. Beer & N. Nohria (Eds.), *Breaking the code of change*. Harvard Business School Press.

When the Crisis Is Triggered   9

Crises are inevitable. Their size, cause and origin may vary, but as a professional communicator you must always be ready to deal with any crises—and preferably prevent them from happening in the first place. This chapter zooms in on the key points of attention and theories in relation to the communication management of crises.

The chapter's case provides insight into the crisis management space in Maersk when Russia invaded Ukraine in 2022, a time that was difficult to navigate as an organisation and showed how global crises today place new demands on organisations.

The chapter's international expert is world-renowned crisis communication researcher Timothy Coombs, who has helped define the field and whose theories can help guide the difficult crisis management in practice.

Crises come like pearls on a never-ending string, so today we are talking about a genuine crisis society (Frandsen & Johansen, 2017). Organisational crises are not only major external crises such as pandemics and terrorist attacks, for which organisations do not bear direct responsibility, but crises can also be triggered by internal factors, such as a whistleblower or a dissatisfied customer whose views are quickly mediatised in a digital society and can take off like a crisis tsunami, striking the foundations of organisations. The pace is fast, and such crises can have major consequences if the professional communicator is not on their toes. Researchers even speak of a so-called 'double crisis' (Frandsen & Johansen, 2007) when communication crisis management fails, thus doubling the crisis.

A crisis is defined as, inter alia, a 'low-probability, high-impact event that threatens the viability of the organisation and is characterised by ambiguity of cause, effects and means of resolution, as well as by a belief that decisions must be made swiftly' (Pearson & Clair, 1998: 60). Pearson and Clair quote Habermas that '[t]he crisis cannot be separated from the viewpoint of the one who is undergoing it' (Habermas, 1975: 58) and emphasise the internal perspective in their definition, whilst for example Coombs (2021) emphasises the stakeholder perspective in his situational crisis communication theory (SCCT):

'SCCT defines crises as occurring when stakeholders experience a violation of their expectations and crisis communication can only be effective when stakeholders accept the crisis accounts offered by the organisation (Coombs, 2019; Pace et al., 2010). SCCT does view crisis communication as an interaction between the organisation and the stakeholder' (Coombs, 2021: 181). A definition that in the age of stakeholder capitalism is essential for the professional communicator to be aware of. The organisational crisis does not have to be perceived immediately as a threat from within, but it can be if the view of the organisation is at stake amongst key stakeholders.

The consequences of organisational crises are multifaceted, with damage to economic, human, social and symbolic capital (Frandsen & Johansen, 2020a: 25). That is why it is essential for an effective communication function to not only be prepared and crisis-ready but also to have strong relationships in the organisation because crises can only be resolved in collaboration with key voices in the organisation, just as the crisis toolbox must be updated so that many channels can be brought into play in the handling of the crisis. According to Frandsen and Johansen, crisis management can be defined as follows:

> Crisis management can be defined as the conceptualisation, implementation, maintenance and enactment of the organisational crisis preparedness, that is, the resources allocated by the organisation to be able:
>
> 1. to detect strong and weak signals indicating that a crisis is building up;
> 2. to prevent that a crisis breaks out;
> 3. to prepare to handle the crisis if it breaks out anyway;
> 4. to bring the crisis to an end and reduce the damage caused by the crisis to the organisation, the industry and external and internal stakeholders as much as possible; and
> 5. to learn from the crises experienced by the organisation and other organisations and to implement the changes made necessary by this organisational learning process (Frandsen & Johansen, 2017: 53).

This means that crisis management involves paying attention to ensure that crises are recognised, prevented, prepared for, managed and learnt from. In today's crisis society, crisis management is an integral part of the professional communicator's field of work. This chapter thus elaborates on crisis types and identifies the theoretical tools that need to be ready for communicative crisis management.

9.1 Risks and Crisis Types

Crises can be caused by many different things, and to begin with the professional communicator must have a high level of crisis awareness and understand the many types of risks and crises. Based on Lagadech's risk civilisation and Beck's sociological perspectives (1986), Frandsen and Johansen define risks as two main types, the old and the new risks (Fig. 9.1).

Old risks	New risks
Local	Global
Actual	Potential
Visible	Invisible
Evident	Not evident or knowledge-based

Fig. 9.1 Two types of risks in the crisis society. Source: Frandsen and Johansen (2017: 26)

The old risks are visible and tangible, whilst the new ones can be much more diffuse and uncertain. The coronavirus crisis is a good example of a global and invisible crisis that was simultaneously also both visible and localised. Whilst classical crisis theory has focused on responses to actual crises, today's crisis communicators have to deal with both old and new risks.

Mitroff (2022) defines the classic crises in the organisational context as:

- Product recalls
- Counterfeiting of product/service/logo
- Sabotage by employees
- Fires, explosions, chemical spills
- Environmental disasters
- Significant decrease in revenue/economy
- Natural disasters
- Loss of confidential/sensitive information
- Terrorism
- Ethical breaches
- Changes in legislation
- Technological change

With an increased focus on stakeholder perspectives, these types of crises can be supplemented with disappointment as a crisis category. Macnamara formulates it as follows: 'It is needed to include at least one additional crisis type that recognises failure of an organisation to meet stakeholder and/or societal expectations even when it is not at fault through intention, or by accident, or involved as a victim. This additional crisis type could be called 'ineffectual' and applied to organisations that are a 'downstream participant'' (Macnamara, 2021a, b: 256). A crisis type that is necessary, amongst other things, because stakeholders today have concrete expectations about, for example organisations' contributions to society in the climate area, and not living up to these expectations can easily trigger a crisis.

The list of potential crises can be very long, but one tool to ensure a systematic look at potential crises can be to map potential crises in a matrix (Fig. 9.2) based on what triggers the crisis (Shrivastava & Mitroff, 1987, in Frandsen & Johansen, 2017: 45).

For example, an IT breakdown would be an internal/technical crisis in the top left box, whilst a hacker attack would be an external technical crisis. A societal crisis such as high inflation is external and would be placed in the bottom right box, whilst

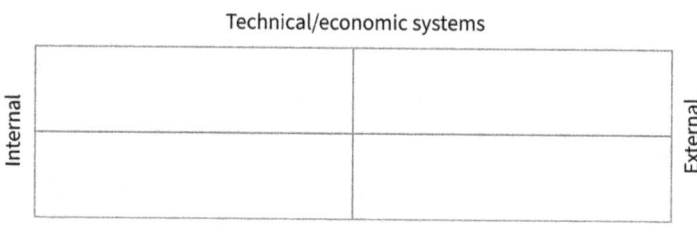

Fig. 9.2 Shrivastava and Mitroff's proposal for a crisis mapping matrix. Source: Frandsen and Johansen (2017: 45)

a fraud case is man-made and internal and would be placed in the bottom left box. Mapping using a matrix such as this can enable the professional communicator to analyse potential crises and work on organisational crisis readiness in relation to very specific potential crises.

9.2 The Strategic Crisis Communicator

Crisis communication theory has historically moved from being about responding to external crises at a rather tactical level to becoming more prescriptive and looking at what to do when a crisis occurs. In recent years, the focus has shifted further to a strategic level with a focus on crisis management, i.e. anticipating, preventing, managing and learning from a potential crisis.

The rise of social media has had a major impact on crisis management because social media has created a whole new area that can trigger the development of crises, because disappointed stakeholders, for example may easily express themselves to a broad public. In this context, Coombs warns that this development should not lead professional communicators to return to working only tactically with crises, because strategic crisis management is crucial, and social media have not fundamentally changed the nature of crises. It has merely expanded the channels and accelerated the pace of crisis management (Coombs, 2021). A point also made by Tkalac Verčič: 'When a crisis occurs in the age of social media, it has a greater reach than it used to have, but so does social media crisis communication. It is a risk, as much as an opportunity' (Tkalac Verčič & Špoljarić, 2020: 29).

The strategic crisis communicator works preventively, anticipating potential crises analytically and ensuring that the organisation is prepared for a crisis. For example, who would represent the organisation in a potential crisis? Have the spokespersons been media trained? Are there updated contingency plans? Is there access to data that could provide useful arguments? There are many preventive, practical measures that need to be ready in a systematic and anticipatory way, and which are very useful to have at hand when a crisis suddenly pulls the rug out from under everyday routines.

9.2 The Strategic Crisis Communicator

In addition, the professional communicator's crisis management consists of being alert and diagnosing potential crisis triggers. This is where some of the organisational listening and data-driven communicator's tools come into play. What is going on with key stakeholders? Is there, for example a simmering dissatisfaction internally that could turn into a leak and a crisis externally? Are there suddenly a lot of critical comments on Facebook or ridiculing posts on TikTok? Only by keeping an eye on stakeholders can the communicator detect potential crises early enough and manage them in time to contain their impact. Or they may be able to influence how crises are actually interpreted by stakeholders so that they do not become real crises (Coombs, 2015). This part of the communicator's work is often quite invisible—because who sees crises that do not materialise? This means that the work is often underestimated, but the absence of crises enhances organisational reputation. In practice, the professional communicator can benefit from ensuring that preventive work is also made clear to internal stakeholders in management, so that it can be prioritised as a natural part of the communication function's work. In theoretical work, it is often called 'strategic issues management' (Heath, 2018a, b) and covers the communicator's work on mapping and acting on the focus areas that are important to the organisation's stakeholders. The communicator must monitor and reduce the discrepancies that may exist between management practices and the expectations of stakeholders in order to create understanding, engage, minimise conflict and explain (Cornelissen, 2020). This work requires the professional communicator to also focus on legitimacy and legitimacy gaps, credibility and trust (see Chap. 3), the role of the 'corporate citizen' (see Chap. 4) and active 'social listening' (see Chap. 6). In a crisis context, it is a natural part both before the crisis and during the crisis to have this practical approach to listening, analysing disagreements and ensuring that relevant, strategic issues are communicated (Brønn & Berg, 2011).

Crisis management is about working on crisis management before, during and after the crisis in order to learn from it before the next one occurs. Crises can be modelled almost dramaturgically, as in Fig. 9.3, where something triggers or initiates the crisis ('initial crisis'), then the crisis grows towards a turning point, and then the post-crisis phase begins with the handling of outcomes and preparing for future,

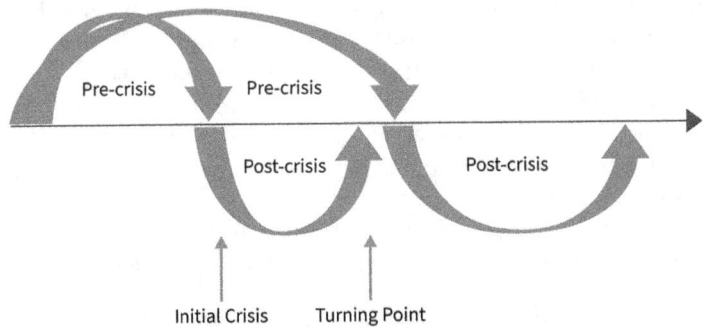

Fig. 9.3 A regenerative crisis model. Source: Coombs (2017), in Gephart et al. (2019: 52)

similar situations. All phases are important areas of work for the professional communicator.

Precisely because crises happen all the time, a potential pitfall for the professional communicator is to breathe a sigh of relief at the turning point of the crisis and slacken the communicative work. The critical voices in the press, on social media and internally may stop immediately, but as Fig. 9.3 emphasises, there is also plenty of work to be done in the post-crisis phase. Partly to ensure that the crisis has not left any damage to key relationships or the organisation's reputation, and partly to learn from the experience before the next crisis wave begins.

9.3 The Rhetorical Arena

Early crisis theorists such as Benoit based their work on the sender, which was later challenged by, amongst others, Coombs and Holladay (2014), who focused on stakeholders. At the same time as this theory formation, the field of crisis theory was further nuanced by Frandsen and Johansen, who focused on the communicative complexity of crises with the development of the theory of the rhetorical arena (Frandsen & Johansen, 2017), which can help the crisis communicator to both map and navigate wisely.

> We wanted to account for the communicative complexity appearing in many crises and to add to the existing research. Thus, we wanted to expand on these first theories, at least in two ways: in relation to (i) the nature of "participants" (stakeholders/actors/voices) involved in a crisis and their interaction in a specific "rhetorical arena," as well as in relation to (ii) the mediation (architecture/forming) of the crisis communication strategies themselves (Frandsen & Johansen, in Coombs & Holladay, 2023: 170).

The theory of the rhetorical arena does away with a linear view of crisis communication and instead looks at all voices in a crisis. Frandsen and Johansen originally chose the term *stakeholder* for the actors but now speak of voices, as there may often be actors in a crisis who do not necessarily have a real 'stake' in the crisis, but who nevertheless step in as a voice in the arena (2023: 172): 'We define the rhetorical arena as a social space that opens up when a crisis occurs, in which multiple voices communicate to, with, against, past or about each other (Frandsen & Johansen, 2020a; Frandsen & Johansen, 2007). The social space opens across public and private spheres and across stakeholders and non-stakeholders'.

Crises are identified at both macro and micro levels. At the macro level, the actors and voices in the rhetorical arena are delimited by the duration of the crisis. The interaction is illustrated as a jumble of interactions within a given period of time, as shown in Fig. 9.4.

In its simplicity, the model can be used by the professional communicator to try to get an overview of the actors in the current crisis and their interactions with one another.

At the micro level, Frandsen and Johansen look at the concrete communication processes each time a voice communicates in the arena and recommend (Fig. 9.5) a

9.3 The Rhetorical Arena

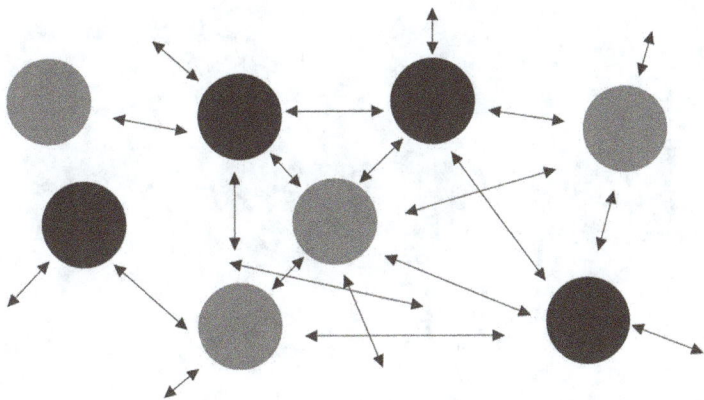

Fig. 9.4 Macro-elements in the rhetorical arena. Source: Frandsen and Johansen (2017: 148)

PARAMETERS	EXAMPLES
Context	Sociological contexts: Situational context (timing, point in time, nature of voices, salience and power of voices, crisis type, crisis victims, etc.) Organisational context (organisation type [private/public], size, leadership, communication culture, organisational culture, etc.) (Inter)cultural and socio-economic context (norms and values, legal, political, and economic factors across regions and borders, including nature of ICT [media landscape, media power]) Psychological contexts: Cognitive schemes influencing perceptions and interpretations of senders and receivers
COMMUNICATION-BASED PARAMETERS	
Medium	Corporate media, print media, audiovisual media (TV), social media, etc.
Genre	Press releases, press conferences, media interviews, corporate statements, social media posts, SMS, etc.
Text	All semiotic resources: words, visuals, actions, artifacts, etc.

Fig. 9.5 The micro-components of the rhetorical arena. Source: Frandsen and Johansen (2023: 171)

focus on context, medium, genre and text, elaborated in the following parameters (2023: 171):

The four elements of the micro-components—context, media, genre and text—help the professional communicator to get an overview of the situational elements and forms of communication in the given crisis. An overview that can help to ensure both the situational anchoring and the orchestration of the best possible channel mix for crisis management. They are visualised in Fig. 9.6.

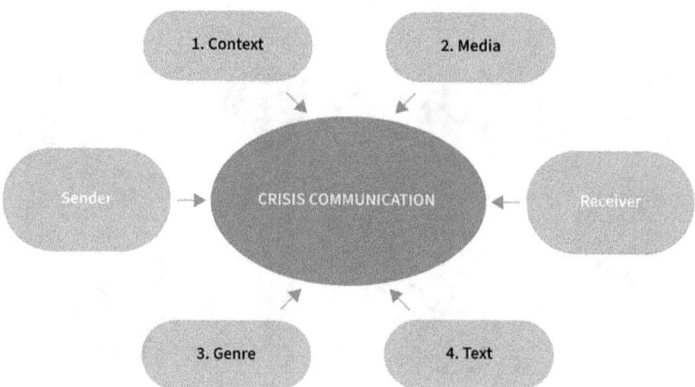

Fig. 9.6 A schematic overview of the micro-elements in the rhetorical arena. Source: Frandsen and Johansen (2007: 284)

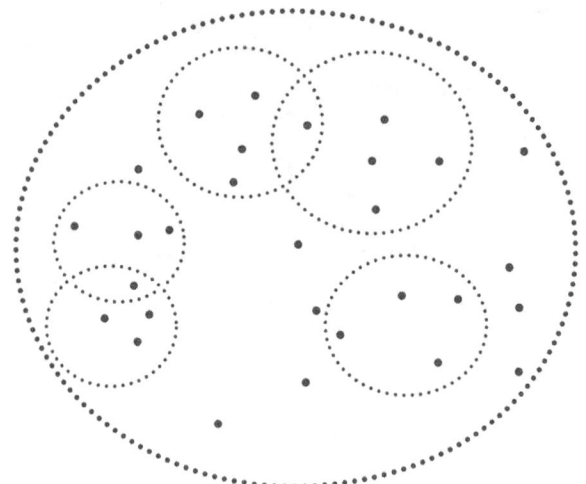

Fig. 9.7 The rhetorical arena with inbuilt sub-arenas. Source: Frandsen and Johansen (2023: 176)

Through insight into the rhetorical arena, the professional communicator can identify the actors and their expressions within the arena. Since the theory of the rhetorical arena theory has been introduced, practice has shown that it makes sense to further nuance the model with sub-arenas. This happens, for example when a subgroup of voices takes up the crisis in a newly defined arena. It may be that a discussion of a TV programme shared on Facebook creates a specific new arena of multivocal voices in the debate. In this case, it is too narrow to consider both TV and Facebook as communication channels, even though it may appear so on the surface, and the debate will typically contain more elements at the micro level than what takes place on Facebook, for example. Frandsen and Johansen illustrate this widening of the arena with this simple Fig. 9.7 that covers the multivocal complexity (2023: 176).

9.4 Response Strategies in Crises

In practice, the rhetorical arena and its sub-arenas can be a very useful tool in the attempt to maintain an overview of the elements and contexts of a crisis. It allows systematically mapping the multiple voices and agendas in a crisis. It can also be used to analyse the crisis retrospectively and learn before the next crisis occurs.

9.4 Response Strategies in Crises

According to Benoit (1995), when the crisis is raging and communicators have to respond intelligently to, for example a direct attack on an organisation's reputation, it is crucial to have an 'image repair contingency plan' based on crisis response strategies drawn from classical rhetoric. He himself summarises his many years of research in a table in Fig. 9.8.

STRATEGY	DEFINITION	EXAMPLE
Denial		
Simple Denial	Did not perform act	Tylenol did not poison capsule
Shift Blame	Another performed the act	Tylenol: a "madman" poisoned capsule
Evade Responsibility		
Provocation	Responded to act of another	Firm left state because taxes increased
Defeasibility	Lack of information or ability	Missed meeting because not informed of changed time
Accident	Mishap	Tree fell after storm, damaging car
Good intentions	Meant well	Sears wanted to provide good auto service
Reduce Offensiveness		
Bolstering	Stress accused's good qualities	Exxon claimed a swift and competent clean-up of oil spill
Minimisation	Act not serious	Exxon: few animals killed by oil spill
Differentiation	Act less offensive than similar acts	I did not steal your laptop; I borrowed it without permission
Transcendence	More important values	Stole food for hungry child
Attack Accuser	Source of accusation not credible or deserved what happened	Accusations are just fake news
Compensation	Reimburse victim	Free dessert if food not properly prepared
Corrective Action	Plans to solve problem or prevent recurrence	AT&T will spend billions to improve service
Mortification	Apologise	AT&T apologised for service interuption

Fig. 9.8 Benoit's typology of responses to reputational crises. Source: Benoit in Frandsen and Johansen (2020a, 2020b: 107)

RESPONSE STRATEGY	SUB-TYPES	MANAGEMENT ACTIONS
Denial	Denial	Claim that no crisis occurred
	Attack accuser	Confront the person or group claiming a crisis
	Scapegoat	Blame some outside person or group
Diminish	Excuse	Deny intent to do harm/claim inability to control events
	Justification	Minimise the perceived damage caused
Rebuild	Compensation	Offer money or other gifts to victims
	Apology	Accept responsibility and ask stakeholders to forgive
Bolstering	Reminder	Tell stakeholders about past good works
	Ingratiation	Thank or praise stakeholders for their help
	Victimage	Remind stakeholders that the organisation is also a victim

Fig. 9.9 Coombs' suggestions for response strategies and management action centred on stakeholders. Source: Coombs (2015: 266)

As the table shows, each response strategy has a way of responding to the incident, from a denial response—'it did not happen'—to more advanced response strategies where the response is to put the crisis in a larger value context—'we had to prioritise safety over xx'. A table like this can show the range of response options and inspire the professional communicator to choose a response strategy according to an assessment of the situation (Benoit, 2020). According to Coombs (2021), this balancing of what is the right thing to do is about assessing the degree to which responsibility can be attributed to the organisation. Coombs distinguishes between three categories of responsibility attribution:

1. Victim: minimal attribution of responsibility
2. Accidents: less attribution of responsibility
3. Potentially avoidable: high attribution of responsibility (Coombs, 2021: 184)

The situational analysis should ensure that the strategically thinking crisis communicator chooses the right response. For example, if the organisation is completely blameless, the communicative approach may be more focused on handling than on apologising etc., although Coombs will always put care for those affected first in the handling (see interview later in this chapter). Coombs also emphasises that the risk of failure in crisis management is greater if you have not analysed whether there is a difference between how external and internal stakeholders understand and frame the crisis (Coombs, 2021). He recommends the following adaptation of response strategies with a focus on stakeholders (Coombs, 2015: 266) (Fig. 9.9).

9.5 Proactive Crisis Management: 'Stealing Thunder'

The response strategies of Benoit and Coombs identify possible responses once the crisis has occurred. But sometimes it is possible for the professional communicator to work more proactively by telling the outside world about a possible crisis and in

9.5 Proactive Crisis Management: 'Stealing Thunder'

this way be transparent and credible, and have a chance to control the origin of the crisis to a slightly higher degree. This proactive crisis response strategy is about not waiting when the organisation discovers a potential crisis but being at the forefront of the scandal. The strategy has been labelled 'stealing thunder' (Claeys et al., 2013) and is, in simple terms, about not sitting on your hands and waiting for a thunderclap when you have seen lightning strike. Research shows that it has a much stronger impact on stakeholders if the organisation itself has the courage and drive to go out and talk about a crisis before it becomes public knowledge: 'When an organisation offers a response that is considered sincere, consumers may be more likely to forgive the organisation for its wrongdoing and evaluate it less negatively' (Claeys et al., 2013: 304).

Furthermore, it seems that it can enhance credibility: '... because sincerity is often considered as a factor in assessing the credibility of a message (Sternthal et al., 1978; Tormala & Petty, 2004), these findings suggest that organisational credibility is enhanced not only by self-disclosing a crisis (Arpan & Roskos-Ewoldsen, 2005) but by expressing sadness as well' (Claeys et al. 2013: 305).

Claeys et al. (2013) gave six reasons for stealing thunder:

1. Credibility—By surprising people by coming out with something yourself, it increases credibility as a source and removes some of the typical bias or bias towards trusting the organisation as a voice in a crisis.
2. Accountability—By playing the hand themselves, the organisation shows its accountability.
3. Attention—Coming out with a crisis yourself is documented to attract less attention because the self-disclosure itself means that it is less possible to cast the organisation as the villain in the same way, which can make it less interesting to cover or talk about.
4. Initial framing—By securing the first initial response to the crisis, it is easier to influence the framing of at least the first wave of publicity.
5. Influence customer behaviour—By managing the crisis proactively, studies show that customers are more likely to return and buy again and spread less negative information.
6. Ethics—By playing the hand yourself, you demonstrate the organisation's integrity.

If 'stealing thunder' as a crisis management strategy is to succeed, spokespersons must be fully present in the communication, and it can be a major challenge as a communicator to prepare employees and managers for this. Many crises can feel unreasonable internally, or spokespersons may have so much at stake themselves that it is difficult for them to step forward with the right humility and accommodate stakeholders' emotions because they are overwhelmed by their own crisis response. That is why an important part of the professional communicator's tasks during crises is to be able to orchestrate the right response—which can sometimes even mean having to exempt otherwise obvious representatives from being spokespersons. Authenticity is a prerequisite for stakeholders' perception of an organisation's crisis management. The right training can often prepare spokespersons for the role and make them more comfortable with the situation, and it can also create the necessary understanding of what the situation calls for. Training situations can also create a necessary opportunity for the spokesperson to verbalise and 'park' their own overshadowing emotions that may otherwise shine through. This is particularly challenging to manage in image-based channels, so authenticity can also be a consideration in relation to the choice of channel and the mix to be implemented.

It can be difficult to know whether it is a good idea to steal thunder and, as the case study in Chap. 4 also showed, it can almost feel unnatural for the professional communicator to go public with a negative case in the media. When the professional communicator has seen the 'crisis lightning' strike, there are three scenarios:

1. Remain silent and observe whether the crisis emerges externally at all.
2. Remain silent and watch as the crisis is eventually revealed by a third party.
3. Proactively go out and put the crisis into words yourself (Claeys, 2023: 108).

Taking a proactive approach to crises is undoubtedly an important part of the communicator's crisis management in order to limit the damage to the organisation's reputation. It requires a mandate from management for real openness, a readiness to communicate sincerely and to be present.

9.6 The Internal Stakeholder in Times of Crisis

Internal communication is often underestimated in crisis management (Johansen et al., 2012) because the external 'damage control' gets extra focus, but the internal stakeholders are nevertheless important both for short-term crisis management and for long-term employee retention. In the short term, because all employees of the organisation are of course potential or actual voices in crisis management in the rhetorical arena. They communicate on a daily basis with all kinds of stakeholders, and they must thus feel able to master individual crisis management. It is not just about sending out an F&Q so that they can answer typical questions mechanically. It is about accommodating their feelings, doubts and possible need for knowledge so that they can respond in a trustworthy and credible way. Only if the internal stakeholders are ready for crisis management will each of them be able to constitute a credible voice in the organisational crisis management chorus. So they must be seen as spokespersons in exactly the same way as a spokesperson to the press. 'In the crisis phase, the initial focus must be on providing employees with fast information through all form of media, even messengers that distribute information in the organisation. A bit later in the process, there will be a need of discussion of the situation in order to make sense of the situation. This is important both for employees as private persons but also in their role as organisational ambassador in external interactions' (Heide & Simonsson, in Frandsen & Johansen, 2020a, 2020b: 272).

An important focus for the professional communicator is to enable the leaders in the organisation to engage in and facilitate conversations that can create meaning and allow employees to interact (Strandberg & Vigsø, 2016). 'Sensemaking is a social process, which according to Weick (2002: 31), means that people' need conversations with others to move towards some shared idea of what meanings are possible. 'Another important leadership act is to question dominant interpretations (Baran & Scott, 2010) by asking questions such as: What is taken for granted, what assumptions should we question? What alternative interpretations can be made?' (Heide & Simonsson, in Frandsen & Johansen, 2020a, 2020b: 269). In other words, the attentive crisis communicator also facilitates a response to the situation the organisation has ended up in. This means, amongst other things, that the professional communicator must engage in active organisational listening internally so that there is a good sense of what needs to arise. It is also an important aspect of crisis management that the internal and external communication are in sync, so there is coherence in the expression and no double crises arise (Frandsen & Johansen, 2011a, b; Heide & Simonsson, 2014).

Internal stakeholder focus is an essential part of crisis management (Bernstein in Špoljarić, 2021). It is a continuous communicative process that takes place between managers and employees and internally between colleagues before, during and after an organisational crisis (Heide & Simonsson, 2019).

9.7 Crisis Awareness of the Professional Communicator

The professional communicator should, as far as possible, detect and analyse crises before they occur by having an active and data-based approach to all stakeholders and by engaging in real organisational listening.

Once the lightning of a crisis has been spotted, it is not a matter of counting seconds to assess how far away it is, but of acting quickly. What kind of crisis is it? Which actors are present in the rhetorical arena and any sub-arenas? Which response options are the wise choice here? Should the thunder be forestalled? Which stakeholders are directly affected—and which indirectly? What is the most appropriate communication plan? Which organisational voices should be brought into play? Why and how? What mix of channels can reach stakeholders where they are?

During the crisis itself, it is not only necessary to send out communicative content but also to constantly listen and keep up a dialogue with all stakeholders in the rhetorical arena, including internal stakeholders.

Whilst it may be tempting enough to collapse exhausted after being caught in a war zone during a major crisis, the crisis is not over once the external focus fades. Long-term credibility and trust from external and internal stakeholders will only be maintained if lessons are learnt from the crises. The communicator has a dual role here—to facilitate the organisation's learning and communicate it, and to evaluate the communication efforts constructively. What has the communication function learnt about crisis management? What would be nice to do better next time? Who needs to be trained? Which roles could be distributed differently etc.?

In today's crisis society, we can be sure that crises do not disappear entirely, but that there is a 'next time' in sight, and communicators need to be ready for it.

9.8 Case 8. Global Balancing Act in Times of Crisis

When Russia invaded Ukraine in February 2022, war in Europe was not only a reality, but it also moved to the top of the agenda in all organisations, bringing crucial issues and dilemmas to the forefront and raising expectations of corporate social and political responsibility in a matter of days. Maersk was no exception. Crucial human, societal and business decisions had to be made with little or no time for reflection.

Russia's invasion of Ukraine was, of course, an externally triggered crisis (Frandsen & Johansen, 2017). At first glance, one might think that the crisis was thus a classic crisis driven by so-called 'old risks', but the crisis was also driven by 'new risks'. Organisations did not only have to deal with actual, visible, local risk factors for employees in Russia or Ukraine. It was also a global crisis for the world's balance of power, and with stakeholder capitalism demanding that organisations step up as 'corporate citizens', there were many more invisible new risks that became part of reality on Thursday 24 February 2022, when Russia invaded Ukraine.

At Maersk, the highest level of crisis preparedness was immediately established, initially with many meetings daily. Hundreds of Ukrainian colleagues were at risk and likewise, our Russian colleagues were caught in between. In addition, there were tens of thousands of containers of clients' cargo travelling to and from ports, mainly in Russia but also in Ukraine. There were endless lists of legal and political issues—sanctions looming and a public mood with a clear expectation of action and attitude from a large global organisation acting as a corporate citizen.

In the media, there was a queue at the microphones, as many people wanted to express their views on the situation, many journalists wanted Maersk's comment, and there was an internal expectation that people would come forward with strong opinions.

However, it was not that simple, as it was important to take into consideration our Russian employees, who were under great pressure from local authorities, who did not hesitate, amongst other things, to issue special laws criminalising cooperation with what they considered to be 'subversive organisations'.

This meant, for example that if a Maersk colleague condemned the invasion on his or her private social media profile with the best of intentions, he or she was asked to tone down the message for the safety of other colleagues.

The principle underlying the first phases of crisis communication was: 'Show, don't tell'. This meant refraining from being vocal about your views, whilst at the same time working hard to evacuate staff and prepare to close down the business in Russia.

In the first week of the war, EU sanctions were implemented, in the second week they resorted to what was called 'over-implementation of sanctions', and in the third week Maersk announced that new bookings of shipments in and out of Russia would be suspended, making it one of the first major players to go much further than the political sanctions required. The Ukrainian ambassador to Denmark was in the media at the time, praising Maersk and recommending that other companies show the same type of leadership.

'The first and most crucial focus of the crisis team was undoubtedly our employees. We had many employees in both Ukraine and Russia, and an evacuation was initiated for Ukrainian colleagues and their families if they wanted to leave the country', says Mette Refshauge, Director of Communications at Maersk, who was part of the central crisis team. The fate of the people was monitored almost hour by hour whilst the evacuation was underway.

The security situation of Russian employees was monitored just as closely: 'Our employees were under great pressure from local authorities. Our actions in the West affected colleagues in the East; and their safety was of paramount concern to us. So we kept quiet, did not answer questions, did not make public condemnations or statements, even though there was hectic activity'. This involved the evacuation of both Ukrainian and Russian colleagues who needed to be protected in the best possible way, both financially and in terms of security, before Russian activities shut down.

Whilst Maersk was quiet as a mouse, acting behind the scenes, the media was up in arms. There were so many emotions at stake, and a Danish tabloid newspaper ran a massive campaign against Maersk over a couple of days.

'It was a bit agonising, of course. There was no room for nuance in those days and in that coverage, and the newspaper made merry, for example, with a front page where they used the Maersk star as a kind of halo on Putin's head and wrote that the company continued to chase profits in Russia, partly because we of course still had ships at sea. Ships filled with our customers' cargo cannot be conjured away in a second, but there was nothing to be gained by retaliating. We paid extra attention to critical voices on social media and in our own internal communication channels. And of course they were there. It is quite understandable that people were also waiting for us to come forward', emphasises Mette Refshauge.

It was a vulnerable time. This was illustrated by the Ukrainian ambassador to Denmark, who shortly afterwards went to the media and accused Maersk of 'helping to kill more Ukrainians', as he was quoted as saying. The reason for the anger was that a Greek tanker was helped by a Maersk-owned tugboat to enter harbour in Kalundborg. It turned out that the tanker was carrying Russian oil. 'We worked through diplomatic channels and held several meetings with the Ambassador to explain our positions and the initiatives we were taking to help and support his country. For example, under the auspices of the UN Logistic Emergency Team, Maersk set up the logistics for the humanitarian aid for the whole of Ukraine. But it was not something we wanted or needed to promote ourselves on in the media', explains Mette Refshauge.

9.8.1 One Step Forward

In the fifth week after the invasion, an opportunity presented itself for communicating more clearly. Maersk held their annual general meeting, where both chairman and CEO were scheduled to speak, and both investors and journalists would have the opportunity to ask questions. It was an obvious 'turning point' (Coombs, 2017) for the crisis communication. By then, evacuations had been carried out, an overview of the many containers that were in or on their way to and from Russia was available, and the plan for the business shutdown in Russia was ready. The silence could be broken and there was an opportunity to speak clearly.

'The good thing about the General Assembly as a framework for our announcements was that we were much more able to ensure that we communicated properly. It wasn't just a response in a newspaper but uninterrupted speaking time where we could explain what we were doing and why', emphasises the Communications Director.

The then CEO Søren Skou took to the podium and put into words what Maersk had done in concrete terms:

> Of course, we cannot continue as if nothing has happened. Russia has attacked a neighbouring country and is now waging war just 1,500 km from Copenhagen. A war that has already cost thousands of lives and displaced millions. On Monday 28 February, we decided to stop all new bookings, except for food and medicine to and from Russia. At the same time, we put a global stop to the purchase of Russian oil for our ships. On Thursday 3 March, we tightened further and stopped all bookings to St Petersburg and Kaliningrad—also for food and medicine. Last week, we decided to liquidate our ownership in Global Ports and to sell all other assets we have in Russia.
>
> Obviously, we cannot be involved in the operation of port infrastructure that is critical to the Russian economy under the given circumstances. We may not return to doing business in Russia for many years to come. But it is a price we can and will pay.
>
> In practical terms, stopping doing business in Russia is not straightforward:
>
> Firstly, when the war broke out, we had over 50,000 import bookings in our network heading to Russia. We will try to deliver these containers as quickly as possible. The cargo inside the containers does not belong to us, it belongs to our customers, which are not only Russian customers. Many containers contain food with a limited shelf life. In addition, there are practical problems of storing containers in already overcrowded harbours on the continent.
>
> We expect that it will take us until the end of April to decommission all containers.
>
> Secondly, we also have 50,000 of our containers in Russia, most of them empty. They are our property, we need them and of course we are not in favour of leaving them in Russia. That's why we still have some port calls in Russia.
>
> Let me conclude by saying that we do not hold our Russian employees responsible for President Putin's invasion of Ukraine. They have been a loyal and integral part of Maersk for decades, and we feel a responsibility for their safety when making decisions.
>
> They are under massive pressure from Russian authorities and new legislation that dictates long prison sentences for activities harmful to the country.
>
> They also naturally fear for their jobs as we withdraw from Russia.
>
> The situation in Ukraine exposes many dilemmas that we have to deal with. It takes place in a public sphere where there are many emotions and many opinion formers in play. The debate can easily become very shrill and black and white.
>
> At Maersk, we have a set of strong core values that guide our decisions. This also applies in this very difficult situation.

In the speech, Søren Skou's response strategy is closest to what Benoit (2020) calls 'bolstering', see also Fig. 9.8, where the situation was explained, stakeholders thanked and the situation contextualised.

After the AGM, media coverage became more nuanced, and the rhetorical arena gained several sub-arenas (Frandsen & Johansen, 2023). This was not only because Maersk had now taken a step forward and spoke more clearly on several platforms, but also because the media coverage entered a phase where more nuances were generally added. Amongst other things, the focus was on the strategic, business and communication nuances and dilemmas associated with the invasion. There was thus a rather rare meta-level in the media coverage, which was decidedly angled on the fact that the situation was not as simple as it might sound. The discussions thus took place in multiple locations and with and between multiple stakeholders in multiple sub-arenas.

9.8.2 The Internal Balancing Act

Internally, too, there were several considerations to balance in terms of crisis management and communication. Everyone at Maersk was affected by the situation, and colleagues needed to hear from management. There was concern for colleagues in Ukraine and Russia, and many also called for Maersk to publicly condemn the war, as a number of other companies (without Russian activities) had done in the first weeks of the war. But with the low profile kept externally, it was important that internal communication did not cause confusion or end up in external media.

It was thus decided to invite all employees to a virtual town hall meeting where the CEO, HR, the chair of the crisis team and the head of the Ukrainian and Russian business areas were informed about the situation and then answered employees' questions. Everything was communicated live and was not recorded or saved. This was because the situation was constantly escalating, and they wanted to avoid fragments of an update being used out of context later on. The turnout for both the first and subsequent meetings was overwhelming, with one question dominating the chat: 'What can we do to help our colleagues?'

In addition to the major joint meetings, frequent updates on the internal media were also part of the internal crisis management (Fig. 9.10). Here, it was a balancing act to provide thorough, factual and caring information about the terrible situation, but without the language becoming too tendentious, partly out of consideration for Russian colleagues who were still employed by the company at the time.

'In writing, we communicated internally in a relatively neutral way. There were certain security considerations, but it was also because of the many emotions at stake', says Mette Refshauge and continues: 'In some cases, we saw a heated debate breaking out between colleagues from different parts of the world on our internal social media—sometimes in Cyrillic script. We did our utmost to monitor it closely and actively moderated the debate'.

There were also a number of well-meaning colleagues who wanted to talk about what Maersk was doing to help colleagues, customers and victims of the war, so here too the moderators were working overtime:

'It was all well-meant, but we were very careful that no one inadvertently appeared to be boasting about good deeds. It quickly comes across as distasteful in

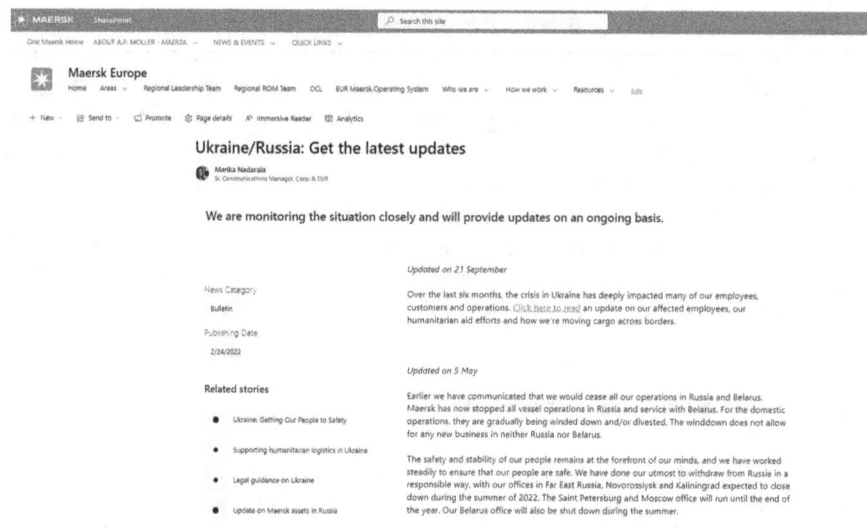

Fig. 9.10 An example of the toned-down but continuously updated crisis communication in the context of Russia's invasion of Ukraine

the context of war and hardship, so we were very cautious—I believe some thought we were bordering on the paranoid', Mette Refshauge explains.

In the internal crisis communication, the General Assembly was a kind of 'turning point' in the crisis management, where all internal stakeholders could also better understand how the withdrawal from Russia was progressing, why it was taking so long and what the management's clear positions were on the war.

In addition, the crisis also meant that Maersk decided to take an extra critical look at the organisation's already planned activities. From product launches to an otherwise large-scale celebration of International Women's Day, it was deemed more appropriate to reduce the level of activity. Everything was toned-down.

9.8.3 With Facts at the Core

To summarise, the communication approach in the initial period of the war was to act on the situation rather than speak about it, as shown in the table in Fig. 9.11. All stakeholders were systematically kept informed on a factual basis at all times. For example, customers received regular updates on what was happening and what was planned. The media received factual answers when they asked. Employees received regular updates at townhalls and on internal media.

The tone and behaviour were initially reactive and without a clear statement of values and attitudes, but gradually the values-based communication was stepped up.

The invasion of Ukraine clearly showed that expectations of organisations today have changed. It is not enough to follow government recommendations, implement sanctions or wait for new measures. Stakeholders expect organisations to take the lead and act when responding to crises.

9.8 Case 8. Global Balancing Act in Times of Crisis   205

Overall Communication tactics: Show, don't tell

Approach	Week 1 Feb 21-27	Week 2 Feb 28-Mar 5	Week 3 Mar 6-13	Week 4 Mar 14-20	Week 5 Mar 21-28
Tone of voice	Reactive, fact-based leader-led comms				Active, value-based mass comms
Key comms initiatives	• Implementing sanctions • Safety and operation • Mainly sharing facts	• Over-implementing sanctions • Customers and society • Safety and operation • Mainly sharing facts	• Going beyond sanctions • Referring to the invasion • Nuancing the dilemmas • Sharing facts	• Value-based communication • Actively communicating wind-down • Managing the dilemmas	• Managing the dilemmas • Refocus external comms • More human touch stories internally
	• CMT activated incl. comms workstream • Initial customer advisories published • Ukraine/Russia comms hub created on One Maersk • Ongoing customer communications • Reactive media handling	• Step up comms support to Ukraine & Russia CMTs • Top 1000 leader call • Daily updates on One Maersk • Local townhalls in Ukraine & Russia • Donation policy launched • Ongoing customer comms • Reactive media handling	• Frequent internal updates on One Maersk • Comms support on Russian asset exit • Local townhalls in Ukraine & Russia • Reactive media issue handling	• AGM speeches and media interviews with Chairman and CEO • Internal focus on wind-down in Russia communication • Step-up in tone-of-voice to become value-driven, preparing to take back initiative in public debate	• All company townhall • Increased focus on humanitarian efforts and support to colleagues • Reactive media handling

Classification: Confidential

 MAERSK

Fig. 9.11 Overview of Maersk's crisis communication tactics in the first 5 weeks after Russia's invasion of Ukraine

'Businesses must lead the way and go further. We need to use our resources and agency to make our mark and find ways to act. This has never been as clear as it was in those weeks, and it is certainly a reality we might as well learn to master. Fortunately, as expectations of companies rise, so does trust, so companies have a credible position from which to act. But it requires a great deal of crisis communication, also because all the stakeholders that surround the companies have so many platforms for expressing their expectations and any dissatisfaction in both words and actions, so we have to listen, communicate and act all at once', concludes Mette Refshauge.

9.9 Interview. Keep Focus on Those Affected!

It is almost symbolic that a small, green, crocheted Star Wars figure peeps out from the shelf in the background next to the globe in Timothy Coombs' office. 'Choose wisely you must!' is one of the most important pieces of advice from the little green Yoda to the young Jedi knight in Star Wars, given at a training session in the film—and that very piece of advice is almost the sum of the crisis researcher's many pioneering studies within crisis management. Professional communicators must act deliberately before, during and after a crisis to handle it wisely and with long-term effect.

It was not in the cards that young Tim would become a pioneering crisis researcher. He studied engineering but got bored, so he switched to communications and public relations. A lecturer assigned him a small task: Study the speech genre when people are sentenced to death. The rest is history: crisis history. This is where Timothy Coombs found a very meaningful field of research: 'I remember that interest really took off at a conference in Las Vegas with both theorists and practitioners on crises—and I sensed that it was more than simply talk in this field. Good communication really made you make a difference. Communicators must act as problem solvers, using communication as a tool and ensuring that those affected by crises are taken care of'.

The fundamental ethical basis of caring for those affected has always been the bedrock of his work for Timothy Coombs, who has just switched from being a professor to being involved with direct crisis management consultancy at the Centre for Crisis & Risk Communications. Motivation to help organisations directly drove him on from academia. He didn't just want to analyse, find coping strategies and train students to help in the long term: He wanted to get back in the middle of the action. So, he now finds himself in the midst of all those organisational crises that overwhelm organisations, from sudden shitstorms to more slowly developing hurricanes that gather over the organisation. Before, as now, his focus is always: 'Think of those affected first. Who are the victims of this crisis, and what can we do for them? It may cost something, but it must be the primary focus, and behaving responsibly will benefit your reputation in the long run', he stresses.

9.9.1 Digital Change: And Yet Not

His research was intensive both before and during the digital transformation of communication channels, so he can speak on studies with and without those opportunities and challenges. 'It obviously has major implications but not for the core of crisis communication. When I developed my Situational Crisis Communication Theory (SCCT) in 2007, I emphasised that crisis management must match the situation, the degree of crisis, the degree to which you can be held accountable and the threat to reputation, and that's pretty much still the case' the professor says.

Professional communicators have to curate a possible crisis based on a situational assessment, and new media have enabled many new ways of monitoring: 'Today, it is possible to scan stakeholder responses in a completely different way than before; for example by monitoring SoMe. The analysis of data, which can also be automated to a certain extent, is becoming increasingly important in order to be able to act proactively on possible crises' he explains. To him, it is important that crises are not defined wrongly. Many make the mistake of too quickly defining the crisis from their own perspective. This may cause a completely erroneous assessment of the crisis from the perspective of other stakeholders.

> As a professional communicator, you should not act on your own experience of the crisis but rather on your stakeholders' assessment of the crisis. And it's often not quite the same, as the internal crisis assessment is sometimes biased.

Crisis management is thus very much about being able to analyse the situation correctly and being able to choose the right response. With all the digital options, that response has, of course, many added possibilities. 'At one time, the only options you had were a media interview or a press conference. Professional communicators can now use numerous channels and act through numerous organisational voices'.

As an example, the professor mentions the power of credibility. Time and again, studies show that credibility is attributed to any ordinary employee who mentions a possible crisis, for example on social media. 'In terms of a communication plan, the choice of words is not always perfect when an employee mentions a situation to his or her followers on social media or in the comments to other people's posts, but their credibility is high' he stresses. 'That inclusiveness for multiple voices is essential in modern crisis management: Employees are also key ambassadors during crises', he stresses.

From Timothy Coombs' perspective, social media should be used mainly for listening—alternatively to smart, strategic communication, but that requires a strong community in the organisation. He smiles whilst telling of a crisis in the aviation industry a little whilst back. The crisis affected both Southwest Airlines and American Airlines. Southwest Airlines actively managed the crisis on their well-functioning social media channels, providing their community with good explanations and clear communication about the reasons that some planes had to stay on the ground to be checked before getting back in the air, explaining what that meant for the traffic situation and each passenger's orientation options. American Airlines probably saw how well it worked and rushed to establish itself on social media.

However, the outcome was somewhat ludicrous; without followers, the only target for their crisis management and communication was themselves. This anecdote points directly to the relational part of crisis management—another important framework of understanding for professional communicators. It is not simply about channel options but about relationships with key stakeholders and the channels in which that relationship exists.

9.9.2 The Hierarchical Fallacy

Crisis management has many built-in pitfalls, according to Coombs. He attributes some of them to hierarchical fallacies: 'Many people think that it's necessarily the CEO's task to speak on behalf of the organisation, but we're not able to document that in research. On the contrary. In a few cases, where famous directors are known by all, it can be a powerful weapon, but fame and the significance of the title are often overrated', he stresses. 'The key is that the organisation takes responsibility and acts, and it can be represented in various ways'.

The professional communicator must decide which people are best suited for the task at hand. For example, should it be an expert within a specific field? Or an experienced employee with a long history, providing perspective? Or a senior manager? 'It's very much about the person and their personal qualifications as a communicator', he says with a twinkle in his eye. 'Some people are much better at making use of the written word than videos or press conferences, for example'. Those are the considerations of any professional communicator as part of the crisis management plan.

9.9.3 Intuitive Decisions Guided by Strategy

According to Coombs, the best crisis responses appear to be those where the communicator allows intuition to influence them, but a clear crisis strategy guides the approach: 'Having some guiding principles for your response is necessary. You have to analyse. But you also have to be able to act in the moment and, for example, have a contingency plan ready to deal with the response necessary, for example on social media. Falling silent, for instance, won't do you any good, but the fact that you can't be everywhere at once will be understood, as long as you remember to let people know', he stresses.

He also makes it clear that you often become wiser and change your behaviour in the course of the crisis management situation. An example of such a successful change could be a crisis at Amazon. They had accidentally given customers access to e-books without the rights being in place. The books were quickly withdrawn, but the explanation was complex, and customers were furious, even though they knew that they would get their money back. Fortunately, someone in the crisis team realised the situation: They did the necessary follow-up and started communicating in a different way.

The intuitive decisions and necessary interaction with other actors, both inside and outside the organisation, require a communicator with a high level of emotional intelligence. Unfortunately, Timothy Coombs has learned that a lot more work has to be put into developing that one aspect amongst communication students than happens in reality right now. 'Unfortunately, I see a decline in personal development, rather than the necessary strengthening of that dimension. In crisis management, you need to know yourself well, understand others and be competent in interacting under pressure', he stresses.

Pride must never overshadow crisis management—that goes for communicators, top managers and professionals alike. 'It's pretty much like teenagers sometimes; they don't listen, they don't understand common sense, and they overreact when they are caught in a crisis that they find unfair', stresses the expert, whilst once again highlighting the emotional intelligence necessary for the communicator to deal with the 'crisis teenagers'.

9.9.4 Nothing Like a Good Crisis …

'There's nothing like a good crisis to create a strong understanding of the importance of communication and the difference professional communicators can make', Timothy Coombs adds. In his close interaction with practitioners in large organisations around the world, he has seen, time and again, how the communication function has emerged stronger from good crisis management.

'Perhaps the communicator was invited into the right meeting forums a little too late in the pre-crisis build-up. But after a well-managed crisis, where the post-crisis is also used wisely, it can change the whole understanding of the communicative aspect in the organisation. The crisis will be the beginning of a new era where the communicator can work more proactively with crisis management in the future, because they will be involved at the right time', the professor concludes.

He is looking forward to spending more time in the engine room as an advisor, making the difference that motivated him back then in Las Vegas to take an interest in crisis management in the first place.

Timothy Coombs

Until 2022, Timothy Coombs was a professor at Texas A&M University, USA, but he now combines his continued research with an affiliation as an advisor at the Centre for Crisis & Risk Communications. He is world-renowned for his research on crisis communication, which has inspired a situational, strategic and ethical approach to crisis management in theory and practice.

He is the author of hundreds of academic articles in internationally recognised journals and of numerous books, most recently the newly edited version of 'The Handbook of Crisis Communication' from 2023 which he wrote with his wife, Sherry J. Holladay.

Timothy Coombs has received numerous awards for his research and has lectured on crisis management around the world.

References

Arpan, L., & Ewoldsen, D. (2005). Stealing thunder: Analysis of the effects of proactive disclosure of crisis information. *Public Relations Review., 31*, 425–433. https://doi.org/10.1016/j.pubrev.2005.05.003

Baran, B., & Scott, C. (2010). Organizing ambiguity: A grounded theory of leadership and sensemaking within dangerous contexts. *Military Psychology., 22*, S42–S69. https://doi.org/10.1080/08995601003644262

Beck, U. (1986). *Risk society: Towards a new modernity*. University of Munich.

Benoit, W. L. (1995). *Accounts, excuses, and apologies: A theory of image restoration strategies*. State University of New York.

Benoit, W. L. (2020). *Image repair theory, crisis communication* (pp. 105–119). Walter de Gruyter.

Brønn, P. S., & Berg, R. W. (2011). *Corporate communication: A strategic approach to building reputation* (2nd ed.). Gyldendal Akademisk.

Claeys, A.-S., Cauberghe, V., & Leysen, J. (2013). Implications of stealing thunder for the impact of expressing emotions in organisational crisis communication. *Journal of Applied Communication Research, 41*(3), 293–308.

Coombs, W., & Holladay, S. (2014). How publics react to crisis communication efforts: Comparing crisis response reactions across sub-arenas. *Journal of Communication Management, 18*. https://doi.org/10.1108/JCOM-03-2013-0015

Coombs, W. T. (2015). *Ongoing crisis communication: Planning, managing and responding*. Sage.

Coombs, W. (2017). *Revising situational crisis communication theory*. https://doi.org/10.4324/9781315749068-3

Coombs, T. (2017). Origin stories in CSR: Genesis of CSR at British American Tobacco. *Corporate Communications., 22*, 178–191. https://doi.org/10.1108/CCIJ-01-2016-0007

Coombs, T. (2019). Political public relations and crisis communication. In *Political public relations* (pp. 208–226). https://doi.org/10.4324/9781351053143-10

Coombs, W. T. (2021). Crisis communication through the lens of strategic communication. In C. H. Botan (Ed.), *The handbook of strategic communication* (pp. 181–193). Wiley.

Coombs, W. T., & Holladay, S. J. (2023). *The handbook of crisis communication* (2nd ed.). Wiley.

Cornelissen, J. P. (2020). *Corporate communication: A guide to theory & practice* (6th ed.). Sage.

Frandsen, F., & Johansen, W. (2007). *Krisekommunikation – når virksomhedens image og omdømme er truet*. Forlaget Samfundslitteratur.

Frandsen, F., & Johansen, W. (2011a). Rhetoric, climate change and corporate identity management. *Management Communication Quarterly, 25*(3), 511–530.

Frandsen, F., & Johansen, W. (2011b). The study of internal crisis communication: Towards an integrative framework. *Corporate Communications, 16*(4), 347–361.

References

Frandsen, F., & Johansen, W. (2017). *Strategic communication*. Wiley.
Frandsen, F., & Johansen, W. (2017). *Organizational crisis communication: A multivocal approach*. Sage.
Frandsen, F., & Johansen, W. (Eds.). (2020a). *Crisis communication* (1st ed.). De Gruyter Mouton.
Frandsen, F., & Johansen, W. (2020b). Advice on communicating during crisis: A study of popular crisis management books. *International Journal of Business Communication (Thousand Oaks, Calif.), 57*(2), 260–276.
Frandsen, F., & Johansen, W. (2023). Corporate crisis management: Managing Covid-19 in Denmark, Sweden and Norway. In I B. Johansson, Ø. Ihlen, J. Lindholm, & M. Blach-Ørsten (red.), *Communicating a pandemic: Crisis management and Covid-19 in the Nordic countries* (s. 173-194). Nordicom. https://www.nordicom.gu.se/en/publications/communicatingpandemic
Gephart, R. P., Jr., Miller, C. C., & Helgesson, K. S. (2019). Crisis communication: The best evidence from research. In *The Routledge companion to risk, crisis and emergency management* (Routledge companions in business, management and marketing). Routledge.
Habermas, (1975). *Legitimation Crisis*. Beacon Press.
Heath, R. L. (2018a). How fully functioning is communication engagement if society does not benefit? In K. A. Johnston & M. Taylor (Eds.), *The handbook of communication engagement* (pp. 33–47). Wiley Blackwell.
Heath, R. L. (2018b). Strategic issues management. In O. Ihlen & R. L. Heath (Eds.), *The handbook of organisational rhetoric and communication* (pp. 383–399). Wiley.
Heide, M., & Simonsson, C. (2014). Developing internal crisis communication. *Corporate Communications, 19*(2), 128–146.
Heide, M., & Simonsson, C. (2019). *Internal crisis communication crisis awareness, leadership and coworkership*. Routledge.
Johansen, & Frandsen. (2007). *Krisekommunikation*, Forlaget Samfundslitteratur.
Johansen, W., Aggerholm, H. K., & Frandsen, F. (2012). Entering new territory: A study of internal crisis management and crisis communication in organisations. *Public Relations Review, 38*(2), 270–279.
Macnamara, J. (2021a). A 'macro' view of strategic communication management: Beyond 'siloes', dominant paradigms and pandemics. *ESSACHESS, 14*(1), 65–91.
Macnamara, J. (2021b). New insights into crisis communication from an 'inside' emic perspective during COVID-19. *Public Relations Inquiry, 10*(2), 237–262.
Mitroff, I. I. (2022). Making strange connections: The challenge of crisis management. *Business and Society Review (1974), 127*(S1), 163–165.
Pace, K. M., Fediuk, T. A., & Botero, I. C. (2010). The acceptance of responsibility and expressions of regret in organizational apologies after a transgression. *Corporate Communications, 15*(4), 410–427.
Pearson, C. M., & Clair, J. A. (1998). Reframing crisis management. *The Academy of Management Review, 23*(1), 59–76.
Shrivastava, P., & Mitroff, I. I. (1987). Strategic management of corporate crises. *Journal of World Business: JWB, 22*(1).
Špoljarić, A. (2021). Managing crisis communication via social media. *Nase Gospodarstvo: NG, 67*(1), 23–32.
Sternthal, B., Phillips, L. W., & Dholakia, R. (1978). The persuasive effect of source credibility: A situational analysis. *The Public Opinion Quarterly, 42*(3), 285–314. http://www.jstor.org/stable/2748294
Strandberg, J. M., & Vigsø, O. (2016). Internal crisis communication: An employee perspective on narrative, culture, and sense making. *Corporate Communications: An International Journal, 21*, 89–102.
Tkalac Verčič, A., & Špoljarić, A. (2020). Managing internal communication: How the choice of channels affects internal communication satisfaction. *Public Relations Review, 46*(3).
Tormala, Z. L., & Petty, R. E. (2004). Resistance to persuasion and attitude certainty: The moderating role of elaboration. *Personality and Social Psychology Bulletin, 30*(11), 1446–1457.
Weick, K. E. (2002). Essai: Real-Time reflexivity: Prods to reflection. *Organization Studies, 23*(6), 893–898. https://doi.org/10.1177/0170840602236011

Skills of the Future

10

What does it take to master the role of a professional communicator in a changing world? The requirements are complex and wide-ranging. It is necessary to have strategic understanding, analytical skills, the ability to design, plan and implement good solutions, as well as an understanding of channel options, technology and strong communication skills. But it is also crucial to be able to stand in the middle of organisational power spaces, to build followership and to work according to a well-calibrated ethical compass. This chapter identifies the competencies necessary for the professional communicator to inspire the constant work of developing communication.

In the chapter's case, Maersk articulates what the organisation has emphasised in the ongoing skills development of their communicators, with a major investment in an academy to match the challenges of the times.

The chapter's international expert is Professor Ralph Tench of Leeds University, who has been following the skills landscape for communicators for decades and has five tips for the professional communicator.

The professional communicator needs many skills. As to what exactly these skills are, opinions abound. A useful division for accessing skills is to distinguish between what you need to know, have specific abilities to do, and what personal qualities you need to possess in order to be able to master the many roles of the professional communicator. The division comes from Tench and Moreno (2015), who define skills as a combination of the individual communicator's ability to have a 'goal-directed, well-organised behaviour that is acquired through practice and performed with economy of effort', i.e. the necessary knowledge and the personal attributes that can promote or inhibit the ability to put knowledge and skills into practice. These three elements constitute the necessary skills in professional communication endeavours, as shown in Fig. 10.1.

The point of this division is that all three elements are necessary to ensure concrete competences in practice: 'the mix of skills and knowledge held by a

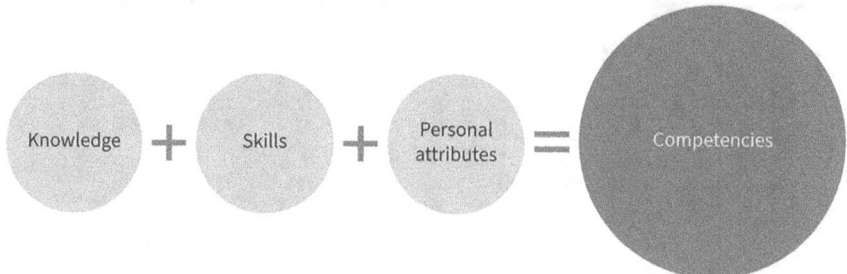

Fig. 10.1 Skills, knowledge and personal attributes constitute competencies. Source: Tench et al. (2017: 141)

practitioner, which combine with personal attributes to produce effective professional behaviours' (Tench & Moreno, 2015: 44). This definition clarifies that developing one's skills does not only happen by burying oneself in theoretical books because knowledge is only one element of the professional communicator's overall competence. It is also crucial to work on your personality and your ability to translate knowledge and ambitions into effective action.

This categorisation can provide a stable framework for developing the skills of the professional communicator, as it is far more unchangeable than, for example the many changing roles that the communicator has to master. As Jeffrey and Bruntons put it: '... roles outline tasks and responsibilities in the job description, in today's dynamic workplace these same roles are likely to change frequently. In contrast, competencies are the underlying foundational abilities that are integral to successfully carrying out the tasks and responsibilities and thus remain a stable blueprint for practice over time' (Jeffrey & Brunton, 2011: 60).

Zerfass et al. (2021) combine the various perspectives and take as their starting point five roles, which are concretised with the skills required for each role. The roles are communicator, coach, advisor, manager and ambassador, respectively, and are shown in Fig. 10.2.

Overall, Zerfass et al. (2021) show that professional communicators in Europe perceive themselves as having mastered very specific communicative skills (77.1%), just as the role of advisor is perceived to be a role that they have the skills to master (57.6%). It is apparently slightly more difficult to be an ambassador (55.4%) and even more difficult to be a coach (53.7%), whilst less than half (49.8%) feel they have management skills.

My best advice is to stay focused on what is needed when you prepare to become a future communication professional. It is very easy to get lost in the latest beauty war on 'so-needed skills'. Find out what you want to contribute with—you cannot become an expert in all fields. Do you want to be a community manager, a data analyst or an expert CCO on crisis communication? Choose your path, know the shared basics but be a specialist as well. Our biggest task as communicators is to help maintain trust by listening to societal voices and encouraging organisations to be present. Communicators of the future need not only sit at the right tables in the organisational hierarchy but use their voices at that table by bringing in facts and knowledge.

– Dr Ángeles Moreno is a leading international researcher and professor at Rey Juan Carlos University in Spain (Spain). She is a former President of the European Public Relations Research and Education Association (EUPRERA).

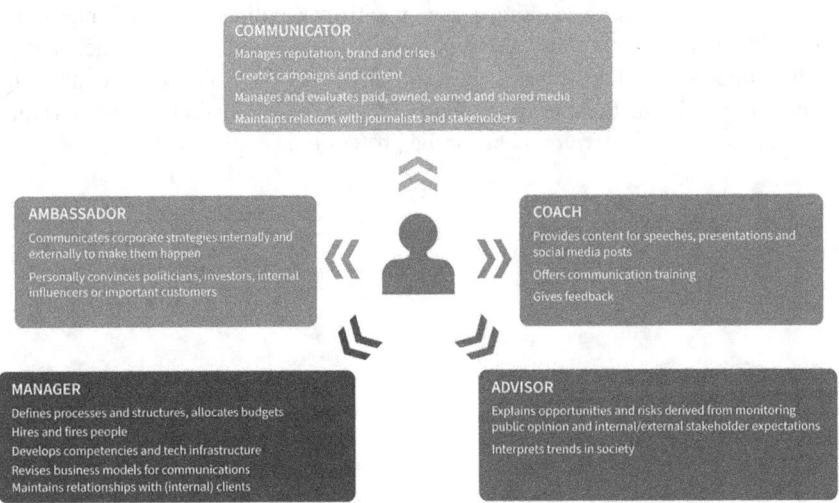

Fig. 10.2 Different roles of the communicator in daily work. Source: Zerfass et al. (2021)

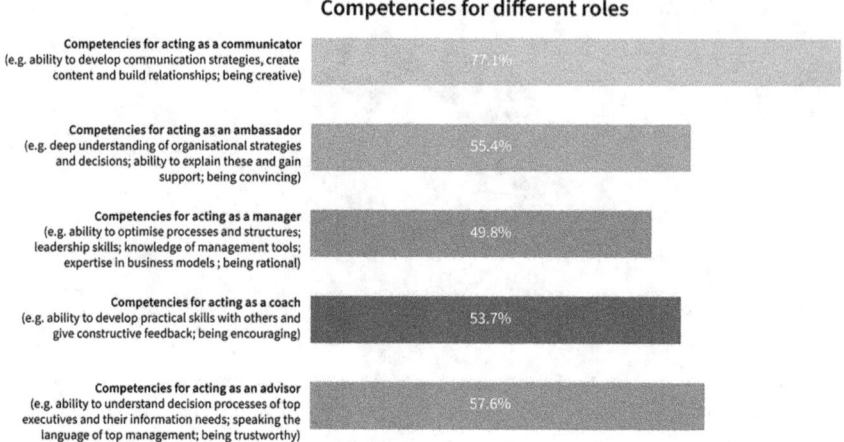

Fig. 10.3 Communicators' perception of their own competencies. Source: Zerfass et al. (2021)

As Fig. 10.3 shows, the survey respondents point out, for example that the advisor must be able to explain opportunities and risks by monitoring stakeholders' expectations and attitudes and understanding trends in society. Perspectives that point to both useful knowledge and individual tools. To get closer to the specific skills of the professional communicator, we may start with the detailed and nuanced overview from Tench and Topić (2018) in Fig. 10.4, which elaborates on how knowledge, skills and personal attributes can be accessed based on the communicator's various roles. The first column of the model lists the six overarching competencies: advising, organising, leading, communicative execution, analysing/interpreting and guiding/supporting. The next columns summarise the knowledge, skills—divided into soft and hard—and personal attributes on which each competency should be based. The table is a very thorough and specific listing of potential focus areas for future skills development for the professional communicator.

10 Skills of the Future

COMPETENCY	KNOWLEDGE	SKILLS - HARD	SKILLS - SOFT (Human & conceptual)	PERSONAL ATTRIBUTES	
Counselling (building relationships, consulting, coaching)	Languages; Intercultural theory and issues; Learning curves of coworkers; Personality profiles	Diversity; Consulting; Consensus building; Negotiation	Team building; Conflict resolution; Persuasive communication; Motivation	Empathy; Trustworthiness; Team minded (worker); Negotiation; Sympathetic; Political intuition; Authenticity; Patience/tolerance	Participative; Sociable; Authority; Calmness; Self-criticism; Responsiveness; Self-awareness; Humour
Organising/executing (planning, making it happen)	Corporate strategy; Financial systems; Planning systems; Project management	Writing; Strategy; Planning; Project management; Time management; Administration; Organisational skills; Creativity with budgets	Strategic thinking; Planning; Decision making	Composure; Energy; Competitive; Leadership; Enthusiasm; Perseverance/resilience	Self-reliance; Multi-tasking; Proactivity; Agility/flexibility; Results orientation
Managing (cross-functional awareness, business focus)	Management; Economics; Branding; Law; Knowledge about own organisation; Business systems; General knowledge; Risk management; Stakeholder management; Public affairs/political dynamics; Change management; Language of the board; Understanding of own business model	Mapping (organisational network systems); Leadership	Negotiation; Influencing; Delegating; Managing people; Sense of timing (when to communicate)	Confidence; Global and strategic vision; Diplomacy; Experience; Courage; Daring/risk taking (and being willing to fail and learn from this); Stress resistance; Adaptability	
Performing and creating (craft e.g., writing, design, presentation)	New technologies; Communication processes; Web 2.0 tools and effects on organisational communication; Media systems and structures; Intercultural aspects of communication messages and products; Global media environment	Writing; Editing; Design skills; Computer writing skills; Multimedia skills; Visioning; Verbal coherence/concision	Communication; Presentation; Creative problem solving; Story telling	Communicative; Entrepreneurial; Polyvalence/supporting diverse and differing perceptions; Initiative; Lifelong learner; Innovative and creative; Enquiring; Openness; Pioneering	
Analysing/interpreting (research, listening)	Research and analysis methods; Human Resources (HR) policies and links to communication; Prediction/forecasting; Monitoring tools; Web monitoring tools; Listening, understanding and interpreting trends, linking them to business strategies; Recognising trends	Critical thinking; Reading comprehension; Research; Social environmental analysis	Forecasting; Listening	Curiosity; Questioning; Good judgement; Strong instincts	
Supporting/guiding (vision and standards, ethics, developing others)	Corporate governance; Ethics/ethical frameworks; Legal issues		Visioning	Ethical and socially responsible; Authority; Integrity; Honesty; Influence; Reputation; Sincerity; Objectivity; Sensitivity/humanity	

Fig. 10.4 Overview of the competencies of the professional communicator. Source: Tench and Topić (2018)

As a communicator, you have to understand how to seize the moments of dialogue in a changing and mediatised world. This means not putting your organisation at the centre of the world, but understanding what is important to the world right now and being able to connect credibly to the ongoing conversation. Dialogue is also not just an intention but a quality of communication itself that all communicators must master in the future. Therefore, it is important to be aware of the world's dialogues, to be able to act quickly, strategically and in a communicatively wise way.

– Professor Øyvind Ihlen, University of Oslo, Norway. Internationally recognised researcher in strategic communication, Corporate Social Responsibility (CSR) and public communication.

Figure 10.4 shows, for example that the advisor role is generally defined by skills in building relationships, counselling and coaching. This requires specific knowledge of language, intercultural theory, learning curves and personal profiles. The advisor's skills must be both hard and soft, where the hard skills are about negotiation and counselling, whilst the softer skills are being able to persuade and motivate. This must be brought into play as competent advice by mastering one's own personal qualities, where empathy, integrity and personality are emphasised. Whilst the analyst requires knowledge of research and analytical methods, HR, forecasting, measurement methods and understanding of trends. The analyst's skills are critical thinking, reading, interpretation, research and analysis (which are categorised as hard skills) and predicting and listening (which are categorised as soft skills). In addition, the analyst role calls for personal qualities such as curiosity, an inquisitive approach, good judgement and strong intuition.

By looking in this way at very specific skills, it becomes clearer where the professional communicator needs to work to strengthen his/her position, depending on the role to be taken in the communication work.

To be a future communication professional you need to have business acumen and to master strategic thinking. This allows you to align business strategy and communication. But first and foremost, you should focus on how to create value for all your stakeholders from investors to employees. In your daily work life, you must be able to prioritise. You are asked to do so many things, but you have to do what is most important for your organisation—something which is very specific in each situation. You must be able to make a convincing argument of why your focus and your way to communicate is the right choice. Don't lean too much on best practices and experiences around you. This is mainly about the past. Instead, be aware of the present and the possibilities of the future with new technology at hand.

– Professor Ansgar Zerfass, Leipzig University, Germany. Internationally recognised researcher in strategic communication and lead researcher of www.commmunicationmonitor.eu

Gone are the days when communication was just simple. It's not just about communicating and using all channels wisely. We need to help organisations deal with paradoxes. We can't just take one issue at a time—it's all interconnected in a new complexity. So we must have the courage to facilitate the big discussions and mediate any conflicts. Communicators must help people understand the ambiguity and accept the uncertainty. We can do this, for example, by helping them to zoom in and out on the issues, frame and reframe to create a nuanced and multifaceted view. This is the prerequisite for creating visions that can be realised.

– Linda Putnam is Professor Emeritus of Communication at the University of Santa Barbara, USA. She is world-renowned for her work on organisational communication, paradoxes and conflicts from the broad societal and organisational perspective, through the human and down to the smallest nuances of language.

10.1　From the Point of View of the Communication Industry

If we ask communicators what skills development should be particularly focused on, data from the European Communication Monitor shows that 'Communication professionals should (1) have a social and empathic antenna, (2) be able to produce and deliver effective messages, (3) have research skills and organisational management skills and (4) have knowledge about society' (Tench et al., 2017: 142).

In addition, there is a desire to strengthen knowledge and skills in technology, business and management: 'communications professionals stated they need more training in technical knowledge, technical skills, business knowledge and skills and management knowledge and skills' (Tench & Topić, 2018: 3).

US surveys of communicators conducted by the Arthur Pages Society suggest that communicators of the future will need to take ownership of the organisation's brand, become more involved in the social contract and move from working solely on internal communication to facilitating a meaningful cultural system. Based on these changes, four paths for the development of the communication function are identified:

- Moving from a digital focus to leading the way with the integrated use of relevant communication technologies (CommTech) that put the organisation in direct contact with stakeholders.
- Moving from defining and creating organisational narratives to securing and managing reputation with true brand stewardship.
- Moving from messaging with internal communication to creating and driving a modern business culture.
- Moving from communicating about CSR initiatives to facilitating societal value creation (Page, 2019).

In the study's projections, to be a role model, the professional communicator must work proactively, be able to handle dynamic content and be able to target relevant stakeholders effectively and accurately. According to Page, this requires, amongst other things, that the professional communicator can work actively with risk analysis and with nuanced data processing.

The importance of having communication technology skills is fundamentally emphasised in surveys, and here communicators themselves are a little flustered or perhaps even a little frightened. Data from the European Communication Monitor 2022 certainly shows that it is an agenda that over a third of communicators admit to not following very closely, as shown in Fig. 10.5—a worrying figure, considering what the future holds.

CommTech is not to be overlooked or avoided by the communicator of the future, but it is not an end in itself; rather, insight into CommTech is fundamental knowledge that the professional communicator must have and be able to put into practice with the right communicative skills. Communication technology must be integrated into the solutions that are designed and developed, both as a channel and as a working tool for development and research, where chatbots, for example offer a lot of new potential. Whereas in the past it was necessary to understand the reader's experience of a leaflet and adapt the communication material accordingly, today the communicator must

10.1 From the Point of View of the Communication Industry   221

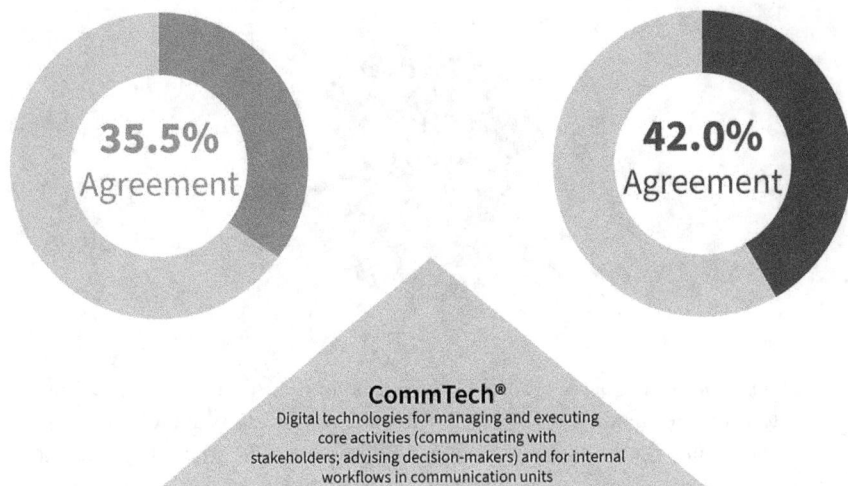

Fig. 10.5 European communicators' own perception of the focus on CommTech. Source: Zerfass et al. (2022)

understand where the key stakeholders are and which channels and forms of communication will work effectively in communicating with them. This requires the use of creative and practical skills, for example when creating an impactful film for LinkedIn, a broadcast for shareholders or a 'reel' for followers on Instagram.

We need to do away with the idea that communication is considered external in too many organisations. Communication is absolutely central to organisations—and only by giving communicators a mandate can organisations handle issues and crises without turning them into double crises or avoiding excessive polarisation, including internally. This requires communicators to have high ethical standards, to be analytical both qualitatively and quantitatively—and not only to communicate but to listen to all stakeholders—including internal ones—in order to safeguard credibility and trust.

– Professor Winni Johansen, Aarhus University, is one of the world's leading researchers in crisis communication

In our research on trustworthiness we have identified four key orientations. People orient to their own and others' truth and honesty, stake and interest, knowledge and ability and consistency and predictability when they work to come across as trustworthy themselves or to decide if they can trust others.
– Professor Mie Femø Nielsen, University of Copenhagen, a leading researcher within international communication & trust

10.2 Prioritised Skills Development

Today, the professional communicator's field of work is so wide-ranging that in practice it can be expedient to look at skills development visualised as a T-shape (Cheetham & Chivers, 1996), which shows the overall breadth of skills as well as the depth of skills in individual areas. The breadth of skills is illustrated in Fig. 10.6 as the crossbar of the letter, which describes the overall approach to being a professional communicator as working analytically, planning, implementing and evaluating with a fundamental professional knowledge. The overall skills are further supported by core skills in a specific field, where you have deep knowledge, experience and high-level craft skills. This is illustrated as the vertical line of the letter.

By working concretely with a T-approach, you can prioritise your skills development to cultivate both generic skills and core skills in areas such as social media, strategic communication or design.

The overall skills include the communicator's analytical and strategic skills. The professional communicator understands organisations, including their driving forces, ambitions and organisational culture, and understands people, communication channels and the interaction in and with society. This knowledge can be applied strategically and analytically. The professional communicator must be able to base his or her efforts on a clear link to the current strategy of the organisation, both on the go and in the design of large, effective initiatives and ensure the impact of the communicative work by analysing all stakeholders. The analytical skills are thus a way of translating knowledge about the business and stakeholders into concrete goals for the initiatives to be implemented.

10.2 Prioritised Skills Development

Too many communication products in organisational practice are evidence that communicators have rushed through the work process or have gotten carried away by a creative impulse or an order from an internal stakeholder. Examples include excessively long films on internal social media, campaigns that are not directly linked to the company's strategy, or advice that becomes too general and not directly targeted to create impact. Many communicators are reluctant to engage in the analytical part of communication work due to their busy schedules. However, an analytical and strategic approach helps to ensure the quality of the communication material and can often be carried out quite effectively by answering the very basic

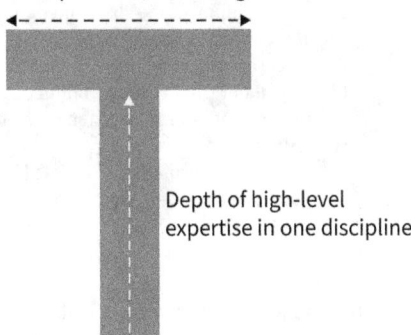

Fig. 10.6 Skills visualised in a T-shape. Source: Model inspired from Cheetham and Chivers (1996)

T-Shaped Skills

Breadth of experience, knowledge & skills

Depth of high-level expertise in one discipline

Today, not communicating is not an option, so we have to prepare for complex and emergent situations. To do that you must lead with purpose. Think of what you want to achieve yourself, then look at the situation in which you communicate. That situation will be complex and you will not be able to anticipate it completely. The best we can do is plan for the process.
– Professor Sine Just, University of Roskilde, Denmark, a leading researcher in rhetoric, trust and digitalisation.

Photo: Christian Falck Wolff/DMJX

> My advice for future communication professionals is to use internal social media for strategic internal communication. With the support from top managers, they should encourage employees to share their knowledge, thoughts and suggestions on internal social media and most importantly they should use internal social media to listen to the concerns of the employees. And here I mean really listen carefully. So, instead of thinking about what we as communicators want to say to the organisation, I think the most important thing is to listen to the employees and respond to their thoughts and suggestions.
> – Associate Professor Vibeke Thøis Madsen, Danish School of Media and Journalism, a leading researcher in internal social media

questions: How is the product linked to the strategy, what is the objective and what do we know about the stakeholders?

Of course, there are situations that require a deeper analysis of stakeholders' attitudes, barriers and desires, but an analytical and strategic approach is a necessary starting point for the professional communicator regardless.

In addition, planning and orchestration skills are key. These skills are often underestimated by the professional communicator. It is very much about taking responsibility for and ensuring that the given task is properly orchestrated. For example, has the right channel mix been chosen to succeed? Is the right team of organisational voices being brought into play? Are the organisational voices ready to deliver at the required quality, or do they need to be trained beforehand? And are the technical and practical elements in place?

It is often about activating both CommTech skills and psychological understanding of how to reach stakeholders in the right way. Planning is crucial, whether it's planning a major change where a change plan is needed to guide the process, organising a virtual town hall meeting with many organisational voices in an event script, or simply planning a text for the intranet where the plan is only a psychologically savvy outline.

The planning and orchestration skills are about mastering strategic architecture to find a good (dynamic) plan for a process that can translate goals and ambitions into reality.

10.2 Prioritised Skills Development

Today's communication landscape is challenging and ever-changing, so prepare for a loss of control but prepare anyway. The urge to control the narrative has always been strong in politicians and CEOs, but control is not possible in today's multi-platform society and probably never has been. So instead, prepare to listen, engage, learn and respond.
– Professor Mark Ørsten, University of Roskilde, Denmark, a leading researcher within legitimisation, journalism and democracy

Even the best plan will not be realised if the professional communicator does not have the communication skills and personality to turn ambition into reality. Here, all elements of competence must be combined: knowledge, skills and personal qualities. If it is, for example a facilitation task that needs to be carried out where the goal is to support a change process over an extended period of time, then knowledge of the effective change, analytical and strategic anchoring skills, planning and, not least, the ability to create good communication products must all come into play. However, you can only succeed in the role of change facilitator if you have the personal qualities and skills that enable you to create trust with key stakeholders and the courage to ensure the right solutions even under pressure.

The same applies if the task is a quick piece of advice in passing—this too will only succeed if the right skills for implementation can be mastered, from the personal relationship to the effective questioning technique, the ability to co-create good solutions and, not least, credible impact that ensures the advisor is followed.

Production tasks also only succeed with both a good plan and the ability to translate it into effective communication, whether it is a mobile video for a personal SoMe presentation for a manager or an opinion piece for a boss. It takes strong critical, analytical ability, a creative mindset and good craftsmanship to produce everything from articles and speeches to catchy posts with mobile videos.

It is in the implementation that the professional communicator really shows his or her worth, and these are skills that require training. With the speed at which organisations work, it is essential that the professional communicator masters both the strategic and the concrete craft in one and the same movement.

Evaluation skills have always been central to ensuring quality and developing both communication and the communicator, but evaluation has become increasingly central to communication work because many communication products can be adjusted and updated. This reinforces the need to be able to distance oneself from the specific product and assess more objectively whether it fulfils the original goal and whether changes in the external environment mean that the plan needs to be adjusted. It may also be that adjustments are necessary due to viewing data or a comment track that is either empty or overcrowded. The evaluation skills have shifted from being reactive or proactive to being constantly active. Evaluation skills are used reactively, for example when there is a need to document success. They are used proactively as a starting point for new development, and they are now also used continuously to ensure an active evaluative preparedness that makes it possible to continuously adjust initiatives.

Evaluation can encompass many methods and possibilities. For example, central 'Key Performance Indicators' that monitor the impact of the communication function, or larger measurements and evaluations involving quantitative and qualitative methods. However, it can also be simple evaluative analyses: How much engagement did my post on Yammer generate? What do people seem to react to positively or negatively? And what can I deduce from that? Evaluation can also be done in, for example, small focus groups with employees who are part of an organisational change, where professional communicators check in to assess the impact of communication in order to improve future efforts.

Common to all evaluations is the need to go beyond one's own bias as part of the solution and take a real look at the quality of the communication effort from the perspective of the intended stakeholder group.

Then there is the individual reflective evaluation, ensuring that you are constantly developing as a professional communicator. This can be difficult to do alone, and it is always a good idea to seek feedback from colleagues and stakeholders. But it is also a mindset. The professional communicator can take small constructive pit stops in everyday life to review the individual feat: What works well, what could be done even better and how? As a professional communicator, you are your own instrument, and it needs to be well-oiled, tuned and maintained.

With the speed of change, skills development is more important than ever before. The professional communicator has a key role to play in the age of stakeholder capitalism. Skills development is a constant and ongoing effort for both individual communicators and organisations to achieve the strongest possible communication functions. As the book has shown, it is about working both strategically and with high quality in the specific communication, so that the professional communicator never fails the core of the communicative DNA: The professional communicator must support the organisation's direction, meaning and reputation by working both in an advisory and an executive capacity. This requires versatile development of competence focusing on knowledge, skills and personal qualities to ensure success because the communicator is his or her own instrument.

10.2 Prioritised Skills Development

While consistency is generally important, I'd recommend not taking the consistency demand too seriously. The trick is to learn to work with differences between what the company is currently doing and what it hopes to achieve. In other words, work professionally with aspirational talk.

– Professor Lars Thøger Christensen, Copenhagen Business School, leading researcher on how organisations make sense of themselves and their surroundings through communicative practices.

An open communication environment is a prerequisite for internal communication. To be successful with your internal communication, you need to understand your organisation's communication environment. If your organisation is characterised by a closed communication environment with little trust between employees and management, it will be difficult to improve the impact of internal communication. In other words, an open communication environment where employees feel comfortable expressing their opinions is a prerequisite for successful internal communication.

– Marianne Wolff Lundholt is a PhD, MA and researcher in corporate communication at the University of Southern Denmark. She is head of the Department of Design, Media and Educational Science.

10.3 Case 9. Future Skills at Maersk

Rapid and radical transformation of an organisation requires more than patient, organic skills development. That is why Maersk decided to make an extraordinary investment in a tailor-made academy for the entire organisation's communication team. The ambition was to create a common frame of reference for what good communication is at Maersk, introduce a shared toolbox and stimulate a professionally curious and learning culture. The aim was to put Maersk at the forefront of the most important trends in communication and corporate positioning.

When Maersk decided to work more systematically with joint competence development, the focus was not only on knowledge but also on skills and personal competences, so that the individual's competence was strengthened as a whole (Tench, et al. 2017). At the same time, there was also an ambition to create even greater synergies across teams, just as quality and speed in the new communicative reality were in focus. In a global communications function like Maersk's, it is obvious to look at skills with a T-shape perspective (Cheetham & Chivers, 1996), because a focus on specialisation is crucial in the communications function. It is important and necessary to have specialists in the individual teams, who are, for example the person you go to for help with the great video, the great graphics or the specialised change advice. At the same time, it is a great strength if the whole unit has the same overall approach to their roles in the organisation, works with the same quality consciousness and coordinates wisely across the board.

The management of the communications function was very keen that the Academy should build on its already solid starting point with the ambition to become even better. Consequently, a great deal of time was spent discussing what the ambitions actually were, what developments they wanted to be at the forefront of, and what direction the Academy should help to set. As shown in Chap. 2, the many discussions culminated in the definition of the 'strategic producer' (Fig. 10.7). Regardless of specialisation, all professional communicators at Maersk had to master this role. As strategic producers, they had to meet stakeholders and communication tasks with the same strategic, psychological and rhetorical mindset, so that they were always strategically anchored, could create followership and deliver high quality at the necessary pace.

The purpose of the Academy was to make the individual communicator even better at creating a real effect from the communicative efforts in a reality with a short 'attention span' amongst all stakeholders, as well as working on the strategic producer's own qualities—i.e. the knowledge of their own strengths and weaknesses and individual work on, for example strengthening their communicative impact. To ensure that the focus was the right one, also from the employees' point of view, an anonymous questionnaire survey was conducted early in the process, where everyone could express how they assessed their own strengths and challenges and what the Academy needed to focus on in terms of knowledge, tools and space for personal development (Fig. 10.8). Individuals could, of course, choose to share their answers with their line manager, but the data was only used for the unit and individual teams.

10.3 Case 9. Future Skills at Maersk

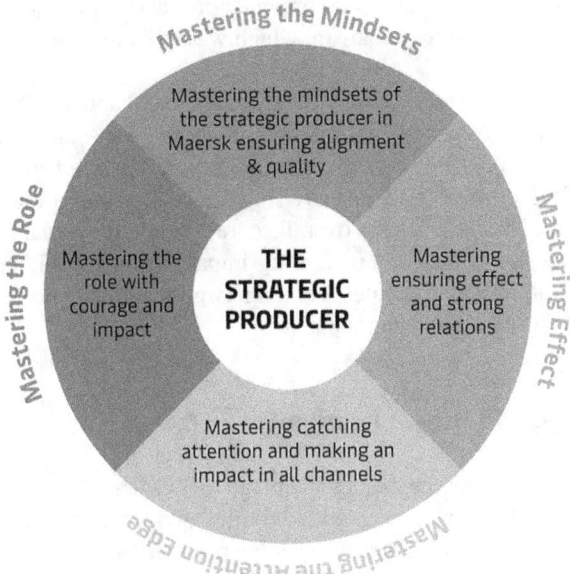

Fig. 10.7 An overview of the Academy's professional elements centred on mastering the role of strategic producer

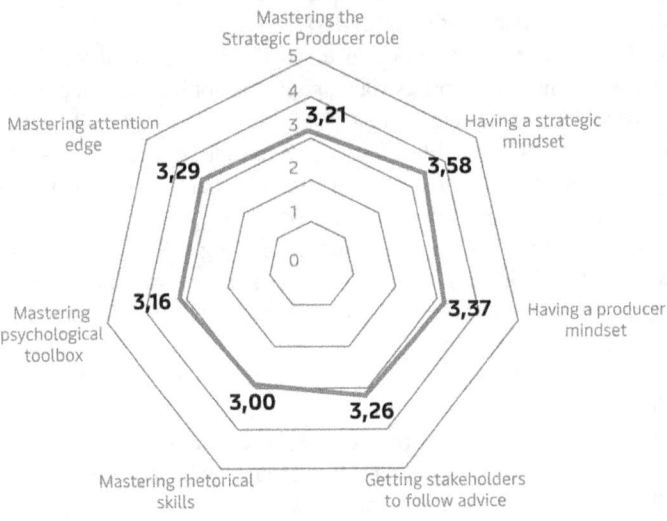

Fig. 10.8 First survey of professional communicators' assessment of their own strengths and challenges

Overall, this survey showed that communicators basically considered themselves to have a high level of professionalism, which was to be expected in a skilled communications function.

At the same time, it was clear that there was a general appetite for improvement, expressed both as a desire for higher scores in various work areas and in the open comments sections of the survey. For example, techniques for mastering the creation of rhetorical followership when advising in a large organisation were requested (scoring 3.0 out of 5 as the lowest overall score). Many individual comments indicated a strong desire to focus on increasing impact and a specific need to become better at moderating panel debates, running large meetings and producing short films as part of the communicator's palette.

10.3.1 Strategic Producer Academy

Based on the ambitions of the management and the wishes of the employees, a final design of the Academy was decided. Activities and methods were numerous to ensure that the Academy was not just a training programme, but that it had an impact on the work culture and made both teams and individuals more competent. That is why the activities of the Academy were not planned to be carried out quickly but over a long period of time—initially a whole year with a lot of coordinated activities. The management group was a key player both at all seminars and along the way, with a continuous focus on the Academy's themes at team meetings, in solving current tasks and in one-to-one dialogues with individual employees. Active work on sparring across teams and disciplines was also an ongoing activity to strengthen interaction across teams and national borders.

Courses in the Academy were organised as intensive seminars in small teams combined across teams and across borders, so it was not just knowledge sharing but real skills development with time for discussions, exercises and exchange of experiences. The Academy was facilitated by an external trainer who ran the entire Academy to ensure continuity and a fresh, external professional perspective. Management was involved in every class and often integrated into the teaching with presentations and sparring on, e.g. solving cases (Fig. 10.9). The seminars were designed with a mix of professional knowledge, simple tools and lots of exercises and sparring, so it was not just talk and each individual experienced how he/she mastered what was in focus.

Between each seminar, each participant completed more in-depth assignments in which the focus area of the seminar was to be applied to a current task for the individual communicator. The tasks were not only presented to the team at the Academy but also discussed in three-person sparring groups, which were also part of the Academy. These were concrete, everyday tasks, but some also had a broader view of examples from other organisations to inspire their work. The first year of the Academy ended with an individual final assignment, where each strategic producer presented a good example of their work that could be collected in a common canon of inspiring internal examples (Fig. 10.10).

10.3 Case 9. Future Skills at Maersk

Fig. 10.9 A role play with a difficult case in the Academy

Fig. 10.10 The end of the Academy's first year was a physical gathering of all the strategic producers with celebration, mutual inspiration and visits from international thought leaders in the field of communication

Data collection continued throughout the duration of the Academy. Not only to evaluate each seminar so that it could be continuously adapted, but also to create data that could be used to keep skills development on the agenda. Data was continuously shared with the management team so that each manager could follow the team's assessments of the Academy and their overall experience of mastering skills, so that it could be brought up based on current data in the ongoing conversations with the team.

Alongside the Academy's work with the overlay of Cheetham and Chiver's (1996) T-shaped skills model, i.e. Maersk's joint skills development of strategic producers, internal workshops were also initiated focusing on some of the specialised skills needed in the communication function. For example, workshops were facilitated on how to be a moderator and how to create mobile videos and catchy social media posts. The specific workshops were based on the Academy's terminologies but focused on individual skills.

10.3.2 A Stradivarius in Play

A world-famous violin became the metaphor for the necessary focus on a communicator's work with themselves as an instrument. 'We know that as communicators we are part of the task solution, even though it is never about us as individuals. So it was a way to inspire us to look at ourselves as the most important and finest instrument in our work. An instrument that you can't just pick up and make it sound like something without preparation, listening, safe storage and careful maintenance', says Mette Refshauge, Director of Communications.

The fact that it was the world's finest, hand-built violin and not some little wooden recorder was both to honour the individual communicator—you are a very special instrument—and to nurture their awareness of self-care.

Individual communicators need to be aware of how each of them could influence the impact of their work, such as which tools would be the right ones for them to use. For example, some had challenges in maintaining impact in a room of power. Others had a tendency to start solving tasks too quickly and thus lacked strategic anchoring when presenting solutions. Whilst others unknowingly came across as cocky or distanced and thus found it difficult to create followership because there was a gap between advisor and stakeholder, but by working with tone or body language, for example new bridges could be built. Individuals received advice to identify their strengths and challenges and were given input to find the tools that could sharpen them.

'The approach in the Academy was at once shared and individualised, so we tried to make each individual more aware of themselves, and the Stradivarius image was a nice, slightly simpler way of talking constructively about it', says Mette Refshauge.

10.3.3 Quality in Production

Naturally, the Academy emphasised that all cases were anchored in Maersk's strategy and purpose, but it was also important not to insist on an inextricable symbiosis between the strategic and the concrete work of delivering high-quality communication products. 'In the world of communication in general, there has been this slide towards separating strategic advice from operational production and perhaps especially focusing on the quality of the strategic work. But the quality of content production is just as critical at a time when the demand for constant production on all channels is challenging traditional production flows. It was a basic idea in our work in the Academy that the strategic and production work should be intertwined, because we all switch between one and the other many times in the course of a day. At the same time, we wanted to learn about new quality requirements from each other and from the best. This meant that we in management had many good discussions about what we thought was good quality in the individual channels', says Mette Refshauge, who in the same period introduced weekly content meetings in the management team, where each manager was assigned changing roles in relation to evaluating and giving feedback on the last week's content productions. The aim was to learn from good examples and promote a self-critical feedback culture.

In the seminars, strategic producers were both inspired by each other with concrete workflows to deliver high-quality communication with the right use of creativity and critical thinking, and were introduced to examples and checklists. Management representatives introduced common quality criteria for all key content formats and communication channels with examples of successful products. What is a good social media post? What does a well-orchestrated webinar look like? And what is a good article for internal media or an opinion piece by a CEO for external media?

In addition, the aim was to inspire high-quality communication through examples from other organisations. To this end, each staff member collected an example from another organisation to create a book of exemplary cases for inspiration.

Similarly, a book of exemplary communication content was to be produced by staff members at the end of the Academy's skills development programme. Each strategic producer thus developed a communicative product that they were proud of. In a few words, they described why it looked the way it did and what impact it had, and this impressive collection was shared for mutual inspiration at the joint wrap-up of the programme.

As one of the participants, Tom Boyd, Media Relations Manager at Maersk North America, summarises it: 'The Strategic Producer Academy gave us the tools to succeed to better handle the myriad of situations we as communications professionals face daily in our line of work. From advising executives to ensuring our messages are crisp and impactful in today's fast-paced, crowded communications space. Most importantly, the Academy showed us the value of a strategic producer mindset and how to build active and trusting relationships that generate better outcomes for our communications goals'.

10.3.4 To Be Continued

The fact that the Academy helped individuals to focus on various areas of work and that communicators felt that they were moving forward is evidenced by the ongoing individual measurements (Fig. 10.11).

The strategic producers have very much embraced the role and at the first-year finals there was an infectious pride, but it was not an easy process. Amongst other things, the Academy was challenged by the fact that the large corporation is (always) busy, so prioritising one's own development could be difficult for many when other deadlines compelled. It was easiest to let down promises to yourself, and it required a steady and persistent focus from line managers, colleagues and the individual to keep development on the agenda. Over the three-quarter duration of the Academy, a collective identity of being 'strategic producers' was created across the department. There was a lot of learning in the communication department, including the use of the same terminology and toolbox and the introduction of constructive feedback on typical everyday tasks, where both strengths and weaknesses are discussed. 'The ambition was and is also to create increased interaction across the organisation—both on the go, where we can play each other stronger, and with constructive

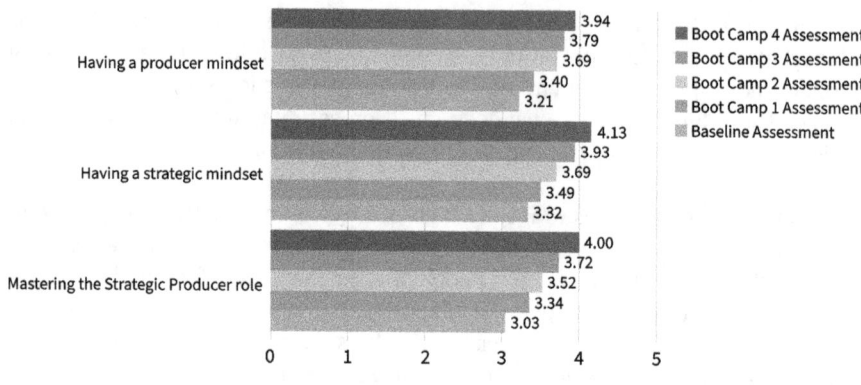

Fig. 10.11 Overview of how the strategic producers assessed the development of their own skills as communicators in the course of the academy

evaluations moving forward, so we constantly improve one another and the quality. With 'always on' transformation, you never reach the finish line, but we are well on the way', emphasises Mette Refshauge.

Although the Academy ended after 1 year, the work continues. There is ongoing onboarding of new colleagues so that everyone in the communication department is familiarised with the role of strategic producer and colleague-to-colleague training with a focus on specific skills, each time also providing an opportunity to revisit the Academy's points. Ad hoc activities are customised for communicators or teams with shared needs. 'For example, we have developed courses for our advisors in major change processes that go deeper into the psychological and rhetorical knowledge of what it takes to master the power space that is professional advice', says Mette Refshauge. It is an initiative that is based on and revitalises the role of strategic producer but now focuses on what is special about being a consultant. Here, too, the ambition is to work with knowledge, tools and the individual counsellor's Stradivarius, so it will be a course with small classes, concrete cases and both collective and individual sparring.

'We also keep a strong focus on feedback and impact data on a daily basis, so that we are constantly developing as individual communicators, as teams and as an overall communications function', she elaborates, 'as well as staying in touch with the latest professional knowledge and seeking inspiration from peers outside Maersk'.

One example of such professional activities is an academic roundtable in September 2022 where Maersk invited leading Danish researchers in the field of communication (Fig. 10.12). Each researcher shared key learnings and inspiration from their work. The audience was by no means limited to Maersk's own communicators. The room was filled with future communication professionals, communication students from all the major educational institutions in Denmark. The students

Fig. 10.12 Photos from the 'roundtable' at Maersk with the participation of leading Danish researchers in the field of communication and a number of students from a wide range of communication subjects

were both inspired by the professors and met with the Maersk communicators for small workshops after the presentations. The workshops aimed both to give the students an insight into Maersk's engine room and to get inspiring input from the students.

'This is an example of something we will continue to do: to give and receive inspiration from interaction with interesting stakeholders in our skills development. It provides us with new insights, gives us a fresh look at our own practice, so we keep moving forward', concludes Mette Refshauge.

10.4 Interview. You Must Link Knowledge, Skills and Personality

Computer sales, live broadcasting as a news reporter and a job at a communications agency: Professor Ralph Tench of Leeds University has been quite busy since those days when his majors were first medicine, then psychology, then journalism. His extensive experience in editorial offices, agencies and organisations is the very thing that enabled him to show a highly application-oriented path for research in strategic communication, with a particular focus on, amongst other things, competences: What abilities do we, professional communicators, need today, and what are we forgetting to focus on?

'Be the "snapper". That was my own first experience of task slippage', Ralph Tench says, quickly elaborating as he sees our confusion, making us think of a big, red fish. 'We called it being the "snapper" when, as a young news reporter out on interviews, I had to take a snapshot myself as I no longer automatically had a photographer with me. Usually, it was just as an outline for something the photographer would later take a professional picture of, but it was my own introduction to the gradual task slippage that the communication profession has undergone'.

Today, a professional communicator must master many facets in order to be competent, but we are mistaken if we think that we must be experts at everything. In the professor's research, competence is about knowledge, skills and personal qualities, together making up competence. We need to work within all three areas to strengthen our competence. The commitment to and belief in the need for the communications profession is evident in the professor. 'Professional communicators must be able to multitask and be present, so that we are constantly contributing to driving the organisational direction, internally and externally. There is a demand for this, now more than ever, and I believe that the pandemic has provided communicators with momentum'.

Both research and experience from Ralph Tench's extensive professional and private networks have convinced him that, although COVID-19 pandemic was bad, it created new opportunities for communicators: 'The pandemic broke down a lot of the barriers in top management. They have not always fully understood the importance of communication. But they do now. They found out during a crisis that affected everyone, and we suddenly had to reinvent and invent ways of being in touch and of taking social responsibility', he elaborates, 'so the opportunities are new and enable even better support'.

That momentum must be seized and keeping a focus on competences, Ralph Tench sees five pitfalls to avoid for this to succeed.

10.4.1 Listen Actively

According to Ralph Tench, professional communicators must listen a lot more in order to succeed. 'Listening is an underrated skill. If we are to help our organisations navigate the ever-changing landscape wisely, we need to shift much of our attention away from communicating ourselves and towards listening', he recommends.

It is both about the ability to listen in specific 1:1 situations with the individual stakeholder but also about listening in a broader sense: 'Being communicators, we must have a deep understanding of all our stakeholders' perspectives and any barriers. We can only gain that understanding by listening to them through all the channels we have available. We often fail to do that on busy days, when our own communication products may end up taking too much of our time'.

10.4.2 Crack the Data Code

Another pitfall for professional communicators is the use of data. 'I sometimes give my students a bunch of numbers to analyse and write an article about. Often someone complains and says they're not good with numbers. But that's not an option today', says Ralph Tench. He does not give them the task to expose them, but to empower them.

'Professional communicators must understand the business and be able to use data actively to plan, monitor impact and evaluate. So being afraid of numbers is not an option. We don't have to be statisticians, but we have to be able to use and read data', he stresses. This is an ability that, in times full of fake news challenges, has become even more crucial, because we need to be able to base our knowledge and recommendations on facts.

10.4.3 Drop the Technology Dazzle

'The fax has just been deleted from the UK rules listing what telecommunications companies must make available to Brits, and who knows what Elon Musk's acquisition of Twitter will mean to the future of that platform', the professor says with a thoughtful smile. 'We must be careful not to be dazzled by CommTech and think that it's the only and most important thing. Technology is first and foremost a tool for communicators'.

The European Communication industry surveys, of which Ralph Tench is one of the researchers, have long tracked the technology focus of communicators (Fig. 10.13). In 2022, it was clear that this helped set exemplary communications departments apart from the rest. Almost 80% of the exemplary, excellent communications departments were innovators, early adaptors or early majority in terms of digital communication, whilst only 54% of the rest helped find and lead the way.

'It's obviously important to master and understand', he stresses, 'but let's not forget that it's not the only thing, but rather one of the tools and channels we need to know and understand how to use'.

10.4.4 Develop Your Understanding of People

'Being communicators, our interpersonal skills are crucial to succeed', Ralph Tench stresses, and he thus warns us that communicators must remember to develop that part of our skills.

'That applies to both simple, practical skills such as networking, something you can train', he explains, 'and to knowledge-based parts of this competence: The understanding of people which you can get, for example, from psychology'. Psychological knowledge can complement communications knowledge and can give us a better ability to navigate in relation to stakeholders, for example in relation to motivation, change and crisis.

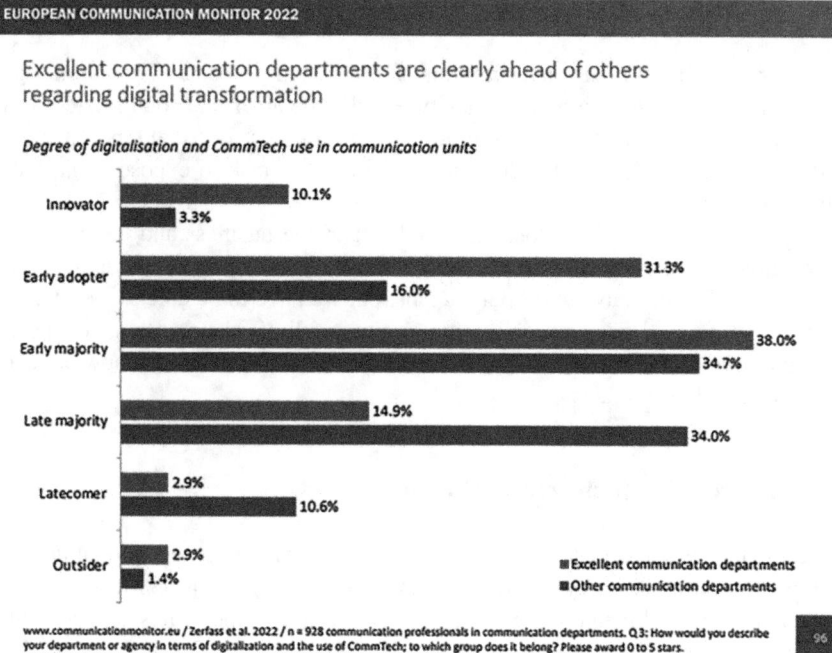

Fig. 10.13 The European Communication Monitor 2022

10.4.5 Look Inwards

Skilled communicators are constantly evolving, curious and ready to ask the dumb questions that make others and themselves smarter. That is why Ralph Tench has no doubt that the most dangerous pitfall is forgetting to be reflective and to look inwards. 'We can't be afraid of being honest with ourselves and must look closely to always ensure the right development. Communicators can't have blind spots in their self-awareness' he stresses.

> I might sound like an old grandma with a slice of apple pie in my hand, but I really do believe that this is the most crucial thing: development driven by self-awareness and curiosity about the world around us, with the awareness to develop knowledge, skills and personal qualities. It differentiates you as a communicator, and it also differentiates the organisations that make room for that development.

Ralph Tench

Ralph Tench, Professor, is the Director of Research at Leeds Business School and an internationally recognised researcher within strategic communication. His research has, among other things, focused on social impact and organisational strategy, behaviour and performance. He is one of the developers of the Communication Monitor, which gauges the temperature of the communication field through the eyes of communicators (www.communicationmonitor.eu).

He is the author of numerous academic articles and more than 25 books, most recently together with Juan Meng & Ángeles Moreno: 'Strategic Communication in a Global Crisis National and International Responses to the COVID-19 Pandemic', 2023.

References

Cheetham, G., & Chivers, G. (1996). Towards a holistic model of professional competence. *Journal of European Industrial Training, 20*(5), 20–30.

Jeffrey, L. M., & Brunton, M. A. (2011). Developing a framework for communication management competencies. *Journal of Vocational Education & Training, 63*(1), 57–75.

Page. (2019). *The CCO as pacesetter what it means, why it matters, how to get there.* Page research report.

Tench, R., & Moreno, A. (2015). Mapping communication management competencies for European practitioners: ECOPSI an EU study. *Journal of Communication Management, 19*(1), 39–61.

Tench, R., & Topić, M. (2018). Strategic competencies. In R. L. Heath & W. Johansen (Eds.), *The international encyclopedia of strategic communication* (pp. 1–14). Wiley.

Tench, R., Vercic, D., Zerfass, A., Moreno, A., & Verhoeven, P. (2017). *Communication excellence: How to develop, manage and lead exceptional communications.* Palgrave Macmillan.

Zerfass, A., Stieglitz, S., Clausen, S., Ziegele, D., & Berger, K. (2021). *Communications trend radar 2021: Denialism, virtual corporate communications, sustainable communications, digital nudging & voice interaction* (IDEAS Working Paper Series from RePEc).

Zerfass, A., Moreno, Á., Tench, R., Verčič, D., & Buhmann, A. (2022). European communication monitor 2022. Exploring diversity and empathic leadership, CommTech and consulting in communications. Results of a survey in 43 countries.

GPSR Compliance

The European Union's (EU) General Product Safety Regulation (GPSR) is a set of rules that requires consumer products to be safe and our obligations to ensure this.

If you have any concerns about our products, you can contact us on

ProductSafety@springernature.com

In case Publisher is established outside the EU, the EU authorized representative is:

Springer Nature Customer Service Center GmbH
Europaplatz 3
69115 Heidelberg, Germany

www.ingramcontent.com/pod-product-compliance
Lightning Source LLC
LaVergne TN
LVHW012248070526
838201LV00091B/153